Security, Audit and Control Features

PeopleSoft®

2nd Edition

A Technical and Risk Management Reference Guide

ISACA®

Serving IT Governance Professionals

ISACA®

With more than 50,000 members in more than 140 countries, ISACA (*www.isaca.org*) is a recognized worldwide leader in IT governance, control, security and assurance. Founded in 1969, ISACA sponsors international conferences, publishes the *Information Systems Control Journal®*, develops international information systems auditing and control standards, and administers the globally respected Certified Information Systems Auditor™ (CISA®) designation, earned by more than 48,000 professionals since inception, and the Certified Information Security Manager® (CISM®) designation, a groundbreaking credential earned by more than 6,000 professionals since the program's inception.

Disclaimer

ISACA (the "Owner") has designed and created this publication, titled *Security, Audit and Control Features PeopleSoft®: A Technical and Risk Management Reference Guide, 2nd Edition* (the "Work"), primarily as an educational resource for control professionals. The Owner makes no claim that use of any of the Work will assure a successful outcome. The Work should not be considered inclusive of all proper information, procedures and tests or exclusive of other information, procedures and tests that are reasonably directed to obtaining the same results. In determining the propriety of any specific information, procedure or test, control professionals should apply their own professional judgment to the specific circumstances presented by the particular systems or information technology environment.

While all care has been taken in researching and documenting the techniques described in this text, persons employing these techniques must use their own knowledge and judgment. ISACA and Deloitte Touche Tohmatsu, its partners and employees, shall not be liable for any losses and/or damages (whether direct or indirect), costs, expenses or claims whatsoever arising out of the use of the techniques described or reliance on the information in this reference guide.

Oracle, JD Edwards, Peoplesoft and Siebel are registered trademarks of Oracle Corporation and/or its affiliates. The publisher gratefully acknowledges Oracle's kind permission to use the trademarks in this publication. Oracle is not the publisher of this book and is not responsible for the content.

Disclosure

ISACA
3701 Algonquin Road, Suite 1010
Rolling Meadows, IL 60008 USA
Phone: +1.847.253.1545
Fax: +1.847.253.1443
E-mail: *research@isaca.org*
Web site: *www.isaca.org*

ISBN 1-933284-46-3
Security, Audit and Control Features PeopleSoft®: A Technical and Risk Management Reference Guide, 2nd Edition
Printed in the United States of America

Acknowledgments

From the Publisher
ISACA wishes to recognize:

The ISACA Board of Directors
Everett C. Johnson, CPA, Deloitte & Touche (retired) USA, International President
Abdul Hamid Bin Abdullah, CISA, CPA, Auditor General's Office, Singapore, Vice President
William C. Boni, CISM, Motorola, USA, Vice President
Jean-Louis Leignel, MAGE Conseil, France, Vice President
Lucio Augusto Molina Focazzio, CISA, Colombia, Vice President
Howard Nicholson, CISA, City of Salisbury, Australia, Vice President
Bent Poulsen, CISA, CISM, VP Securities Services, Denmark, Vice President
Frank Yam, CISA, CIA, CCP, CFE, CFSA, FFA, FHKCS, FHKIoD, Focus Strategic Group, Hong Kong, Vice President
Marios Damianides, CISA, CISM, CA, CPA, Ernst & Young LLP, USA, Past International President
Robert S. Roussey, CPA, University of Southern California, USA, Past International President

The Deloitte Touche Tohmatsu Research Team
Mark Sercombe, CISA, CA, Sponsoring Partner
Iain Muir, CISA, CRP, CISSP, CA, Engagement Advisor
Richard Higgins, Project Manager

Expert Reviewers
Bradley Artigue, KPMG LLP, USA
Antoni Bosch-Pujol, CISA, CISM, Institute of Law & Technology, Autonomous University of Barcelona, Spain
Claudio Cilli, Ph.D., CISA, CISM, CIA, CISSP, University of Marche, Italy
Shahvez Jaywant David, CISA, Tower Insurance Limited, New Zealand
Ikechukwu Charles Eke, CISA, FCA, Nigerian Security Printing and Minting Plc., Nigeria
Daniel Mayer, CISA, Israel
Edward J. Pelcher, CISA, Office of the Auditor General, South Africa
Sunil Rajan, CA, CIA, PricewaterhouseCoopers LLP, Canada
Parvathi Ramesh, CISA, CA, India
Vivek Shrivastava, Air New Zealand, New Zealand

From the Authors
The authors wish to acknowledge the contributions of:

Richard Rudnicki, Deloitte Touche Tohmatsu
Richard Wilson, Deloitte Touche Tohmatsu

Table of Contents

Foreword

Enterprise resource planning (ERP) systems such as PeopleSoft®, SAP®R/3® and Oracle® are now pervasive in large organizations worldwide. An ERP system is a packaged business software system that allows an organization to:

- Automate and integrate its core business processes
- Share common data and practices across the entire enterprise
- Produce and access information in a real-time environment
- Provide a single access to enterprise data

ERP systems have transformed enterprise business processes by automating manual tasks such as authorizations, empowering users to initiate transactions and monitor performance online. As a result, the integrity framework supporting these business processes has also been transformed. The level of automated controls and the importance of logical access security and configuration controls have increased. The current trend to web-enable ERP systems and the integration of back-end ERP systems with front-end e-business systems will further transform business process and technical infrastructure risk/control frameworks.

PeopleSoft is one of the developers of enterprise applications. This technical reference guide on PeopleSoft audit is the second edition in a series of technical reference guides providing information relating to the world's three major ERP systems. The other two guides in the series focus on SAP R/3 and Oracle Applications.

The purpose of this research is to document current best practices and identify future trends in ERP risk and control. The objective is to enable auditors and risk and security professionals (IT and non-IT) to evaluate risks and controls in existing ERP implementations and facilitate the design and building of better practice controls into system upgrades and enhancements. The publication is designed to be a practical how-to guide.

There has been a need for a series of definitive audit guides for these products for some time. By using a definitive approach, the authors sought to provide detail on testing techniques within the ERP products and their execution, rather than generic descriptions of the audit tests to be performed.

Sections covering the introduction to ERP, strategic risk management in an ERP environment and directions in ERP audit will be common to all three guides. The remaining sections covering ERP product-specific characteristics and auditing techniques are unique to each of the respective technical reference guides.

1. Executive Introduction

An ERP implementation and its associated business process changes transform the critical elements of an organization. Prior to ERP systems, an organization's legacy systems were typically organized around functions or departments (e.g., sales, purchasing, inventory and finance), not the business processes (e.g., Purchase-to-pay, Order-to-cash). Functions evolved independently of other functions. ERP systems, on the other hand, have a business process focus. Their relational database tables are designed around a complete set of core functions rather than disparate modules that merely pass transaction data from one module to another. Traditional paper-based audit trails can be lost as the internal control structure is transformed to support ERP-enabled business processes. Controls shift from detective to preventive, and traditional matching reconciliation controls are automated in the ERP software. Consequently, it makes enormous business sense to ensure that adequate controls are properly integrated into the reengineered ERP-enabled processes.

Senior management support of the project is crucial. This decision is certainly one of the most important that executives can make. The business case for an ERP system needs to be carried through implementation—guided by detailed work plans, milestones and benefit scoreboards. Business process owners who will ensure effective communication of the dependencies of processes need to be established. Configurable options need to be thoroughly explained to users and documented in the business requirements, design or blueprint documentation. Changes in the system of business controls need to be considered early in the implementation process and included in the design to minimize the cost of retrofitting controls at a later time. System performance must be tested to ensure that the application and related infrastructure can handle the typical transaction loads processed by the organization. Business continuity management plans need to be revised, taking into consideration the ERP as a single point of failure. An online, real-time system also needs an online, real-time business environment to effectively monitor and deal with exceptions. The IT infrastructure requires the same planning as the business processes. Data conversion is an area of key importance for an organization and its auditors.

Audit can contribute to an ERP implementation in a number of ways. Audit can become involved from the earliest stage of the project, assisting the project team with the designing and building of the controls. A preimplementation review of controls design can point out issues to be resolved before the system is operational. A postimplementation review focuses on the implementation of controls. The most complex role involves the performance of a quality assurance audit. This requires audit participation throughout the project, focuses on the overall quality of the business process reengineering program and considers specific deliverables at each project milestone. Involvement throughout ERP implementation allows audit to contribute to the establishment of the most effective control environment possible; however, an independent party may then be needed to perform a postimplementation review.

The implementation of an ERP system can introduce new risks and alter an organization's risk profile. Risk and control assessment requires a framework covering the areas of business process controls, application security, program interface and conversion controls, technology infrastructures, and project management. When control issues are identified, the auditor should attempt to uncover and report to management the causes of the problem and his/her recommendations. In this respect, the IT Governance Institute's (ITGI's) *Control Objectives for Information and related Technology* (COBIT®)[1] can help to meet the multiple needs of management by bridging the gaps between business risks, control needs and technical issues. It provides good practices across a domain and process framework and presents activities in a manageable and logical structure. COBIT's good practices provide a measure to judge against when things do go wrong and can assist in identifying problem causes.

The first-year audit of organizations that have implemented ERP systems needs to be carefully scoped, as there is often a combination of centralized accounting controls and decentralized operational controls. A detailed knowledge of ERP is necessary to effectively understand security and control issues over application areas, and the technical environment and automated diagnostic tools are required for application security and data integrity assurance.

In the e-enabled ERP environment, control solutions for risks associated with e-business must be developed. The traditional control framework must be extended to include identity management, content quality, privacy, collaborative commerce and integrity.

Between the covers of this book, readers will find all the details needed to confidently plan and execute a detailed review of risks and controls in a PeopleSoft environment.

This is one in a series of three technical and risk management reference guides dealing with security, audit and control features of enterprise resource planning systems. This series of guides is intended to be considered collectively. Consequently, common business processes and the related risks and control features are not covered in each and every guide. This guide covers the Human Resources and Payroll components of PeopleSoft 8.

ISACA's IS Auditing Standards, Guidelines and Procedures offer additional guidance to IS auditors.[2] Guideline G21, Enterprise Resource Planning (ERP) Systems Review, is particularly relevant.

[1] IT Governance Institute (ITGI), COBIT 4.0, USA, 2005, *www.itgi.org*

[2] ISACA, IS Auditing Standards, Guidelines and Procedures, USA, *www.isaca.org/standards*

What Has Changed With the Second Edition

Since the original publication of this guide in 2003, a lot has changed in terms of new product features, new releases and various regulatory compliance requirements for organizations. This second edition aims to ensure that the audit programs, risks and controls are functional and relevant with current research for PeopleSoft HRMS release 8.8.

This guide also updates the audit plans to incorporate CobiT® 4.0. In addition, chapter 11, New Directions for PeopleSoft and ERP Audit, discusses the changing compliance landscape, tools to assist with compliance and Oracle Fusion, and the pathway for PeopleSoft installations.

How the Book Is Organized

Introduction to ERP Systems

The evolution of ERP software is described from its early beginnings in material requirements planning packages centered on manufacturing, to the present-day systems that provide enterprisewide, integrated solutions and extensions to suppliers and customers beyond traditional organizational boundaries. The benefits and characteristics of ERP systems are discussed.

Introduction to PeopleSoft Applications

The PeopleSoft organization and the innovation surrounding the development of the PeopleSoft ERP application system are introduced. Major PeopleSoft modules, products and functionality are overviewed, and guidance on navigating PeopleSoft is provided. The manner in which an ERP implementation and its associated business process changes transform critical elements of the business, including the control environment, is outlined.

Strategic Risk Management in an ERP Environment

Strategic-level business risks (e.g., business process, application and technical infrastructure security, data conversion, program interface, and project management risks) and key management controls for ERP implementations are outlined, leading to a discussion of the importance of establishing an integrity framework for ERP environments. The impacts on audit following the implementation of an ERP system are also described. The purpose of this chapter is to help organizations minimize the risk of not obtaining the significant benefits that can flow from a well-executed ERP implementation.

ERP Audit Approach

Audit impacts arising from the implementation of ERP are detailed, and frameworks and methodologies for auditing and testing in a PeopleSoft environment are provided. These include a recommended PeopleSoft audit framework, guidance on adopting a risk-based audit approach to ERP, an overview of the PeopleSoft authorization concept, how to test PeopleSoft security, configurable controls and segregation of duties/excessive access. The need to identify the causes of issues arising from audit or control testing and a technique to assist in identifying the cause of issues with using the CobiT framework are also described.

Auditing PeopleSoft

The relationship between PeopleSoft and the major business cycles operating within organizations is explained. The core business cycles, i.e., Human Resources (HR) and Payroll, for a manufacturing organization and their integration are overviewed. For each of these business cycles, the functionality of the PeopleSoft business process and its subprocesses is described from a controls perspective. Specific risks are identified, potential automated controls are outlined, and sample testing techniques are suggested. Techniques for testing user access to business cycle functions and segregation of duties are also described.

New Directions for PeopleSoft Audit

The guide concludes by looking at the various stages through which ERP audit has progressed and looks ahead at two major new directions that are emerging for ERP audit—continuous assurance techniques (e.g., application security assurance and data assurance) and extension of the traditional ERP control framework in response to the growing e-enabled ERP environment. The available tools for continuous assurance in a PeopleSoft application's environment are overviewed, and a sample control framework for the e-ERP environment is provided. The changing compliance landscape and PeopleSoft applications' solutions are profiled from a controls perspective. Finally, a discussion on Oracle's Project Fusion and the implications for PeopleSoft installations are presented.

A well-executed ERP implementation can provide significant benefits to the organization. Senior management support and audit involvement in the project can help ensure full benefit realization of an ERP system.

Who Should Read This Book

This publication has been written with the business manager in mind. IT and assurance professionals will also find it highly informative and helpful. Other audiences include security and risk management professionals. Parts of the publication are written for those looking to learn more about how PeopleSoft applications work, as well as the strategic and risk management issues. However, for the most part, the book assumes that the reader has a fundamental working knowledge of PeopleSoft.

What Makes This Book Different

Although there are many books that have been written on PeopleSoft, they are more narrowly focused on the implementation, business aspects or how one of the PeopleSoft modules actually works. This publication is unique in that it deals with aspects of risk management, audit, security and control over PeopleSoft. These are important aspects that have not been dealt with previously in a comprehensive manner in one publication. The book is also unique in that it contains audit programs, audit suggestions and internal control questionnaires (ICQs) for the business cycles addressed within the publication.

2. Introduction to PeopleSoft and ERP Systems

Prior to ERP systems, an organization's systems were typically set up around functions or departments (e.g., sales, purchasing, inventory and finance), as depicted in **figure 2.1**, not the business processes (e.g., purchase to pay, order to cash). Functions evolved independently of other functions. Each function may have had an individual application system or a number of disparate systems to support it, with or without interfaces between the systems. This resulted in the maintenance of a series of disparate and decentralized systems, with duplication of data and inconsistent implementation of security and controls across an organization. Frequently, business controls had a high manual component.

Figure 2.1—Traditional Environment

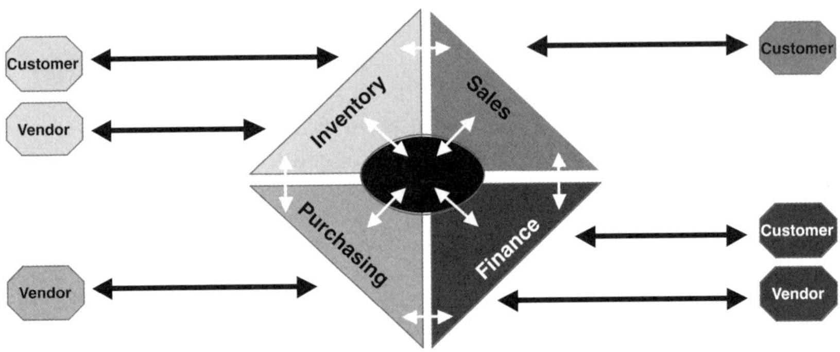

- Functions are separate.
- Interface and communication links with other functions
- Variety of systems
- Each function maintains its own master data.
- Duplication of data entry

Prior to the widespread use of ERPs, it was common that:

1. Purchase orders (PO) were approved when generated
2. When the invoice arrived, the PO was either printed out again or retrieved from filing and stapled to the invoice
3. The invoice was approved for payment
4. Once again, the documents may have been scrutinized and approved during the check payment process

Non-ERP systems also suffer from a design problem in that they are typically designed around disparate and independent modules that transmit transaction data among themselves by means of "interfaces," where the information is normally summarized (e.g., totals or balances only) in nature. In cases like these, further details of such transactions are often difficult to ascertain, unlike the ability to drill down provided by ERP systems such as PeopleSoft.

ERP systems, on the other hand, have a business process focus. ERP systems grew out of the integration of separate materials resource planning (MRP) systems (used to integrate material requirements to production, demand and capacity) and financial accounting systems in manufacturing organizations. The integration of these functional capabilities into an online and real-time application system, designed to support end-to-end business processes, enables organizations to plan and optimize their resources across the whole enterprise. Their relational database tables are designed around a complete set of the core functions for an enterprise rather than disparate modules that merely pass transaction data from one module to another.

An ERP environment operates in line with the business—online and in real time. Management has access to online and up-to-date information on how the business is performing. Common and consistent information is shared simultaneously among application modules and among users from different departments. For example, following implementation of an ERP system, organizations typically report completion of period or year-end closes in one or two days as opposed to two to three weeks under their legacy system environments. Another key change brought about by the implementation of ERP systems is that the systems are owned and driven by business process owners/end users, with the technical support of information technology, rather than being owned and driven by information technology alone.

Organizations implementing ERP systems can achieve significant benefits, such as:

- Reduction in inventory
- Redeployment of personnel into more value-producing activities
- Productivity improvement
- Order management cycle improvement
- Financial close/cycle reduction
- IT cost reduction
- Procurement cost reduction
- Cash management improvement
- Transportation/logistics cost reduction
- Hardware and software maintenance reduction
- On-time delivery improvement

The intangible benefits delivered by an ERP implementation—while difficult to quantify—can deliver significant business value through improved organization capabilities, including:

- Information/visibility (e.g., drill-down capability and consistent, reliable information across business areas)

- New/improved processes
- Improved customer responsiveness
- Integration and standardization of processes, policies, security and controls
- Flexibility
- Globalization

The PeopleSoft system was developed in the late 1980s, focusing on the nonmanufacturing functions of human resources (HR) and payroll. Since the ERP generation grew out of the manufacturing industry from disparate legacy MRP and financials systems, HR and payroll capabilities may not have been provided by these systems or some of the competitor ERP systems.

The 1990s saw PeopleSoft branching out to develop its financial and distribution modules, while other ERPs developed their HR and payroll functionality. Although ERP systems have been advertised as "enterprisewide" and "fully integrated," the Internet revolution has resulted in ERP systems becoming increasingly web-enabled, providing a more flexible and wider-reaching solution to cater to customers, vendors and employees. This globalization of ERP products has brought on additional considerations for the main ERP vendors. PeopleSoft 8 has introduced global payroll to cater to a number of European countries in addition to the existing support of North America and Canada. In line with this global rollout, version 8 also has translated versions in Dutch, French, Canadian French, German, Japanese, Portuguese and Spanish.

The introduction of the euro currency gave rise to the problem of euro conversion. Although most systems are capable of dealing with foreign exchange transactions, organizations were forced to run multicurrency systems. This is now history. The euro became the definitive currency for the Eurozone countries on 1 January 2002, and all the individual currencies for those countries were consigned to history.

Today, PeopleSoft has more than 4,700 organizations in 107 countries running e-business applications, encompassing Human Resources Management, Financial Management, Supply Chain Management and, more recently, Customer Relationship Management modules.

Major PeopleSoft Modules and Functionality

Although PeopleSoft may be better known for its human resources functionality, it has provided financial applications for almost 10 years. The initial solutions were developed in the early 1990s and were composed of the General Ledger (GL), Payables, Receivables, Assets, Purchasing, Inventory, Billing and Projects modules. Developments since that time have resulted in PeopleSoft financial management applications, providing a more diverse solution with the ability to support e-procurement and business-to-business Internet functionality.

In PeopleSoft Enterprise Financial Management Solutions 8.9, the main modules include:

- Asset Lifecycle Management
- Financial Analytics
- Financial Management
- Profitability Management for Financial Services
- Treasury
- Industry Enterprise Financial Management Product

In PeopleSoft Human Resources Management 8.9, the main modules include:

- Absence Management
- Benefits Administration
- Candidate Gateway
- Directory Interface
- eBenefits
- eCompensation
- Manager Desktop
- eDevelopment
- ePay
- ePerformance
- eProfile
- eProfile Manager Desktop
- Global Payroll
- HelpDesk for Human Resources
- Human Resources
- Learning Management
- Payroll for North America
- Payroll Interface
- Pension Administration
- Services Procurement
- Stock Administration
- Talent Acquisition Manager
- Time and Labor
- Workforce Planning
- Workforce Rewards
- Workforce Scorecard

PeopleSoft also provides a suite of supply chain management (SCM) applications. These are divided into four main groups: customer order management, logistics, manufacturing solutions, and supply chain planning. PeopleSoft 8 incorporates e-procurement and e-store functionality with web-enabled requisitioning, receipt management and inventory management. These are integrated with the Financial Management modules to further develop and enhance business-to-business capabilities. The main modules include:

- Customer Order Management
- Logistics

- Manufacturing Solution
- Supply Chain Planning
- Additional SCM Product Modules

PeopleSoft provides specific capabilities to cater to industry-specific requirements. In addition, PeopleSoft industry solutions are complemented by subsolutions to provide for the different types of organizations within an industry. For example, the Financial Services industry solution allows the differentiation of banking, insurance and brokerage firms. Currently, PeopleSoft can be tailored for the following industries:

- Communications
- Consumer products
- Education and research
- Engineering and construction
- Financial services
- High technology
- Industrial manufacturing
- Natural resources
- Professional services
- Public sector
- Retail
- Travel and transportation
- Utilities

The release of PeopleSoft 8, with its emphasis on Internet capabilities, has led to the development of a fully integrated customer relationship management (CRM) system linking Customer, Financial, Supply Chain and Employee modules. In 1999/2000, PeopleSoft also acquired the Vantive Corporation, a CRM vendor. The PeopleSoft 8 Internet Architecture (described in chapter 9, PeopleSoft Application and Technical Infrastructure) means that no code is retained on the client. Only a standard web browser (e.g., Internet Explorer) is required to access the information, making it more accessible to both internal and external (third-party) users. CRM aims to track and analyze customer behavior by using information stored in relation to sales and marketing, field service, and help desk and support.

PeopleSoft CRM includes:

- CRM Field Service
- CRM Help Desk
- CRM Help Desk for Human Resources
- CRM Sales
- CRM Mobile Sales
- CRM Support
- CRM Support for Customer Self Service
- Customer Portal
- Mobile Field Service
- MultiChannel Communications

More recently, PeopleSoft has deployed release 8.9 into the marketplace, building upon the Internet-based architecture and improving online, real-time collaboration with suppliers, customers, partners and employees. At the time of publication of this guide, the following have been released:

- PeopleSoft Enterprise Financial Management Solutions 8.9
- PeopleSoft Enterprise Supply Chain Management 8.9
- PeopleSoft Enterprise Customer Relationship Management 8.9
- PeopleSoft Human Resources Management (or Human Capital Management) 8.9
- PeopleSoft Enterprise Portal 8.9

The specific audit implications are dependent on the way each of these products is implemented. However, key risk and control considerations will continue to focus on the increased user base (customers, suppliers, partners and employees) and the additional entry points into the PeopleSoft environment, resulting in an increased emphasis on data quality and Internet security to ensure confidentiality/privacy.

As discussed in the executive introduction, this technical reference guide is part of a series of three guides. The series of guides is intended to be considered collectively; consequently, common business processes and the related risks and control features are not covered in every guide. For example, risks and typical controls associated with inventory and revenue business cycles are considered in the SAP R/3 technical reference guide. This guide covers in detail the key risks and controls associated with the core HR and Payroll products of PeopleSoft release 8.8. However, many risks dealt with in the other guides may be applicable to the core functional modules not covered in detail in this guide. For example, the following lists focus on some of the risks associated with the more common applications, such as revenue and expenditure, and these could be considered when planning an audit. These lists should not be considered exhaustive and will be dependent on the implementation and processes within the organization.

Financial Management Solutions Risks

Risks to payables include:

- Changes to the vendor management master data may be invalid, incomplete, inaccurate and/or untimely.
- Master data may not remain current and pertinent.
- If amounts posted to accounts payable do not represent goods or services received, unauthorized payments may be made and the organization may incur a financial loss.
- Accounts payable amounts may not be calculated completely and accurately or recorded in a timely manner.
- If accounts payable amounts are not recorded completely and accurately, suppliers may not be paid in full, possibly damaging supplier relations.
- Disbursements may not be recorded accurately, affecting cash flow decisions and causing reconciliation difficulties. The nonrecording of disbursements may also result in duplicate payments.

Risks to the GL include:
- Invalid journal entries may be booked to the GL.
- Journal entries may be posted more than once to the GL.
- Not all journal entries may be posted to the GL or in the correct period.
- Valid GL account balances may be excluded from the financial statements.
- Financial statements may be inaccurate and may not reconcile to the GL.
- Closing procedures may be inadequate to prevent any further postings to that period and may inaccurately reflect the transactions that took place in a given accounting period.

Navigating the PeopleSoft System

Logging On

The sign-in page requires a user to enter his/her user ID and password, which are both case-sensitive. The language is also chosen on this page, as shown in **figure 2.2**. PeopleSoft's online security will validate the user ID and password against the database. PeopleSoft also allows authentication to occur against an organization's LDAP directory server (e.g., Microsoft's Active Directory or Novel NDS). If either the username or password does not match, an error message is displayed, as shown in **figure 2.3**. Once a user is logged on to the PeopleSoft application, the user profile associated with the user ID determines the menus, pages and action types the user may access. PeopleSoft security is discussed in more detail in chapters 9 and 10.

Figure 2.2—Sign-in Page

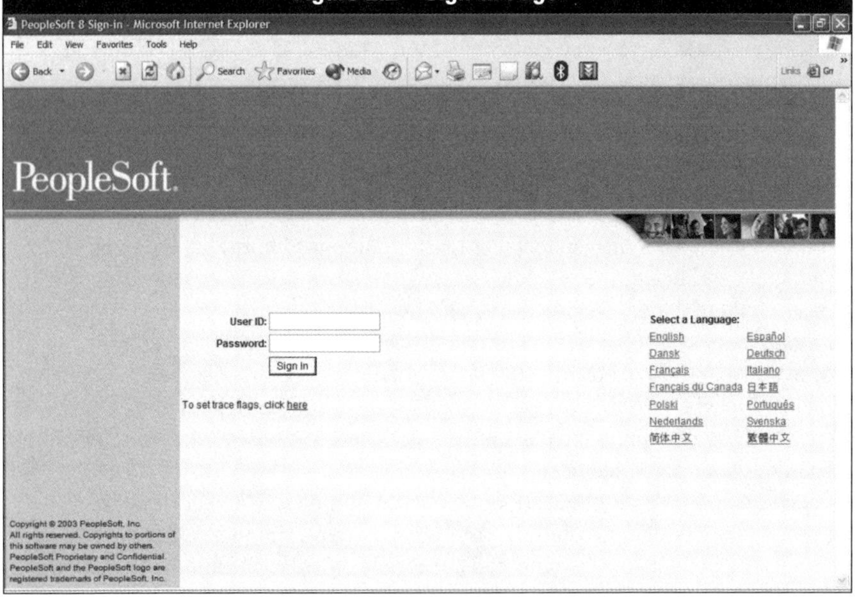

Figure 2.3—Sign-in Rejection

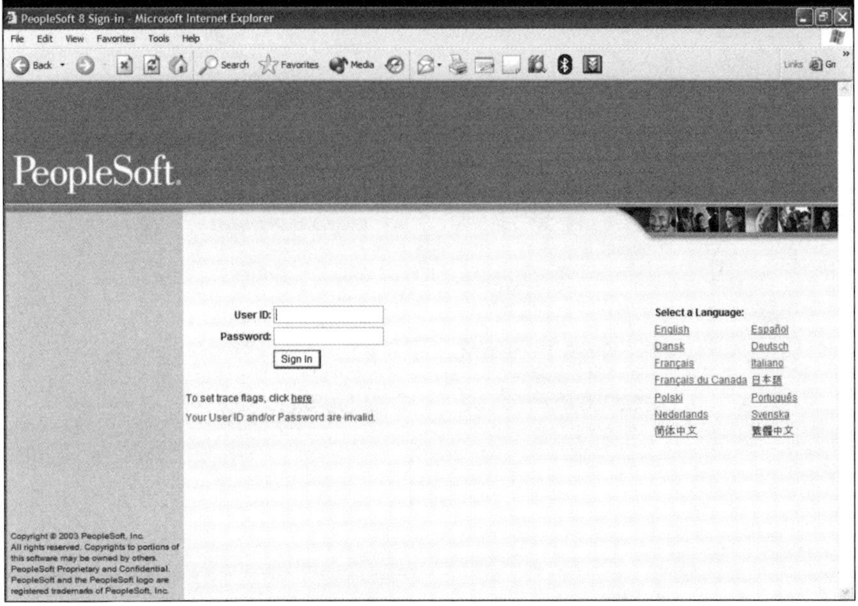

Screen Layout and Information

PeopleSoft 8 is built on the principles of a client-server, Internet-based architecture, called pure Internet architecture. The user environment is completely Internet-driven and can be personalized to the user, depending on whether he/she is an employee, customer or supplier. All screens, called pages, are in Hypertext Markup Language (HTML) format.

The PeopleSoft 8 graphical user interface (GUI), as shown in **figure 2.4**, consists of the following:

- Application portal—A web site that helps the user navigate to other web-based applications and content. This is usually the entry point when the web browser is launched. This can be customized to include PeopleSoft application, external and intranet links.
- Navigation header—The header area in PeopleSoft Internet Architecture (PIA) that remains static as the user navigates through pages. The navigation header contains links back to the initial home page and a sign-off button. The navigation header also has categories, favorites and search features.
- Page—The individual display and data-entry screens for each part of the PeopleSoft application. Pages appear in the browser window.
- Menu—A navigation list that contains menu headings and links by which a user can move between the pages of the system. The menu will expand and collapse based on a user's selection.
- Component—A group of related pages that pertain to a specific task. Users access components from the menu. Components contain folder tabs with each tab containing a related page.

Figure 2.4—PeopleSoft GUI

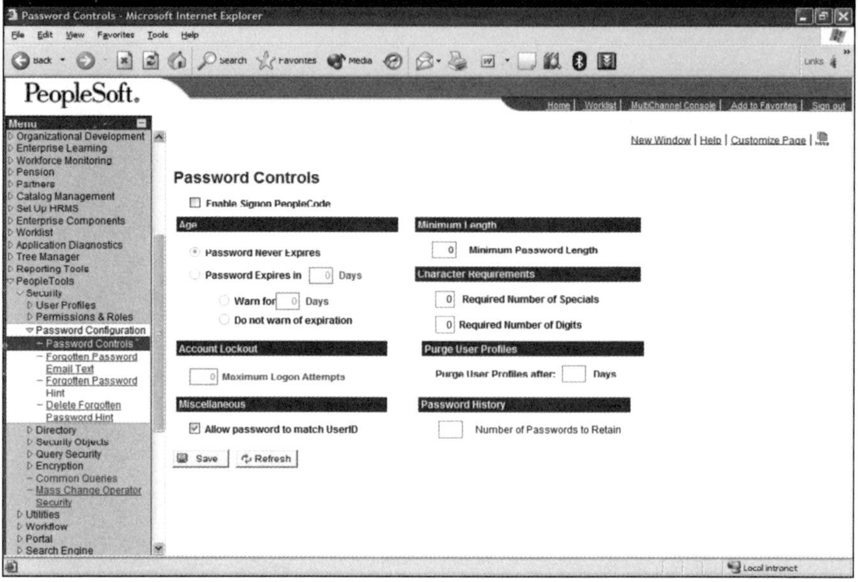

• Keys—The display-only fields that uniquely identify the data. To display a page, the user enters the keys so the system can retrieve the correct row of data from the database tables.

Navigating Menus

PeopleSoft provides a number of methods for a user to navigate and access application pages, such as:

• Menu navigation
• PeopleSoft Navigator

Menu navigation is the default method for accessing menus and pages and is organized around PeopleSoft functionality. PeopleSoft Navigator (or business process navigation) provides the user with a graphical depiction of a business process, designed to represent the sequential tasks and relevant pages required to complete an activity. This provides the user with an overall understanding of the procedures surrounding a business process.

Menu Navigation

PeopleSoft's browser-based interface provides an intuitive way of updating or viewing data in the database. The menu columns are set up as lists of links that enable the user to navigate to the desired component or page. The menu structure is the primary means of navigating the PeopleSoft application. It consists of a series of right facing triangles with accompanying menu heading. The main column, also known as "home," contains a general list of the areas in the application. A right-facing triangle before a menu heading indicates that there are sublevels to view under that heading. Sublevels are viewed by clicking the triangle or the menu heading. This will expand the heading, causing the triangle to face downwards and reveal any sublevel menu items. A minus sign (-) indicates that the lowest sublevel has been reached.

Menu navigation changed significantly in PeopleSoft 8.8 and subsequent releases. In previous releases of PeopleSoft, the menu expanded into three navigation columns, whereas menus in the current release of PeopleSoft are contained in a single column, with submenus indented below the parent menu, as seen in **figure 2.4**.

PeopleSoft Navigator (Business Process Navigation)

Another method of navigation is via the PeopleSoft Navigator. As previously discussed, this provides the user with a graphical representation of the steps or tasks and associated pages required to carry out an activity or complete a business process. The Navigator home page is accessed via PeopleTools. It shows the business process map in a tree format on the left side of the screen and the graphical representation on the right side of the screen, as shown in **figure 2.5**.

Figure 2.5—PeopleSoft Navigator

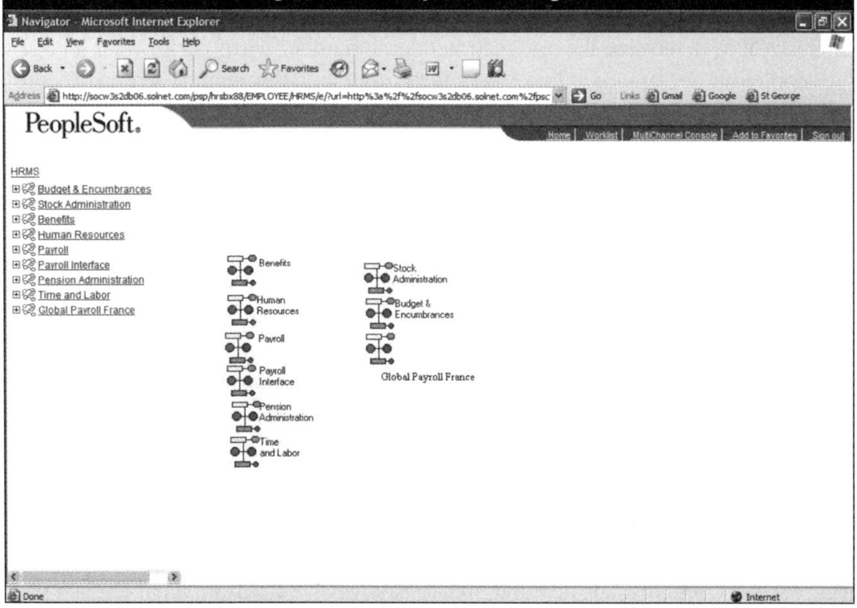

The Navigator hierarchy comprises three levels. **Figure 2.6** shows the various tree and map icons used.

Figure 2.6—Navigator Hierarchy

Tree Icon	Map Icon	Name	Description
	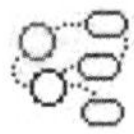	Business Process	A complete business task consisting of one or more activities or of other business processes. A business process might include work that is done by multiple users and work that occurs over time in several stages.
		Activity	A subprocess of the business task, consisting of one or more steps. Normally, activities are made up of steps that are all completed by a single user in a relatively short time.
		Step	A discrete step in the activity corresponding to a single transaction executed on an application page or through an external program

Application Release Number

It is useful to determine the application release number when performing an audit of PeopleSoft applications. In a browser environment, this cannot be done by the usual Help→About path since this returns the release number of the browser itself. Instead, if CTRL+J is selected on any active page, a new window appears showing the details of the page in which the user is currently working, including the:

- Browser
- Operating system of the client machine
- Tools release
- Application release
- Service pack
- Page
- Page component
- Page menu

Executing Commands and Online Pages

Pages act as the main interface with users for the processing of data in PeopleSoft. Users display, add and update data via the fields on a page. Each page displays related data from one or more tables in the underlying database tables. Action types with regard to user access are discussed in chapter 4, ERP Audit Approach. However, it is appropriate at this stage to introduce the concept of action page options and effective dating, which allow users to work with historic, current and future data.

Effective dating allows changes to certain data to be stored and tracked. When data are changed by a user through a page, the original data are typically replaced in the database by the entered data. However, when the effective date feature is enabled, the original data are retained in the database and a new row is created to hold the new data.

Certain pages have action options in the bottom right corner that define which data will be retrieved from the database. These are:
- Update/Display—Retrieves only current and future rows. Only future rows can be changed. A new current row can be added.
- Include History—Retrieves all rows. However, changes can be made only to future rows. A new current row can be added.
- Correct History—Retrieves all rows and allows any row to be changed and corrected. New rows can be inserted, regardless of the effective date or sequence number.

Reporting

There are a number of methods and tools that enable data and analysis of data to be run and viewed by a user:
- Standard online reporting
- PeopleSoft Query Manager
- Crystal Reports
- PS/nVision
- Tree Manager
- Cube Manager
- Structured Query Report Writer (SQR)
- Process Scheduler
- Process Monitor
- Report Manager

PeopleSoft reporting revolves around the submission of process requests via the Process Scheduler and viewing the result using the Report Manager functionality. The process of printing a report has four major steps:
- Selecting the appropriate report
- Entering the required parameters for the report
- Specifying where and when the report is to be run
- Defining the report output type and distribution method

Report activity is accessed primarily through the menu navigation Home→ Reporting Tools→Report Manager, as shown in **figure 2.7**.

Figure 2.7—Access to Report Activity

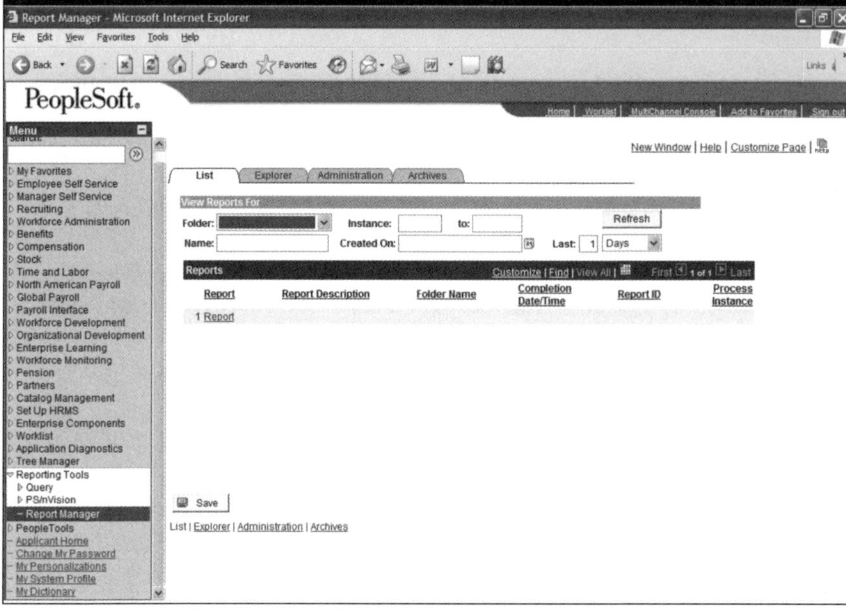

Every report must have parameters set by the user to define when the report is to be run and its destination, in addition to the content of the report. These settings are recorded as a run control and saved in the database. Run control IDs are associated with the profile/logon ID of the user. One user cannot see the run control ID list of another user from his/her own logon ID. Users do not have to reenter the report parameters each time the report is requested; instead, the Run Control ID is entered and the system retrieves the report definition from the database. This applies to both online reports and offline process requests. Process requests are submitted in the Process Scheduler request page. Users are restricted to the type of processes they are permitted to run by the roles and permission lists assigned to their user IDs. PeopleSoft 8 also provides the capability to select the format of the report and establish distribution lists for the reports, such that the output can be e-mailed to recipients in a variety of formats, including Excel and HTML.

Users will accumulate a number of reports and processes that they run during the course of their job functions. These report and process definitions are held in a personal area within the Report Manager functionality in PeopleSoft. This essentially represents the reports and processes to which a user has access. This list is accessed via Home→Reporting Tools→Report Manager.

PeopleSoft Query

PeopleSoft Query provides the ability to interrogate the database to extract data without the user having to write detailed SQL query statements. This is done via the user's web browser, and the output is downloaded into a variety of formats, including Microsoft Excel and comma-separated values (CSV).

Crystal Reports

Crystal Reports is a report formatting tool commonly used in conjunction with PeopleSoft Query Designer to create reports, mailing labels or forms. PeopleSoft recommends that Crystal Reports be used when:

- Special formatting of the report is required (including color, images and fonts)
- Repeated values in the result set need to be suppressed
- Multiple report lines per row of the result set need to be created
- Mailing labels need to be created
- The display and sequence of the columns of data need to be controlled without changing the original query
- Report breaks and totals need to be controlled

The Structured Query Report Writer

The Structured Query Report Writer is a tool that can extract data from any SQL-based relational database and download it in a prescribed format. A Structured Query Report (SQR) can be used to create tabular, single- or multi-page reports, and form letters and flat files compatible with audit software. In addition, SQRs can be used to update the databases, load and unload tables, and perform interactive queries. Standard SQRs are provided with the PeopleSoft system, and it is possible to customize these to suit the reporting requirements of the organization. The standard SQRs are stored in the \PS\SQR directory. The reports can be output in text, HTML or Acrobat (.PDF) file formats. PeopleSoft recommends using SQR for reporting if:

- The user needs the procedural logic of a programming language
- The database data need to be updated
- Reports need to be run on a server, rather than in Windows

PS/nVision

PeopleSoft provides the nVision reporting tool that can be used to define and deliver reports in Microsoft Excel. nVision offers report formats that summarize information from the underlying databases and also provides a drill-down facility that allows the user to view the supporting details. A report created and designed by one user of a particular business unit can be easily adopted by another business unit without having to define the report parameters. Users working remotely are able to run and view reports via an Internet browser, which still provides for the drill-down facility.

E-mail options allow nVision reports to be sent to individual users or roles. PeopleSoft recommends using nVision when:

- Users want to build summary reports using aggregate functions, such as SUM
- Query data and criteria form a matrix of rows and columns
- The same report layout and corresponding queries need to be used several times, e.g., for a number of different business units
- The user requires a drill-down facility to view the supporting details
- Charts or graphs of the data are to be created

Logging Off

A user can log off from the system in two ways. Either the user deliberately signs off the system, or the system automatically logs the user off after a specified number of minutes. The time-out period can be specified at the permission list level via Home→PeopleTools→Security→Permissions & Roles→Permission Lists. By selecting the general tab, a parameter can be defined to indicate the number of minutes of no screen activity after which the system will automatically log off the user, as shown in **figure 2.8**. An administrator can choose the default Never Time Out option; however, it is important that this setting be defined, as the Never Time Out setting ensures additional security. This parameter can also be defined at the web server level.

Figure 2.8—Time-out Setting

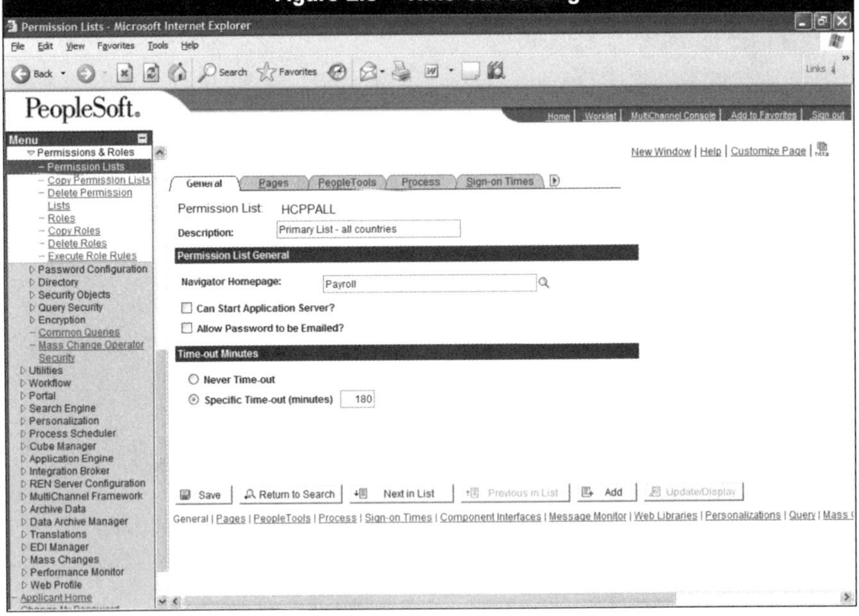

Fundamental Changes in Business Controls

An ERP implementation and its associated business process changes transform critical elements of the business. Some reasons for the change include the following:

- Decisions taken on erroneous real-time information often are irreversible or costly to set right.
- Batch-oriented controls are not the focus in an online, real-time environment.
- Traditional (paper-based) audit trails are lost.
- Access requirements have expanded vastly to include field personnel and, increasingly, suppliers and customers.
- Master data changes can have a significant impact on transactional data.

As a result, the integrity and control structure supporting ERP-enabled business processes also must be transformed. ERP systems can change internal controls in three fundamental ways:

- The method of control—From rechecking and revalidating paper-based records to online monitoring and measurement
- The point of control—From multiple validations of transactions, often based on printed outputs and source documents, to a single validation at the point of creation, often an online approval
- The amount of control—From many redundant, process-impeding controls to fewer automated, strategic controls

Consequently, it makes enormous business sense to ensure that these enhanced controls are integrated into the reengineered and ERP-enabled processes.

3. Strategic Risk Management in an ERP Environment

While the implementation of an ERP package may provide significant benefits for an organization, it also may introduce new risks and changes in the organization's risk profile. This chapter outlines:
- Strategic business risks and key management controls
- The importance of establishing an integrity framework

Key Business Risks and Key Management Controls

In his chapter, the strategic business risks associated with the implementation of an ERP package are described in terms of the following four areas:
- Project management and project governance
- Business process/functional
- Applications security and technical infrastructure
- Data conversion and program interfaces

Immediately following the description of each strategic risk area is a summary of the key management controls that, when executed, may remove or mitigate the risk. The identified risks may apply to any ERP implementation and are not specific to a PeopleSoft implementation. The benefits resulting from a well-executed ERP implementation may be significant, and the purpose of this chapter is to help organizations minimize the risks of not obtaining those benefits.

Project Management and Governance

The major concerns for ERP implementations involve organizational issues rather than technological issues.[3] This section discusses the risks of and key controls for an ERP project, including:
- Organizational change management and training
- Planning and problem management
- Lack of executive sponsorship
- Reliance on third parties
- Project cost blowout

Organizational Change Management and Training: Risks

Organizational change management and training often rank as the primary areas of risk for organizations implementing an ERP system.[4] During the initial budgeting and business case phase for a project, these areas are often descoped or downscaled to reduce costs. However, literature on enterprise systems confirms

[3] Manual, J.E.; *Definition and Analysis of Critical Success Factors for ERP Implementation Projects*, 2004, *http://professores.ie.edu/jmesteves/thesis_research.htm*

[4] Deloitte Consulting, *ERP's Second Wave: Maximizing the Value of ERP-Enabled Processes*, USA, 1998

that failure to address the human and organizational aspects of change all too frequently contributes to poor outcomes in such investments.[5] Staff members often defer their involvement in the ERP development, even though it may significantly affect the way they perform their roles in the new ERP-enabled organization. In addition, staff members require considerable training on changed business processes and hands-on exposure to the system to adapt to the new processes and systems. An important aspect of change management that is sometimes inadequately emphasized is the role of the users and the impact that their actions have on a single integrated enterprisewide application. Another key factor concerns the retention of staff, once they are trained in new processes and systems.

Organizational Change Management and Training: Key Controls

A project sponsor should be established who should ensure that the organization has the same vision as the original motivations for implementing ERP-enabled processes—the targeted capabilities and the targeted benefits. Aligning on the true destination (as opposed to the initial go-live phase) is a hearts-and-minds issue, which requires special focus on communication, management expectations, education and senior management support. The change management and training program must reach affected people at all levels and provide them with the skills and knowledge required to participate appropriately in the development, understand the changes to their job role in the post-go-live environment and contribute to the next milestone. Typically, this is not an area where the budget can be trimmed successfully. Organizations need to establish business process owners and champions who own the business processes and understand the impact of the actions of one group on another. A key success factor for the business process owners often revolves around how early and to what extent they obtain hands-on experience on the new or redesigned processes and the new ERP system. These owners and champions should ensure that the dependencies among processes and modules are effectively communicated.

Planning and Project Management: Risks

Key challenge areas for an organization implementing an ERP system include detailed planning and project management of the people, process and technology factors. Approximately 50 percent of the issues and obstacles facing an ERP implementation concern people factors[6] such as:

- Prioritization
- Resource allocation
- Teams/project structure
- Discipline
- Ownership
- Communication

[5] Lau, Linda (ed.); *Managing Business with SAP: Planning, Implementation, and Evaluation,* Idea Group Publishing, 2005

[6] *Op. cit.*, Deloitte Consulting, 1998

Failure to place sufficient emphasis on these factors, as opposed to process and technology factors, often leads to disappointment with the implementation outcomes.

Planning and Project Management: Key Controls

Organizations need a strong business imperative to implement ERP so their projects do not stop in midstream and end in disillusionment. This imperative needs to be embodied in the business case and carried through to an effective implementation plan and design with appropriate user involvement. Successful projects are guided by detailed work plans, milestone plans and rollout plans. Key dates and deliverables are spelled out, dependencies are synchronized, benefit scorecards are created, and results are tracked and communicated. There is a need for a professional project manager with the ability to:

- Integrate IT and business users into joint decision making
- Facilitate significant and difficult decisions, such as whether to implement processes enabled by the ERP package or whether to implement the ERP package for reengineered or redesigned processes

The bright star of going live—large as it looms at the time—is only a point in time. It is not the point where the full constellation of business benefits is realized. It is the beginning of a journey. Benefits such as improved cost structures, faster response to customers and more effective business processes are why the journey starts, and they should be milestones on the way to the full power of the integrated enterprise. Successful organizations may miss a scheduled milestone or a date to go live, but they never miss an expected benefit.

Lack of Executive Sponsorship: Risks

Project management and users may become frustrated and effective change may not be achieved if there is no sponsorship or if active involvement of executive management is lacking. Project resources may be redirected to other priorities and the project may stall in the middle. Conflicts may arise between the business areas and IT (or among business areas), and effective resolution may not be achieved. The right level of investment may not be maintained, and the project may lose its purpose.

Lack of Executive Sponsorship: Key Controls

Senior executive buy-in and sponsorship are needed to achieve the right mix of business and IT involvement in the project and to resolve conflicts. Business process reengineering needs championing, and systems architecture needs investment. Risks must be managed and business controls must be designed and deployed effectively. To succeed, these aspects need executive support. During implementation, the responsibility for going live on time and on budget usually rests with the project lead. However, going live is only an interim destination. In successful organizations, there is no mystery about the accountability for results. An unambiguous responsibility and accountability should be set up for the benefits of the project, and this should be communicated to the entire organization.

Reliance on Third Parties: Risks

While consultants bring valuable experience and methodologies to a project, their presence alone does not guarantee success. The organization may overly delegate to consultants or third-party suppliers of ERP solutions, expecting them to intuitively know their business requirements and effectively test and implement the solution. A major pitfall may also involve the payment of large sums of money on the delivery of documents, such as designs and flowcharts, without any tangible delivery of the computer system solution. Often organizations focus so much on going live as the end product, that the need for a postimplementation stabilization phase and benefits-realization phase are ignored or not well understood. This results in the consultants or the project team being let go too early, skills and knowledge not being effectively transferred to the organization, and inadequate support being available in the postimplementation environment. Another consequence of funding or remunerating consultants upon going live may result in the organization being pushed to go live irrespective of its readiness.

Reliance on Third Parties: Key Controls

Business process owners who understand the organization and its business requirements need to be appointed. These business process owners must gain hands-on experience with the solution and champion the cause to ensure effective testing and implementation of the solution. The organization needs to contract effectively with its suppliers to ensure the quality of deliverables and effective postimplementation support. This may take the form of warranties or retainers until the delivered product is proven in production. Effective transition planning and training are required to transfer skills from vendors or consultants to appropriate staff. Retention plans are required to ensure that staff members, once trained and marketable, remain with the organization. Each key member of the team should have a backup staff member with similar training and experience.

Project Cost Blowout: Risks

Some of the major causes of project cost blowout have been discussed already. These include change management, training and a lack of software functionality. In addition, the customization and integration of software packages can make up a considerable component of total implementation costs. Changes to the vendor-supplied software or customizations usually build in upgrade costs, since additional testing of the changes is required during the upgrade. Generally, it is better not to customize. However, the organization needs to be sure that the vanilla solution can handle the major parts of its business. Other areas that are often underestimated include program interfaces, data conversions, report changes, integration testing, process rework and consequent increases in consulting fees. Unexpected project costs also may be hidden in business-area desktop computing budgets or in other IT infrastructure budgets.

Project Cost Blowout: Key Controls

The nature of the change management and training challenge (involving an understanding of the integration among business areas, the data flow through the organization and the impact of one area's actions in the system on another) that accompanies an ERP implementation needs to be presented to, and understood by, executive management. These programs need to be targeted and funded appropriately. Project cost overruns need to be identified early through effective reporting to the appropriate governance mechanism.

The business case should not be a static, one-time exercise intended to secure funding. On the contrary, the business case needs to be a dynamic and evolving management tool—one that should live beyond the go-live phase through the benefits-realization phase. Successful organizations use the business case tool in a variety of ways, including:

- Justifying the program
- Validating the design
- Setting postimplementation targets and managing them
- Prioritizing postimplementation change initiatives

Too often, the business case for an ERP implementation consists of a high-level mission statement or description of intangible, unquantified business benefits. A proven business case template should be employed and tailored to the organization's environment. Factors that should be considered include:

- Total cost of ownership, factoring in, for example, the additional cost of upgrading as a result of making software customizations
- Appropriate due diligence in determining benefit and cost items involving the input of variables and formulas for determining inventory, people savings, and conversion and integration costs
- A cash flow analysis, including appropriate risk factors and cost of capital

Measurements need to be initiated in the legacy system's environment to baseline costs and benefit streams so the improvements in the postimplementation ERP environment can be measured effectively.

Business Process/Functional

Business Process Reengineering: Risks

For users who are familiar with the functional orientation of a legacy system environment, it can be challenging to embrace the notion of an integrated ERP environment based on business processes. As with any integrated environment, errors in one part of the process may have effects throughout the processes. Reengineering of the business processes will most likely also result in structural and job role changes within the organization. Staff members who worked within the legacy environment for an extended period of time may find it difficult to adapt to new roles and, as a result, certain business functions may not be properly performed in the postimplementation environment. Also, there is a risk that the reengineered business processes may not have been configured properly, resulting in incorrect processing (e.g., incorrect tax indicators) or inadequate business controls (e.g., three-way match on purchases being bypassed).

Business Process Reengineering: Key Controls

The change management and training program needs to provide users with an appropriate overview and understanding of the impact of their actions on the process, system and others. Users need to be trained sufficiently, and the appropriate procedural controls need to be defined so users are able to execute their new roles in the new and integrated processes and system on the first day of going live.

Organizations, even those successful at implementing ERP, usually experience a temporary dip in performance after going live. Going live with an ERP is a significant change for any organization. The dip will vary among organizations, depending on how well they were prepared for the introduction of the new system. Most users need to walk before they run, and after mastering the basics on the live environment, they may require refresher training on the more advanced topics. The organization needs to be prepared for contingencies and the considerable effort often involved in correcting errors made in an online, real-time environment. This may require additional trained data entry or programming resources to correct data errors.

Configurable options need to be explained thoroughly to users and documented appropriately in the business requirements, design or blueprint documentation. Changes in the system of business controls need to be considered early in the implementation process and included in the design to minimize the cost of retrofitting controls at a later time.

Software Functionality: Risks

Organizations often find when they get down to the detail—or worse, when in the production phase—that the ERP solution cannot handle the major parts of their businesses. While the organization perceived that the vendor or reseller said that the solution could meet the business requirement, the requirement may not have been clearly specified or effectively detailed. Whatever the reason for the misunderstanding, if there is a fundamental mismatch between the system and the business need, the consequences may be costly.

Software Functionality: Key Controls

Management needs to take the time needed to effectively complete its due diligence on the new system. Appropriate software selection guidelines should be utilized, and factors to consider include:

- Others in the industry using the solution
- Particular local requirements
- Legislative or compliance requirements (e.g., tax, statutory reporting, industrial awards/agreements)

- Foreign currency handling (e.g., financial vs. management accounting treatment and reporting through time on a transaction and across country borders)
- Particular reporting requirements (e.g., external reporting and reconciliation needs)
- Impact that the loss of specific legacy system functionality may have on customer service (However, caution needs to be exercised prior to replicating legacy functionality; only if it is the best, or at least the better, process should the organization consider replicating it. It should not be replicated only because the organization is used to it.)
- Stability of the current software release
- Specific operational needs (e.g., handling fresh produce or livestock)
- Marketing needs (e.g., bulk discounting across product lines)

Further along in the implementation, adequate user acceptance, system and integrated testing need to be performed to ensure that the system performs as anticipated. System performance is another critical area that must be tested to ensure that the application and the related infrastructure can handle the typical transaction loads processed by the organization.

Application Security and Technical Infrastructure

Single Point of Failure: Risks

Within the legacy environment, the impact of a component failure within a system has limited, if any, impact on other systems. This is so, even in the case of a total loss of a particular application system. For example, a purchasing system could, in most cases, be managed through manual workarounds. In an ERP environment, where the whole enterprise may be reliant on the system, the loss of the system for any extended period of time is likely to have significant effects on the organization's operations and significant financial implications.

In the legacy system environment, systems could typically be unavailable for a few days before offsite and contingency facilities had to be invoked. In an ERP environment, the period of time between when the system is unavailable and when the contingency plan needs to be invoked is typically measured in hours.

Because the organization has moved to operating in an online, real-time mode, its business operations may be disrupted when the system is unavailable. For example, a distributor of perishable food went live with its ERP, utilizing a legacy front end that processed orders from field personnel using handheld devices. The process consisted of field personnel entering data into a legacy front end that, in turn, updated the ERP's back-end system. When the front-end legacy system failed—unable to handle the volume of data—the organization was forced to use manual data entry for orders completed by field personnel. The customer service personnel, with no experience in entering orders, made errors when entering the data. Orders were incorrect and out of sequence, and this played havoc with the back-end warehousing operations of the business. The warehousing personnel, also new to the system, had considerable difficulty dealing with incorrect order details, returns and corrections. Incorrect deliveries were made, inventory information became inaccurate and the entire episode resulted in a significant write-off.

At the core of the PeopleSoft system is a single relational database. This database utilizes complex technology to ensure that it can feed the system the necessary information to complete all business processes. The complexity of the database and the amount of information that is fed in and extracted from it requires careful controls to be instituted.

Single Point of Failure: Key Controls

Business continuity management plans need to be revised, taking into consideration the ERP as a single point of failure. Four characteristics of ERPs that may impact business continuity planning (BCP) are:

- The large number of modules that cover a broad range of the enterprise's business processes
- A large, integrated database
- The physical and logical intertwining of all modules and data, which may necessitate recovery at the same time
- An increase in the direct interface among ERPs suppliers and other third parties

Because of these characteristics, rapid recovery may necessitate a complete rethink and redesign of the organization's BCP arrangements.

Another point to consider is that an online, real-time system also needs an online, real-time business environment that can monitor effectively and deal with exceptions before they turn into significant problems and impact other areas. System maintenance and version control also are important in terms of maximizing system availability and integrity.

Distributed Computing Experience: Risks

Although it is sometimes overlooked, the IT architecture may be totally overhauled with the implementation of ERP. The organization may move from a centralized mainframe environment to a distributed client-server environment. New skills are required to manage and maintain this environment, and the impact of this change is often underestimated.

Figure 3.1 illustrates how complex an ERP technical environment can become. This environment is indicative of the environment on which PeopleSoft applications and legacy applications can be run (a client-server computer architecture). Depending upon the IT architecture used in the implementation, the audit may be centralized or decentralized. Extra care needs to be taken in scoping the first-year audit of organizations that have implemented ERP systems. In this type of environment, there is often a combination of centralized accounting controls and decentralized operational controls.

Figure 3.1—Complex ERP Technical Environment

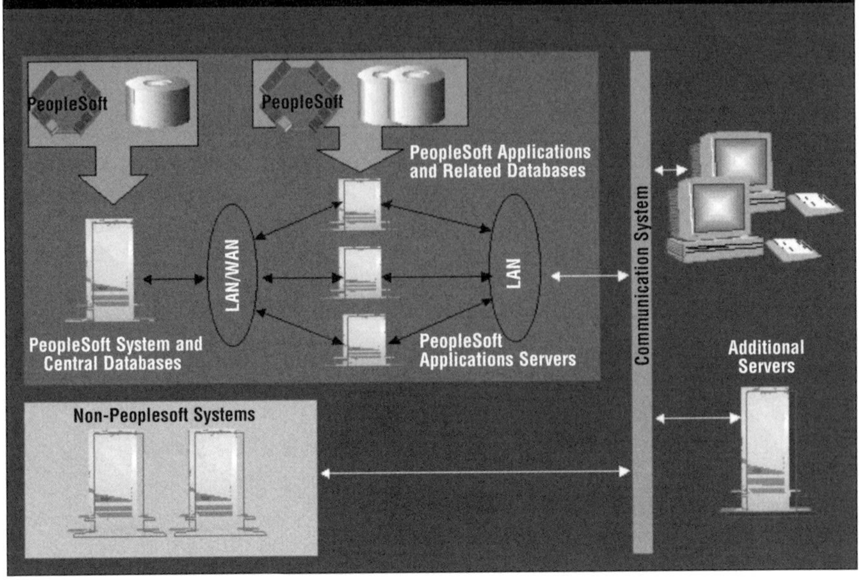

Distributed Computing Experience: Key Controls

The IT infrastructure requires the same planning as the business processes. IT staff may require training and may also need to develop new skills. These areas are often underestimated in the initial planning for an ERP implementation. IT staff may become extremely marketable following training in the new environment and, for that reason, it is advisable to consider retention and succession plans.

System Access: Risks

Bringing a number of the organization's applications together into one enterprisewide application potentially gives users more access to additional information and processing functions. Recent releases of certain ERP systems are designed to allow wireless or remote access for field and sales staff and, if necessary, customers and suppliers. This level of direct access to the system from remote locations allows the system to be kept up to date in real time. Yet, increased remote access may create an environment in which the system is far more susceptible to hacking or other malicious tampering. It may also increase the likelihood that incorrect data are introduced into the system.

System Access: Key Controls

PeopleSoft contains a number of security parameters covering passwords, intruder lockout, superuser access, etc., that, when set appropriately, serve to secure the system. Other ERP systems have varying degrees of security functionality; some require add-on packages to adequately secure them. User access to the system should be designed and built in accordance with the organization's security policy or needs. Some of the factors to be considered include:

- The segregation of access/duties

- The provision of access to only the transactions or objects required by users to perform their jobs or process roles
- The provision of access based on risk assessment of the consequences of providing the additional access vs. the cost of implementing tighter security (e.g., access to view all plants vs. maintaining separate security profiles for users in each plant)

Security is covered in greater detail in chapter 4, ERP Audit Approach.

Data Conversion and Program Interfaces

Data Quality: Risks

As an ERP system may be reliant on a single, central database, the integrity of the data within it is paramount. Data fed from legacy systems may be inaccurate, incomplete or duplicated, resulting in operational difficulties in a more automated and integrated environment. For example, a higher education institution converted its supplier master file complete with fax numbers for each supplier. In the new ERP environment, it moved to online faxing of purchase orders on approval by the appropriate delegated authority. As some of the fax numbers were out of date, a number of faxes were misdirected or lost. Further, the organization had implemented the ERP solution with a third party's middleware and was unable to receive fax completion or OK messages without logging off the ERP system and logging on again. Data can also be locked away in the complex data structures of ERP systems. Finally, as e-business opportunities increase and prevail, the ability to unlock the data within the ERP will become increasingly important. Data quality is also becoming more important in the e-enabled ERP environment, as external parties access invoice and financial information via the Internet.

Data Quality: Key Controls

All data should be effectively cleansed prior to loading them into the organization's ERP system. Cleansed information should be secured while awaiting conversion to the ERP environment. Control techniques, such as control totals (often embodied in ERP conversion and load utilities) and data editing criteria, should be employed as appropriate. Mock conversions should be performed and financial reports reconciled between the two systems during the mock and final conversions to confirm the completeness and accuracy of the data conversion. Data conversion is an area of key importance for an organization and its auditors.

Program Interfaces: Risks

While ERPs enable many different types of functions to be completed, some organizations have requirements that are not met by an enterprise application program or need to transfer information with suppliers, customers and financial institutions. As a result, program interfaces are established to transfer transactional information among these systems. If interfaces are not controlled effectively, there is a risk of inaccurate, incomplete, unauthorized or untimely information being fed into the ERP system or extracted from it.

Program Interfaces: Key Controls

Controls over program interfaces are similar to those operating over data conversions, except they may be performed in an interactive manner rather than in batch mode. Further, the timing of the program interface can often be significant, particularly where there are a number of program interfaces that must be executed within a short processing window.

The Importance of Establishing a Control Framework

A control framework for an ERP environment can create a robust management tool and methodology for ascertaining the risks associated with an ERP environment and a standard for defining the established controls. This can be achieved by:
• Establishing an organizational control framework
• Defining the control framework for an ERP environment

Establishing an Organizational Control Framework

The Committee of Sponsoring Organizations of the Treadway Commission (COSO) developed a model for evaluating internal controls with the objective of helping organizational management improve its entity's internal control systems and provide a common understanding of internal control among interested parties. This model has been adopted as the generally accepted framework for internal control and is widely recognized as the definitive standard against which organizations measure the effectiveness of their internal control systems. The framework defines internal control as:

> *...a process, effected by an entity's board of directors, management and other personnel, designed to provide reasonable assurance of the achievement of objectives in the following categories:*
> • *Effectiveness and efficiency of operations*
> • *Reliability of financial reporting*
> • *Compliance with applicable laws and regulations.*[7]

The framework defines five interrelated components of internal control:
• Control environment
• Risk assessment
• Control activities
• Information and communication
• Monitoring

The COSO framework is an effective starting ground for defining an organization's internal control framework and methodology with regard to an ERP environment. It can then be used for defining the elements of a control environment that are specific to an ERP implementation.

[7] COSO, *Internal Control—Integrated Framework*, 2004

Defining the Control Framework for an ERP Environment

The implementation of an ERP system can introduce new risks and alter an organization's risk profile. As a result, an organization needs to redefine its approach toward risk management and control assessment to cater to the different risks in an ERP environment and achieve complete coverage of the associated management controls. A framework is required to facilitate the assessment of risk and the completeness of controls. There are several frameworks that can be adopted to model the ERP control environment. One that is consistent with the ERP business process-driven approach and works well in practice is outlined in **figure 3.2**.

Figure 3.2—The ERP Environment and Process and System Integrity

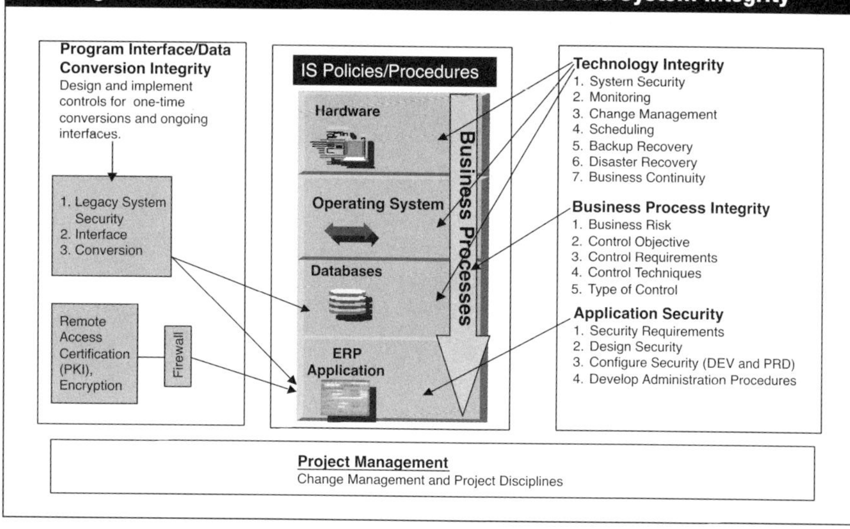

The control framework consists of the following five areas:

- Business process controls, which include automated (e.g., online approval, three-way matching of purchase order amounts, goods receipt quantities and invoice particulars) and manual (e.g., reconciliations, manual approvals, review of exception reports) controls within the reengineered business processes. Business process controls are most cost-effective when incorporated from the beginning of the project throughout the design and development phase. Retrofitting controls after the implementation is often costly.
- Application security, which includes maintenance of roles and permission lists that provide access to application functionality and system services. It includes user, system and security administration procedures, and it incorporates the setting of security parameters (e.g., password lengths) and the granting and removing of user access to the PeopleSoft application system.
- Program interface and conversion controls, which also need to be considered within the framework to address the risks associated with converting or interfacing data from legacy or external systems

- Technology infrastructure, which includes controls surrounding the technology platform on which the application resides. The technology infrastructure consists of the servers, operating system, database and network layers.
- Project management, specifically the aspect of the control framework relating to change management and project disciplines discussed in this chapter in the Project Management and Governance section.

Summary

This chapter outlined key risks and controls associated with the implementation of ERP systems. Key risks include change management, cost blowout, single point of failure and data conversions. Associated key controls include executive sponsorship, training, backup and recovery, data cleansing, and control totals. This chapter also introduced the increased emphasis on governance and the importance of establishing a framework of internal control. This led to a conclusion regarding the need for organizations to redefine their approach to risk management in an ERP environment and the importance of establishing a control framework to facilitate the assessment of risks and the completeness of controls.

4. ERP Audit Approach

Audit Impacts Arising From the Implementation of ERP

The nature and manner of auditing an organization that has implemented or is in the process of implementing an ERP system may need to change dramatically. Based on the organization embracing an ERP package solution, it is more important than ever for audit to address the new environment through or in the following ways:

- Change management
- Audit methodology
- Auditor role
- Audit involvement in the project
- Audit responsibilities

Change Management

Audit needs to manage the change to an ERP environment focusing on two key aspects:

- Staffing—The complexity of the environment usually requires a staffing model with a higher ratio of information systems auditors. Traditional financial and operational auditors must transform to become integrated auditors understanding the nature of ERP and dependencies among different subprocesses. The audits of complex and technical areas may need to be supplemented by skilled and experienced resources.
- Training—Auditors need to learn security and control implementation methodology and may need to attend ERP training, join ERP user groups and learn new tools to effectively audit ERP. A detailed knowledge of ERP is necessary to effectively understand security and control issues over application areas and the technical environment. Extensive training is necessary to adequately understand the new environment.

Audit Methodology

Significant reengineering of the audit approach needs to be undertaken within the new ERP environment. The organization's concept of its audit universe may need to change to audit the new system effectively. A risk assessment should be performed, and the audit approach should be modified accordingly.

Integrated audits covering business process and security aspects are necessary in the ERP environment. Segregation of duties and security management come together in risk management of the new reengineered business process. Trade-offs in separation of duties are made and compensated by automated controls, such as object-level security, release strategies, master data validation and tolerance levels. Further, effective audit practices in the ERP environment require new automated diagnostic tools. ERPs have powerful and complex security arrangements, and testing security is not just a matter of looking up the security matrix of users to functions. Composite security profiles may be used, and unravelling these to find out who has access to what often requires the use of automated diagnostic tools available from third parties.

PeopleSoft software is flexible, yet complex, and can be customized to fit each organization's environment. The configuration of business processes and degree of customization, the scope of the implementation, and the version of PeopleSoft software all contribute to the uniqueness of the environment. Therefore, it is not possible to design one standard audit program that will work in every PeopleSoft environment.

Role of the Auditor

There are a number of opportunities where audit can and should contribute to the organization's ERP implementation. The role(s) chosen will depend on the circumstances and the organization's audit charter/strategy. The different levels of involvement that audit may have in the project may be characterized as follows:
- Project assurance
- Preimplementation review
- Postimplementation review
- Quality assurance

Project Assurance

Organizations using the integrated method focus on the design and implementation of controls for the new systems. This approach requires audit to be involved from the earliest stage of the project, helping the project team design and build the controls. It considers project risks and business process risk assessment and requires auditors to perform testing to ensure that controls have been implemented properly and benefits have been pursued.

Preimplementation Review

The preimplementation review approach allows the auditor to conduct a review of the controls design and implementation plans at an appropriate time before going live. It usually involves a review of:
- The business case
- Project risk
- Application security design
- Data conversion and program interface controls
- Business process risk assessment and controls design

The preimplementation review may also include project management aspects, such as a review of:
- Performance measurement criteria
- User readiness to go live (e.g., adequacy of training provided, quality of user operating procedures)

A preimplementation review is obviously sensible, as issues generally can be addressed before the system is put in place. This is usually a far more cost-effective approach than reconfiguring the system after it is operational.

Postimplementation Review

Another role that the auditor can undertake in the project is to conduct a postimplementation review. It focuses on the implementation of controls for the new system and, as the name suggests, is conducted after the system has been implemented. This type of review considers:

- Control assessment of business processes
- Application security assessment
- Data conversion and program interface controls
- Achievement of project objectives and business case
- User satisfaction and outstanding issues

Audits in the first year after implementation may be particularly complicated if the auditor has no prior involvement. This is because the organization is in a state of significant change, with the organization conducting business in a markedly new way with the implementation and acceptance of an ERP system. New systems and processes need to be documented, and this may be time consuming, depending on the availability of existing documentation from the user team. Further, it may be challenging to get all of the information that is needed to conduct an audit because:

- Critical information may not be known
- Resources may not be available
- There may be processing problems, if all things were not considered during implementation
- The system may have some defects that could affect data integrity

The process of auditing may be further complicated by the fact that little knowledge of or experience in auditing this new environment exists within the organization. In particular, audit tools and methodologies may not be sufficiently mature or robust for the new environment.

Change management is a key consideration, particularly during the early stages after the go-live date when many changes may still be proposed (and made) to the implemented system. Adequate, structured change management processes should be in place to support the authorized and appropriate development, testing and migration of changes through to the production environment. These processes should include the existence of adequate policies, procedures and control mechanisms surrounding the implementation of changes such as:

- Restriction of access to the separate instances to maintain segregation of duties
- Lock down of production instances
- Formal change requests with justification, impact analysis and back-out plans
- Appropriate approval
- Stakeholder involvement in the design of test plans

- Program, integration, stress and user acceptance testing
- Approval of testing results and migration to production

A postimplementation review should ensure that such processes and mechanisms have been followed. Furthermore, it is important that policies and procedures are made available covering all aspects of the system administration to help maintain its ongoing integrity.

Quality Assurance

The final and most complex role that an auditor may undertake is in the performance of a quality assurance audit. This approach requires the auditor's participation throughout the life of the project and, as such, is the most comprehensive approach. It focuses on the overall quality of the business process reengineering program and considers specific deliverables at each key project milestone.

Audit Involvement in the Project

While the approach that is adopted will vary according to the organization implementing the ERP, the most effective approach usually involves audit having an extensive and active involvement during the implementation project. Involvement throughout the implementation allows audit to contribute to the establishment of the most effective control environment possible, as controls are built in during configuration, along with other changes. If this approach is adopted, an external or independent party may need to be called on to perform any postimplementation review.

New security, audit and control tools may need to be developed/acquired to facilitate the effective implementation, operation and review of the control environment. Whichever approach is adopted, it is worth reiterating that it is far more cost-effective to address issues during implementation than to reconfigure the system after implementation. It is also worth noting that audit's role remains ongoing after the implementation, during the stabilization phase and continuing into the review of future enhancements.

Audit Responsibilities

Each environment needs to be evaluated on an individual basis from a risk perspective. A combined team needs to decide on the extent of involvement from the financial, operational and computer audit groups. In addition, subject matter specialists, such as tax personnel, may be needed to supplement the team. There are no hard-and-fast rules to split roles and responsibilities among the internal audit groups. An evaluation needs to be made as to how the roles and responsibilities should be defined. The important issues are that users and management should have a seamless and efficient audit and a well-integrated and knowledgeable team.

However, external auditors should carefully observe relevant auditing guidelines, regulations and laws, such as the US Sarbanes-Oxley Act, to consider the possibility of potential impairment of professional independence and conflict of interest in accepting the level of involvement in the implementation.

Recommended PeopleSoft Audit Framework

In the last chapter, the need for a control framework to facilitate the assessment of risk and the completeness of management controls was identified. The audit framework in **figure 4.1** shows the key components of an ERP environment from an audit perspective.

Figure 4.1—Audit Framework

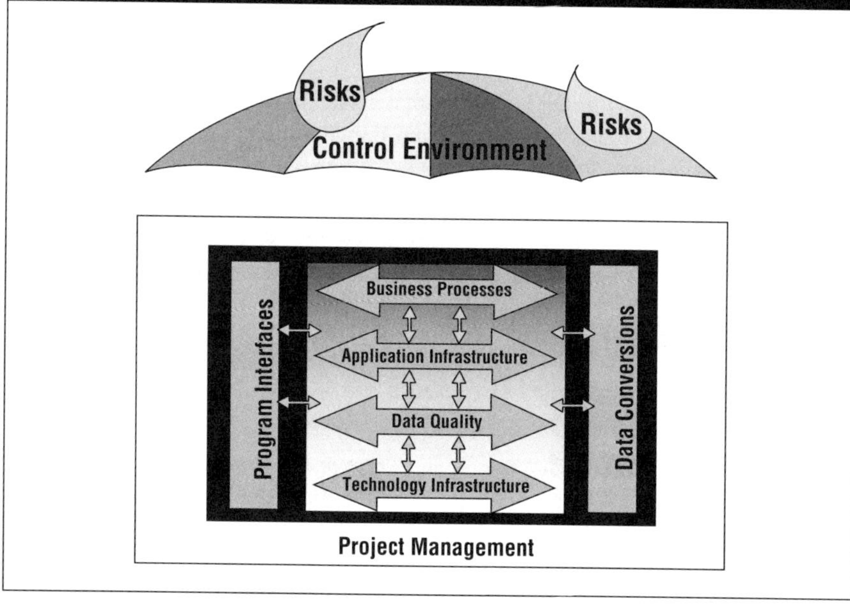

The first component of this audit framework is business processes (also referred to as business cycles). As noted earlier in this guide, PeopleSoft is an integrated application system, so it is important to assess the end-to-end business processes when performing risk and control assessments.

A PeopleSoft enterprise control environment will have controls driven by the business cycle that are more automated and focused on prevention (rather than detection). Compare this with a legacy IT system where controls may have been manually intensive, detective in nature and dispersed across different departments. An ERP system is pervasive throughout the organization and the whole framework of controls needs to be considered. A risk at the beginning of the process may be mitigated by a key control at another point in the process or a series of compensating controls throughout the process. While the primary concern when auditing a PeopleSoft system should be with the business process, the auditor then needs to know what system functionality needs to be audited. For that reason, it is important for the auditor to obtain an understanding of the relationship between audit business processes or business cycles and the PeopleSoft applications.

Note that the definition of business cycles may differ among organizations. For example, the Expenditure and Inventory cycles may be combined into a larger cycle called Purchase-to-pay. In this case, however, assessing it separately may be preferable since the Expenditure cycle links to other cycles, such as Asset Management. The Revenue cycle is sometimes referred to as Quote-to-cash. However, service organizations may have a derivative of the above, e.g., a higher education institution may refer to the revenue cycle as Enrollment-to-cash, and instead of an Inventory cycle, it might have a student education cycle involving Admission-to-graduation.

Organizations dealing with large projects may have a Project Accounting cycle, which essentially combines the Revenue and Expenditure cycles and tracks the revenue and expenditure for particular projects to completion. **Figure 4.2** illustrates these relationships.

Figure 4.2—Linking Audit Cycles to PeopleSoft Applications

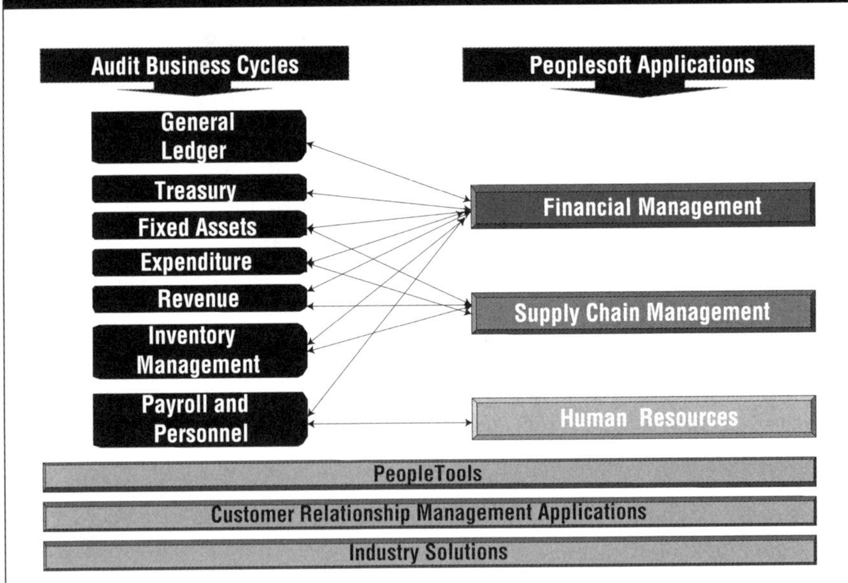

The Financial Accounting cycle (involving the setting up of the chart of accounts, the processing of journal entries and the preparation of the financial statements)

and the Treasury cycle (involving borrowing, managing cash and investments, and managing derivative transactions) link directly into the Financial Management applications (e.g., GL, Cash Management, Deal Management) in PeopleSoft. The operational business cycles of Human Resources and Payroll (discussed in more detail in chapters 5 through 8) link to the Human Resources Management System (HRMS) and the Financial Management applications. The Revenue, Expenditure and Inventory cycles link to the Financial Management applications (e.g., receivables, purchasing and payables) and the Supply Chain Management applications (e.g., order management, production management and inventory). The PeopleSoft Industry Solutions do not relate to individual audit business processes; rather, they function across all the business processes. For example, the PeopleSoft for Higher Education industry solution encompasses student administration, HRMS, and financial management for education and government (within the Financial Management application). Other functions that cross over all audit business processes are the tools and utilities contained within PeopleTools and the web portals that may be implemented.

Figure 4.3 illustrates the relationships among the business cycles. Sales are made in the Revenue cycle, generating a demand for the production of finished goods from the Inventory cycle. Production of goods necessitates the purchase of raw materials through the Expenditure cycle. All of this activity is recorded online in real time in the Financial Accounting cycle and secured within the Application Security Infrastructure component.

Figure 4.3—Core Business Cycles

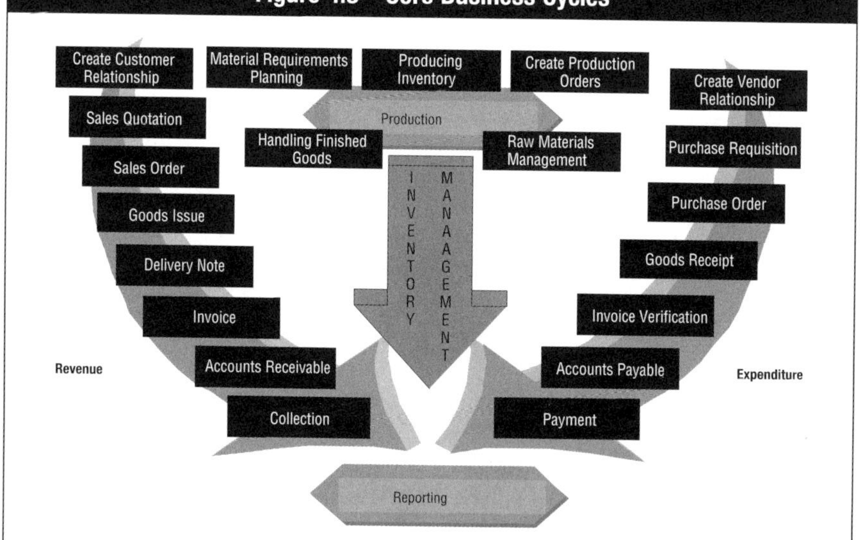

By way of example, auditing the core HRMS business cycles is described in chapter 6, Auditing PeopleSoft HR Business Cycle, and chapter 8, Auditing PeopleSoft Payroll Business Cycle.

The application infrastructure components (see **figure 4.4**) can be broken down into major subcomponents relating to application infrastructure functions and the PeopleTools used.

Figure 4.4—Application Infrastructure Components

Function	PeopleTools and Utilities
Development and integration	• Application Designer • PeopleCode • Business Process Designer • Application Engine • Workflow Administrator • EDI Manager
Data management	• Cube Manager • Data Mover • Tree Manager • Mass Change
Operations	• Process Schedule Manager • Process Monitor
Security administration	• Maintain Security

Auditing the PeopleSoft Application Infrastructure tools and utilities illustrated in **figure 4.1** is described in chapter 10, Auditing PeopleSoft Application Security. The other major components of the control framework can be broken down in a similar manner. Audit of these other components is not unique to an ERP environment and is covered in other ISACA and ITGI publications, such as COBIT 4.0.[8]

Adopting a Risk-based Audit Approach

Having broken down the control framework into its components and subcomponents, a risk-based audit approach can be undertaken. (This guide assumes the adoption of a contemporary risk-based audit approach to the audit of the PeopleSoft environment.) This may involve:
- Gaining an understanding of the environment
- Identifying the significant risks in the PeopleSoft ERP environment
- Determining key controls required
- Testing those controls to confirm their adequacy

Techniques for gaining an understanding of the business process or function of the component or subcomponent under review include:
- Reviewing systems implementation or process documentation
- Interviewing implementors and others knowledgeable in the area
- Developing process flow diagrams and descriptions

[8] IT Governance Institute, COBIT 4.0, USA, 2005

Once an understanding of the area under review has been obtained, there are many techniques for identifying significant risks. Some techniques that may be employed include:

- Utilizing a checklist approach (This technical guide will provide a checklist for risks, controls and testing techniques in the areas of core business cycles and the PeopleSoft Application Security Infrastructure component in chapters 6, 7, 8 and 10.)
- Using history or past experience (The risks included in this technical guide are based largely on past experience.)
- Determining objectives for the implementation and assessing of potential or existing barriers
- Analyzing the regulatory requirements and adherence to policy or procedures
- Adopting and applying the CobiT framework
- Utilizing a systems audit approach that considers inputs from the system, processing or calculations, and outputs from the system
- Adopting a quality management perspective
- Performing a strategic analysis (e.g., a strengths, weaknesses, opportunities and threats [SWOT] analysis or applying portfolio theory analysis)
- Questioning assumptions being made for implementing the ERP system
- Assessing the needs of various stakeholders and the extent to which they are being met by the implemented system
- Evaluating hot spots (e.g., looking at the best and worst instances/population strata, key person dependencies, security issues, going concern or business continuity issues, integration or conversion difficulties, valuations, accountabilities, and reconciliations)
- Ascertaining that updated patches have been applied to the system and assessing the potential risks of errors in system processing and operations due to unapplied patches

After identifying the significant risks, key controls need to be determined. Determining the key controls involves:

- Understanding the controls culture of the organization (e.g., a just-enough-control philosophy is employed consistent with the pursuit of an overall cost leadership position in the industry, or a belts-and-braces philosophy is employed consistent with the pursuit of a position of differentiation based on image, product, distribution or service characteristics that needs to be protected)
- Exercising judgment to determine the key controls in the process or function and whether the controls structure is adequate (Any weaknesses in the control structure need to be reported to executive management and resolved.)

There are four basic types of control in an ERP environment:

- Manual controls—Management controls, such as report monitoring and manual reconciliations or approvals

- Inherent controls—Controls built into the operation of the system, such as edit and validation routines and certain password controls preventing the reuse of the last five passwords, passwords containing any three-character string contained in the user ID, and passwords beginning with three identical characters
- Configuration settings—Customized options at installation or at a later time that control and direct processing operations in the system
- Logical access security—Restricted access to computer system functions based on the ERP and technical infrastructure security authorization techniques

These key controls need to be tested to confirm that they are operating effectively and as intended by management. The control testing techniques described in this guide focus on configurable controls and logical access security because:
- Manual controls are not unique to an ERP environment, and testing techniques already have been covered in other forums and literature
- Automated controls, such as inherent configuration settings and logical access security, tend to be more pervasive in an ERP environment
- Inherent controls are essentially built into the PeopleSoft software and, therefore, do not require controls testing

PeopleSoft Configuration Concept and Testing Configurable Controls

As with other application packages, configuration settings allow organizations tremendous flexibility to customize and direct the operation and processing of PeopleSoft software in their environment. The PeopleSoft application programs read the configuration settings, and processing is directed accordingly. Configuration settings are stored as values in tables within the PeopleSoft software.

Testing of configurable controls may be performed by:
- Inspecting specific data held within pages (e.g., password parameter settings can be viewed via Home→PeopleTools→Security→Password Configuration→Password Controls)
- Running reports utilizing PeopleSoft Query Manager or SQR

PeopleSoft Security Authorization Concept

Within the PeopleSoft software, the security permissions concept provides for the protection of programs and data from unauthorized use. Access to the system is defined through the use of user profiles. In many cases, the security requirements of groups of users may be common, and roles and permission lists are created to aid the administration of individuals' access security rights. **Figure 4.5** shows how users are assigned roles that determine the specific access granted.

Security administration is performed using the security component of the PeopleSoft PeopleTools tool set.

Figure 4.5—Security Authorization Concept

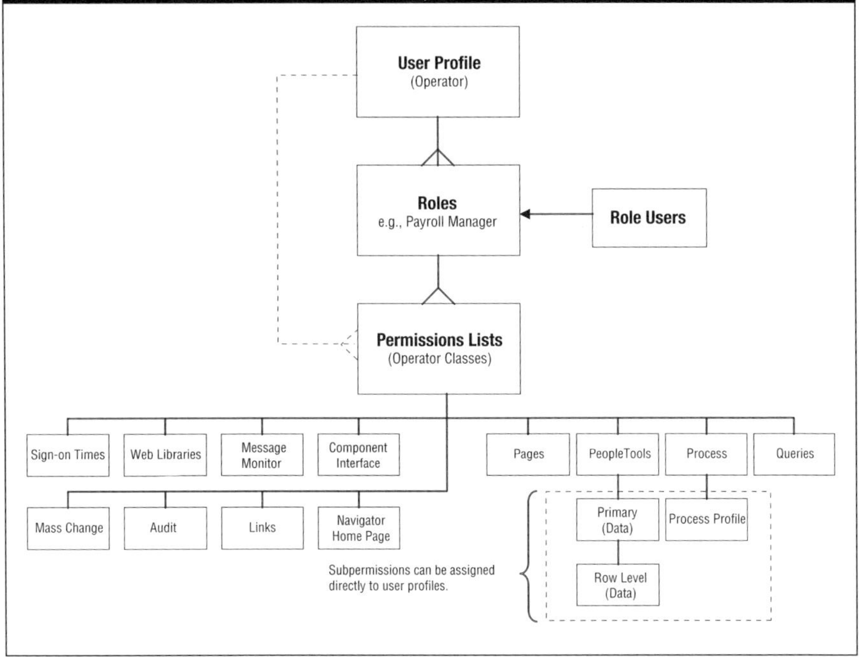

User Profile

A user profile is a set of data that describes a particular user of the PeopleSoft system. A user profile is identified by a user ID. Security-related information, such as passwords and general attributes (e.g., e-mail ID and language code), are maintained in the user profile. It is also here that workflow information is administered. Workflow attributes are assigned for situations when a user is not available (e.g., on vacation). This allows alternate user IDs to be assigned worklists (tasks to complete) while the primary user is away. An effective time period can be specified, and pending worklists can be reassigned to the alternate user. From an audit perspective, it is important to determine whether the alternate user is an appropriate user to ensure that he/she complies with the policies and procedures of the organization.

It should be noted that a user has no access by default, and access to pages and functions must be explicitly granted by the security administrator through the assignment of roles and permission lists described in the following section.

Workflow enables the integration of the automated processes within PeopleSoft with the business processes of an organization. The tasks of individual users are normally part of a larger business process involving multiple users, potentially across multiple departments. Workflow enables the results of these tasks (workflow items) to be routed to the subsequent user in the process (e.g., a purchase requisition once approved by one user is then automatically routed to the purchase order clerk for submission to the supplier).

Role

A role relates to a function(s) or job(s) within a business (e.g., accounts payable clerk, payroll manager). One or more roles may be assigned to a user profile depending on the responsibilities and functions performed by that user. A role is a collection of permission lists that provide access to the functions and subfunctions required to perform a job role.

Role users are user profiles or users who have membership to a particular role. Users inherit most of the permissions from the roles assigned to the user profile. Administration of roles can be decentralized using the Role Grant function. PeopleSoft also provides the ability for members of one role to grant other specified roles to an existing user profile. This functionality is useful if, for example, a manager of a business unit has some devolved security administration responsibilities for his/her business unit.

That manager will be granted security privileges to be able to assign a specific set of roles to other users. A security administrator should set the Role Grant function to ensure that the manager cannot grant roles greater than or outside of his/her own system access privileges. In this situation, the manager will not be able to grant himself/herself additional access.

Auditing of PeopleSoft should take this into consideration as part of a review. It is important to ensure that the Role Grant function can be applied only to subordinates in the security hierarchy (i.e., a manager should be able to update only an employee's user profile— maybe within his/her business units—not his/her own profile or the profiles of other managers).

Permission Lists

Permission lists are linked to roles and should be aligned with the business processes and functions to which a specific role requires access. They provide the basic mechanism by which access is restricted and segregation of duties is enforced. PeopleSoft comes packaged with a number of predefined permission lists. However, these generally provide more access than most users require in a production environment. Some of these predefined permission lists, such as ALLPAGES, provide very high levels of access, and these should be examined by organizations to determine if they are appropriate for use in their environment. It is considered better practice for an organization to define its own permission lists, as opposed to using those that are delivered predefined.

Through the administration of permission lists, access to the following functions and subfunctions is provided:

- General
- Pages
- PeopleTools
  - Application Designer Access (Object, Tools, Miscellaneous)
  - Data Mover Access
  - Object Security Access
- Process
  - Process Group
  - Process Profile
- Sign-on Times
- Component Interfaces
- Message Monitor
- Web Libraries
- Personalizations
- Query
  - Access Group Permissions
  - Query Profile
- Mass Change
- Links
- Audit
- Permission List Queries

While permissions are normally linked to user profiles via one or more roles, it is possible to assign permissions lists containing the following functions directly to user profiles:

- Navigator Homepage (This determines the initial business process map displayed.)
- Process Profile (This determines the access to run batch processes in the Process Scheduler.)
- Primary and Row Level Security (These determine the user's access to data. Whether the primary or secondary permissions are used is dependent on the application.)

Permission lists control which pages a user (or role) can access. The type or level of access (i.e., display, update) related to the permission list is defined through action types, discussed in the following section. This determines what a user can actually do with the information and data accessible through a particular page.

Permission lists also determine other parameters, such as the time of day that the user may log into the system or the maximum period of inactivity before the user is automatically timed out. These are described further in chapter 9, PeopleSoft Application and Technical Infrastructure.

Pages and Page Security

Pages are the individual screens that a user sees and interfaces with when using PeopleSoft. These allow users to access data in the database without performing SQL commands. A page group is a logical grouping of related pages. The group normally forms the items on a menu. Security within PeopleSoft is controlled by restricting user access to menu items or pages (screens). Since access to a page is obtained via a menu, restricting a user's menu options (either an entire menu or specific menu items) restricts the information the user can access via a page. Access to pages is defined within the related permission lists (see **figure 4.6**). The actions that users are able to perform on the information or data to which they have access can be restricted (see **figure 4.7**). In considering the different actions that can be assigned to a user and the associated audit risks, it is important to take into account the timing factor. Certain action types within PeopleSoft allow historic (as well as current and future) information to be viewed and edited.

Figure 4.6—Page Access Defined

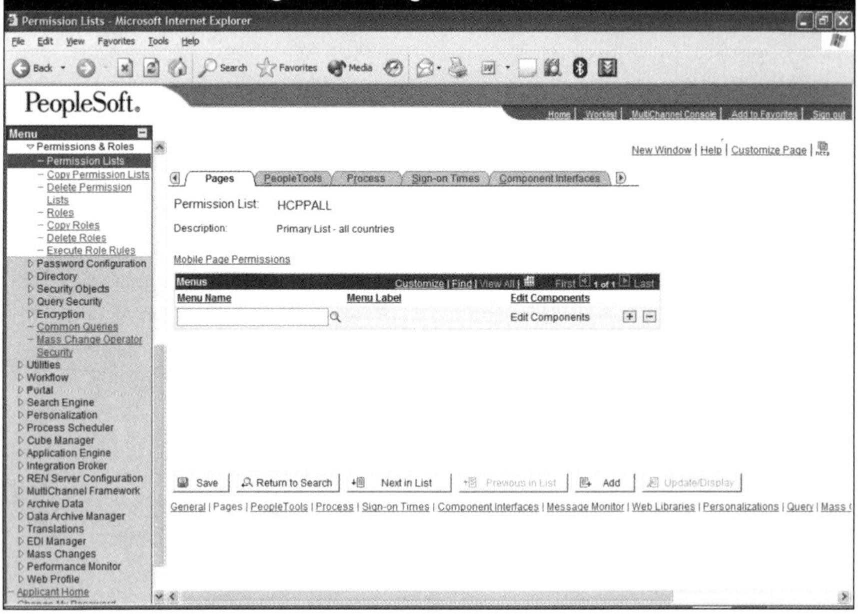

The following action types may be assigned:

- No Access—A user does not have access to change or view data.
- Display Only—A user has access to view current and future information but not to edit that information.
- Add—A user has access to add new future data (rows).
- Update/Display—A user has access to view current and future information held on a page, but has the access to edit future-dated data only.
- Update/Display All—A user has access to view historic, current and future information held on a page, but has the access to edit future-dated data only.

Figure 4.7—User Restrictions

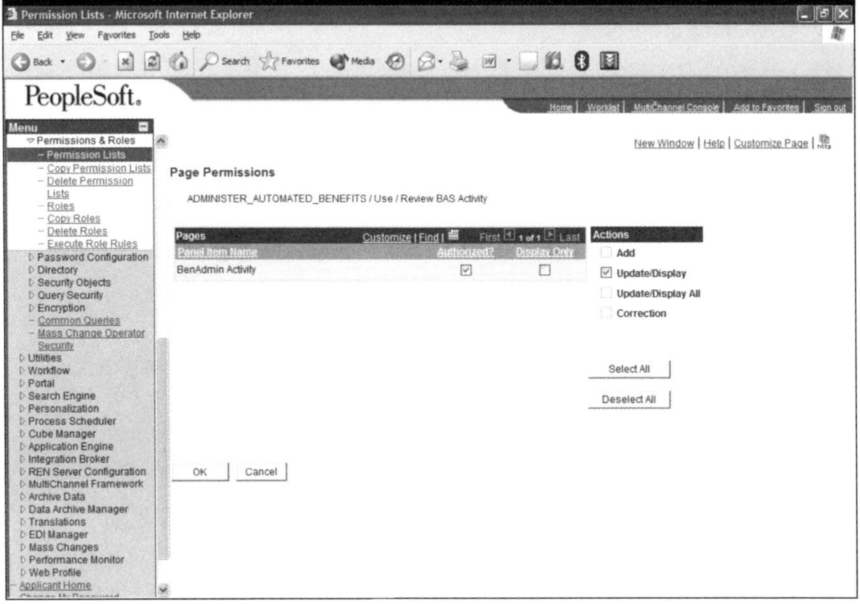

- Correction—A user with correction mode access has access to view and edit all data irrespective of the date of creation. This allows changes to historic, current and future-dated data. This type of access may have a potential impact on historic reporting from the system and, as such, should be granted only in special circumstances.

Access to default permission lists, such as ALLPAGES and HCPPALL, should be examined, and it is important to restrict access to them. The role and permission lists definition should be performed based on the access requirements of a job or function (e.g., payroll manager) rather than the user's perception of his/her access requirements. It should also be noted that where more than one permission list provides access to a particular page, the greatest level of access is provided to the user.

Process Security

A process within PeopleSoft may be a program, a batch job, a report, an interface transfer or any activity that requires a number of tasks to be performed within the system. Such processes are run and managed by the Process Scheduler within PeopleSoft. It is possible to restrict access to certain processes within PeopleSoft by establishing process groups. A batch process is assigned a process group when created. That process group is then linked to a permission list, as shown in **figure 4.8**. The permission list is then assigned to a role and, subsequently, a user ID. A process profile is also linked to a permission list. A process profile defines the settings for the process scheduler/monitor for users who have been assigned that permission list.

Figure 4.8—Process Group Link to Permission List

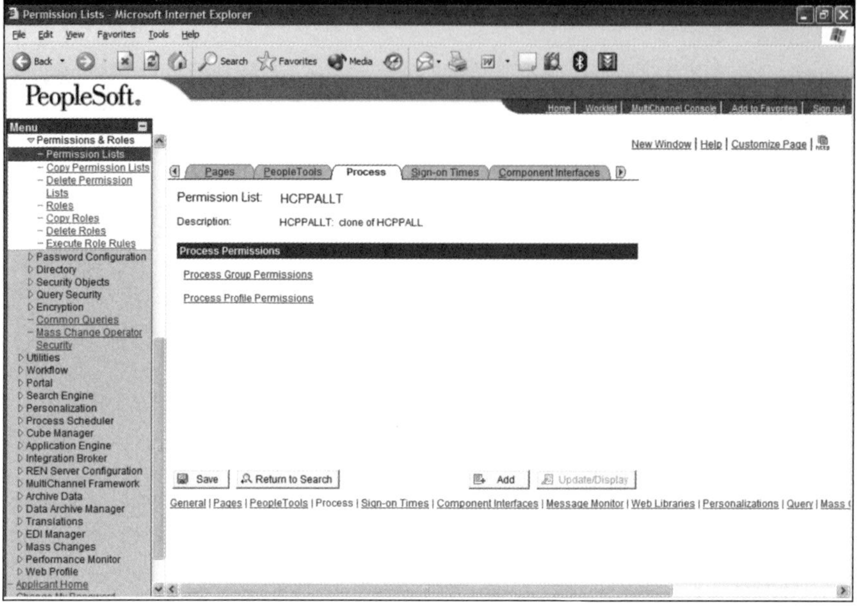

Query

PeopleSoft provides the ability to run *ad hoc* queries to access data (in the form of SQL queries), in addition to the information generated via standard reports. This is done via the Query tool. It may be necessary to restrict access to not only the Query tool function, but also the data records upon which queries are run. Query users should have access only to the information to which they would normally have access via menu options and pages. This is done by setting up query access groups and linking these to query trees and permission lists, as shown in **figure 4.9**.

Audit

Audit provides a facility to track the last change to a permission list, including the date and time of the change and the user ID responsible for the change, as shown in **figure 4.10**.

Links

The Links page details a list of links to other security settings outside the security area of PeopleSoft to which the specific permission list has access. The Links page allows links to be added easily to other pages within a PeopleSoft system that pertain to a particular permission list. For example, a PeopleSoft application may require a specific security setting to be attached to a permission list. If the application-specific setting appears on a page, a link can be added to the permission list, so that anyone updating the permission list can quickly and easily navigate to it.

Figure 4.9—Query Access Group Links

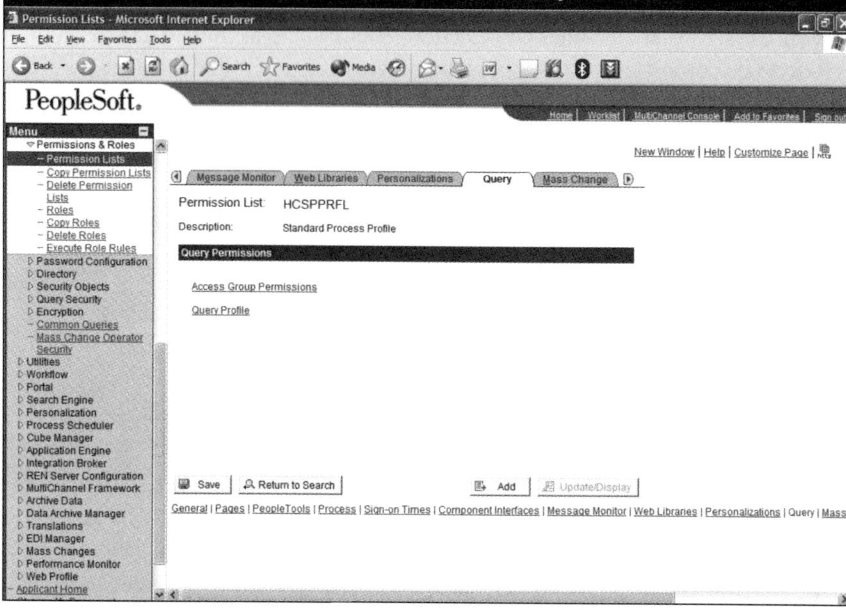

Figure 4.10—Permission List Audit Trail

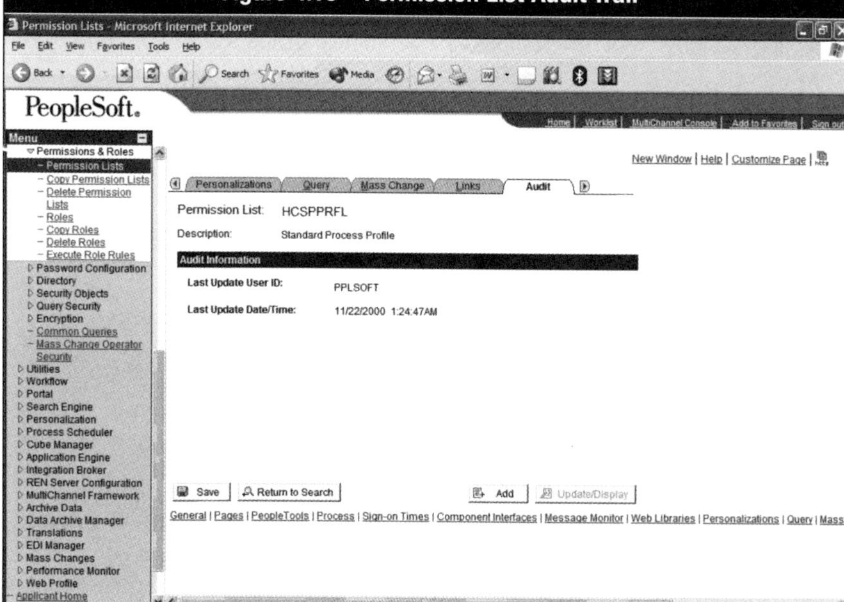

Component Interfaces

Component Interfaces provide access to a PeopleSoft application from another system. Therefore, if a business transaction requires data to flow to another system to be completed, the user must be provided access to the relevant component interface. This particular function lists the component interfaces that the permission list has access to use.

Message Monitor

Message Monitor provides the user with access to application messages in the system. These application messages detail the status of processes running in the system, e.g., a report request.

Mass Change

Mass Change contains a list of mass change templates to which the permission list has access. Mass Change is an SQL generator used to perform updates to large amounts of data.

Object Security

Object Security controls/administers access to the database object definitions (e.g., tree structures, records and fields) held within rows at the table level within PeopleTools. These are created using the Application Designer, and PeopleTools stores the definitions in the underlying PeopleTools tables. Object groups or group IDs are defined and linked to permission lists. An object group is a collection of one or more objects that form a logical group for security purposes. Objects need to be protected so that unauthorized users cannot alter data within the database. Object Security prevents/restricts changes to the application by limiting user access record definitions. Object security can be applied only to object groups—not to individual objects. To ensure comprehensive object security, every object must be assigned to at least one object group. If an object is not assigned to any object group, anyone with access to the PeopleTools menu items will have update access to it.

Application Data Security

Application Data Security is addressed by trees, row security and field access restriction.

Tree Manager

PeopleSoft trees are objects that can be used to define and graphically represent the hierarchy that exists within a department or organizational unit. These objects can be used for security and reporting purposes. A tree is linked with query security, where database record components (which can be one or more rows of a table) are grouped together and represented under the nodes on the tree. Users are assigned to query access groups associated with a particular node, and they have access only to the data held within the records associated with those nodes.

Row

Access to data within PeopleSoft database tables can be restricted via Row Security. This allows, for example, two groups of users to access the same pages (or menu options) via the standard permission list security, but at the same time restricts access to the different sets of data obtained through those pages. For example, in PeopleSoft HRMS, user access to update employee data is restricted to the employee's own department or business unit. Two user IDs may have the same role assigned to them and, as a consequence, the same primary permission lists (defining the menu options and pages), but a secondary permission list is assigned where the specific business unit, project, analysis group or pay cycle is defined to restrict the data that are accessed, as shown in **figure 4.11**. This data restriction could also include restricting access to the user's own records in the database.

Figure 4.11—Secondary Permission List

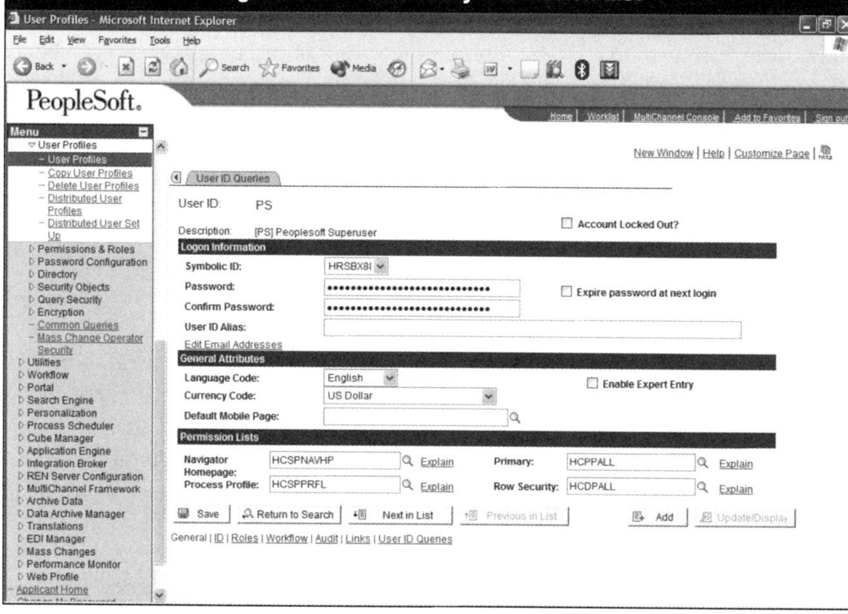

Field

PeopleSoft security can be further extended to restrict user access to specific fields on a page. For example, it may be necessary to grant access to certain HRMS pages but restrict access to sensitive information, such as employee salary. This is done by customizing the PeopleCode (PeopleSoft programming language) to control the display of information on a page.

PeopleSoft Internet Architecture

PeopleSoft is composed of a number of different application modules, and it is likely that users in the course of their day-to-day tasks will require access to one or more of these different modules or systems. PeopleSoft 8 supports e-business processing, including single sign-on functionality. This allows users to access multiple modules or systems while having to log on only once and, therefore, remember one user ID and password combination. Once a user successfully signs on to a PeopleSoft application, referred to as a node (e.g., HRMS), the application server generates a web browser cookie containing a single sign-on token. When the user requires access to another application, the token is used by the application server to identify and authenticate the user without the sign-on prompt being displayed again.

The introduction of the web increases the audit risks with potential access by a much wider user base, and an audit or review should consider the controls in place to mitigate these risks. The new Internet architecture provides additional entry points into the PeopleSoft environment, which calls for proper analysis to understand the risks and techniques to mitigate those risks. In addition, different types of users or identities may access the application from myriad physical and logical locations, and integration of the directory or web single sign-on requires additional configuration and synchronization of user information. Since PeopleSoft is now accessed using a standard Internet web browser, there is an increased emphasis on Internet security. Security, encryption and extended password controls have been introduced with release 8, including Secure Sockets Layer (SSL) encryption between web server and browser, password aging, expiration, minimum password length, and optional special character and number requirements.

Audit Implications

In an ERP environment, it is common for a large number of the controls to be automated using access security or configuration settings. An understanding of the PeopleSoft security authorization concept and the PeopleSoft application infrastructure tools and utilities (e.g., PeopleTools) is essential in identifying the risks and understanding the controls and the techniques for testing them. An understanding of the PeopleSoft architecture and an organization's particular system landscape is also essential in determining an effective audit approach. Under PIA, the nature, number and access paths for users have expanded significantly. As a result, there is an exponential growth of application security exposures, and collaboration with trading partners requires an increased focus on PeopleSoft application security to address confidentiality and transaction validity issues. Improved user identification and authentication controls in PeopleSoft release 8 need to be factored into audit plans and testing, along with greater emphasis on access path determination and Internet security and encryption. Furthermore, due to the potentially expanded user base, nonrepudiation, confidentiality and privacy issues need to be addressed.

Some of the audit aspects that the previously described factors may impact include:

- Testing of security parameters (Is there more than one application server and/or database server?)

- Infrastructure testing requirements (How many systems are there? Which systems are running as production servers?)
- Testing under rotation plan (Is an audit rotation plan operating? If so, what systems are relevant? What business cycles are due for testing under rotation, and on what systems or platforms are they running? What countries are they supporting?)
- Specific identified risks (Have systems been upgraded? Have there been any localizations/changes to the standard software to meet country-specific requirements?)

Testing PeopleSoft Security

The logical access controls within PeopleSoft, as with most ERP systems, are designed to be preventive in nature. Permission lists and roles are designed as part of security and should be assigned to users IDs in accordance with their job function requirements. As described earlier, user access to PeopleSoft is controlled by restricting access to menu options and pages. Each page can be thought of as a row in the underlying database tables. It is appropriate at this stage to revisit the concept of action page options and effective dating, which allows users to work with historic, current and future data. Effective dating allows all changes to data to be stored and tracked, provided that the data are effective-dated (not all types of data are effective-dated). When a user changes data via a page, the existing data remain in the database tables and a new row is created, holding the new data. Certain pages have action options in the bottom right corner. These are listed in chapter 2, in the Executing Commands and Online Pages section.

A full list of action page options, sometimes referred to as action types or activity codes, is detailed in **figure 4.12**.

The menu items to which a user ID has access is based on all permission lists assigned to that user ID. If a permission list grants more access to a particular page than another permission list, the highest level of access is granted to the user ID. Although a user may not have been explicitly granted access through roles or permission lists to a particular function, he/she may nevertheless have inadvertently been given access through the combination of permission lists, menus options (pages) and action types by virtue of the combination of these across the whole range of the roles or permission lists assigned to them. Consequently, the auditor should test logical access to the specific permission lists, menu options and action types to which a user has access, rather than simply preparing and testing access based on a matrix of users with their access to roles or permission lists.

It is also not uncommon for roles and permission lists to initially have been built with very broad access (e.g., by using the action type Update/Display All or even Correction) to minimize disruption to operations during the initial implementation. For this reason also, it is important to test access to the PeopleSoft software at the permission list, menu items (pages) and action type levels, rather than at simply the role or permission list assignment level.

Case Study

To more fully explain this concept, as well as to understand the necessary steps needed to test logical access security in the PeopleSoft software, the following case study is presented as steps to follow.

Step 1: Identify High-risk Transactions

This can be achieved through a combination of the following:

- Interviews/questionnaires with the appropriate line of business management
- A review of process flow and security documentation
- The auditor's knowledge of the business, the PeopleSoft software and related risks
- Organization chart of employees within the department under review

Security reports within PeopleSoft are not normally available as standard. This requires reports to be developed and maintained according to the needs of the security and audit functions. Similarly, audit trail flags must be manually set up to log changes to records and fields. Access to perform functions in PeopleSoft revolves around a user's access to pages. Since access to a page is determined by access to a menu, access to a page can be restricted by restricting access to that menu and specifically a menu item (remembering that a menu item corresponds to a page). Permission lists control access to specific pages and the functions a user can perform on a particular page. The page permissions of a permission list (Home→Security→Permissions & Roles→Permission Lists) detail the components (menu names), e.g., ADMINISTER_WORKFORCE, available for assignment. Consequently, it is possible to identify the permission lists associated with high-risk functions.

Step 2: Identify Relevant Authorizations

A number of methods may be employed to identify the necessary permission lists, though they may have varying degrees of accuracy:

1. Security documentation—If security has been sufficiently documented, the project team may have captured all the relevant roles, permission lists and associated menu items and action types as part of the security implementation. When relying on security documentation, the auditor should consider independently corroborating with at least two members of IT/security management that the documentation has been maintained accurately and is up to date. Results should be confirmed with management also. Note that assessing access based on the roles created by the organization is unlikely to yield accurate results either, since they may have been created with additional permission lists that provide excessive access, or through the combination of roles and permission lists, users may have inadvertently been provided with access to functions contrary to management's intentions. Remember that menu-level (and, subsequently, page) access is based on a combination of all permission lists, so the access is finally granted for the permission list with the highest level of access.

2. Extract the information directly from PeopleSoft—PeopleSoft does not provide any standard security reports containing a complete list of users with their access to specific pages and the level of access granted. Consequently, any such analysis must be done by writing specific SQL queries using Query Manager in the PeopleTools tool set (Home → Reporting Tools→Query→Query Manager, as shown in **figure 4.12**), followed by the selection of Create New Query. The query should then be built and run, and the results analyzed offline. If the query is exported to Microsoft Excel, it should be noted that the column names are exported, but the query name and source table names are not. If multiple query scripts are being run, each Excel file should be saved with an appropriate name to avoid confusion. Permission list definitions are contained in the PSAUTHITEM table and user ID information is contained within the tables PSOPRDEFN and PSOPRCLS in the database. It is necessary for an auditor to analyze both of these tables to determine which user IDs have access to the relevant menu items in question. The query written to extract the authorizations must link the PSOPRCLASS (role) and OPRID (user ID) fields in the PSOPRDEFN (operator definition) table, to the MENUNAME, PNLITEMNAME (panel item name, i.e., page) and AUTHORIZEDACTIONS (action types) fields in the PSAUTHITEM table, together with the MENUGROUP in the PSMENUDEFN table.

Figure 4.12—SQL Query

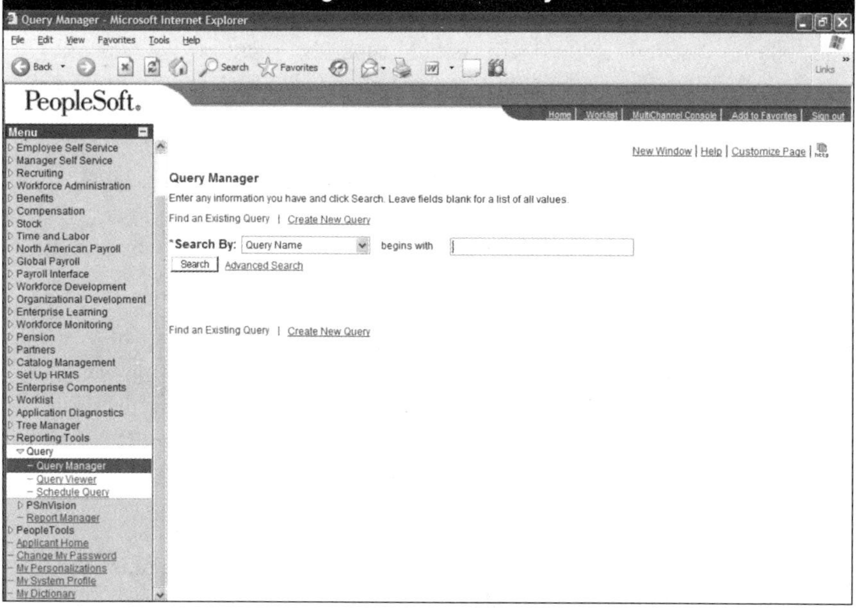

3. The results can be downloaded in Excel format and will list the users with access to the different menu items, i.e., pages, and the action types (e.g., Add, Update/Display, Correction) granted to those users. The auditor can analyze the data to determine which users have access to specific high-risk menu items (or

components) already identified in step 1. With the data available for offline analysis, an auditor can determine not only the users with access to specific menu items but also the permission lists and roles that have been assigned to users. A high-level review of these may yield inappropriate role and/or permission list assignment, which could in turn lead to potential segregation of duties issues. Subsequent discussions should be held with security administrators and management to discuss the findings from the reports and determine whether users should have access assigned to them in the PeopleSoft system.

A typical SQL query that can be used to generate a list of user IDs and the permissions and action codes granted is:

```
SELECT A.OPRID, A.OPRDEFNDESC, A.ACCTLOCK, B.ROLENAME,
C.CLASSID, D.MENUNAME, D.BARNAME, D.BARITEMNAME,
D.PNLITEMNAME, D.DISPLAYONLY, D.AUTHORIZEDACTIONS

FROM PSOPRDEFN A, PSROLEUSER B, PSROLECLASS C, PSAUTHITEM D

WHERE A.OPRID = B.ROLEUSER
AND B.ROLENAME = C.ROLENAME
AND C.CLASSID = D.CLASSID

Order by A.OPRID, B.ROLENAME, C.CLASSID, D.MENUNAME.
```

The authorized actions column will contain values that represent the type of actions (action types/codes) that the user is authorized to perform. **Figure 4.13** summarizes the actions available.

Testing Segregation of Duties/Excessive Access

A breakdown in segregation of access stems from the assignment of an inappropriate combination of page permissions. A dummy user may be generated with no roles assigned in the Test or Quality Assurance instance, and then the required roles that would constitute a breakdown in segregation of access could be added. Testing whether this dummy user is able to perform the conflicting functions would confirm the inappropriate role assignment. Having downloaded the security information from PeopleSoft, the auditor should analyze the data using Audit Command Language (ACL), Microsoft Excel or Microsoft Access to search for the conflicting combinations in the actual security setup.

Traditional systems of internal control have relied on assigning certain responsibilities to different individuals or segregating incompatible functions. Such segregation of duties is intended to prevent a person from having both access to assets and responsibility for maintaining the accountability for the assets. For instance, in an inventory management system, different individuals are typically responsible for duties such as:
• Initiating or requesting a purchase
• Placing and inputting purchase orders

- Receiving goods
- Custody of inventories
- Maintaining inventory records and/or authorizing adjustments to costs or quantities, including authorizing disposal or scrapping
- Making changes to inventory master files
- Performing independent inventory counts
- Following up on inventory count discrepancies
- Authorizing production requests and/or materials transfers
- Receiving/transferring goods into/from manufacturing
- Shipping goods

Figure 4.13—Activity Codes Conversion Table

Action	Action Code	Action Description
0	Action	Action
1	A	Add
2	UD	Update Display
3	AUD	Add and Update Display
4	UDA	Update Display All
5	AUDA	Add and Update Display All
6	UDUDA	Update Display and Update Display All
7	AUDUDA	Add, Update Display and Update Display All
8	C	Correction
9	AC	Add and Correction
10	UDC	Update Display and Correction
11	AUDC	Add, Update Display and Correction
12	UDAC	Update Display All and Correction
13	AUDAC	Add, Update Display All and Correction
14	UDUDAC	Update Display, Update Display All and Correction
15	AUDUDAC	Add, Update Display, Update Display All and Correction
128	DE	Data Entry
129	ADE	Add and Data Entry
130	UDDE	Update Display and Data Entry
131	AUDDE	Add, Update Display and Data Entry
132	UDADE	Update Display All and Data Entry
133	AUDADE	Add, Update Display All and Data Entry
134	UDUDADE	Update Display, Update Display All and Data Entry
135	AUDUDADE	Add, Update Display, Update Display All and Data Entry
136	CDE	Correction and Data Entry
137	ACDE	Add, Correction and Data Entry
138	UDCDE	Update Display, Correction and Data Entry
139	AUDCDE	Add, Update Display, Correction and Data Entry
140	UDACDE	Update Display All, Correction and Data Entry
141	AUDACDE	Add, Update Display All, Correction and Data Entry
142	UDUDACDE	Update Display, Update Display All, Correction and Data Entry
143	AUDUDACDE	Add, Update Display, Update Display All, Correction and Data Entry

Further, physical counts of inventory should be performed by someone who does not have custody of inventory and who has no access to inventory records. An individual who is independent of the custody and recording of inventory should also follow up discrepancies noted in the comparison of the counts to inventory records. If one individual has responsibility for more than one of these functions, that individual could misappropriate assets and conceal the misappropriation.

For example, if one individual had both the ability to process sales orders and access the inventory management master files, that person could modify product-selling prices and process unauthorized sales. Legacy system environments necessitated and facilitated segregation of duties because of the predominantly manual control framework surrounding them. The fragmentation of legacy systems also facilitated segregation of duties, since purchasing systems, warehousing systems and general ledger systems were all separate.

However, the traditional notion of segregation of duties needs to be refined in a fully automated PeopleSoft environment. ERP systems have shifted the emphasis to user empowerment, enabling users to have access across business functions or, alternatively, to handle physical assets and record their movements directly into the computing and accounting system. As discussed earlier in this guide, along with this, transition controls have moved "up front" in the process and have become increasingly more automated with online release, automated matching of transactions, increased integration, etc.

The notion of the segregation of duties control needs to be developed to include a risk management perspective and a trade-off or balance between functional access and security in the new ERP environment. The ERP environment should be assessed from a risk and controls perspective. Key control steps should be modeled for each business process in the organization, and appropriate trade-offs should be made between empowerment and the need to minimize the risk of fraud or unauthorized transactions.

Figure 4.14 shows a model of the expenditure cycle. In the model, a goods receipt is considered in the same way as an invoice approval, since the entry of a goods receipt in many cases completes the matching process and gives rise to an authorized payment. From a segregation of duties perspective, users may present a risk at the following levels:

- Low—Users who have access to a single step in the process (i.e., the individual must collude to effect a fraudulent or unauthorized transaction)
- Medium—Users who have access to two steps in the control model (i.e., the individual must influence at least one other to effect a fraudulent or unauthorized transaction)

Figure 4.14—Expenditure Cycle

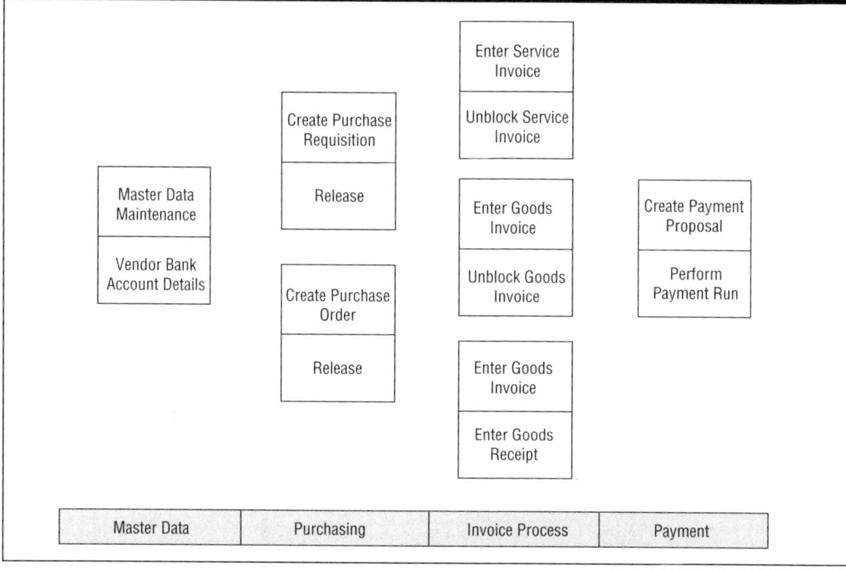

- High—Users who have access to three steps in the control model (i.e., the individual can most likely effect a fraudulent or unauthorized transaction that may go undetected, at least for some time). For example, a user who can enter and release a purchase order and perform a goods receipt can misappropriate goods.

Specific techniques for testing automated controls (i.e., access security and configurable controls) in the PeopleSoft application are described in chapters 5 through 10 and deal with testing the PeopleSoft core business cycles and application infrastructure. Depending on the level of risk and the amount of testing required, audit testing rotation plans may be established for each of the components or subcomponents of the audit framework.

Risks and controls vary in organizations, depending on external and internal factors, the configuration, and the release in use for the PeopleSoft system. This guide does not attempt to comprehensively address legal and regulatory compliance risks falling under a specific jurisdiction. The primary focus for controls is on automated controls that are unique to ERP or the PeopleSoft environment. Auditors should already be familiar with manual controls, such as reconciliations, manual approvals and dual signatories. Specific assurance techniques vary from organization to organization, depending on the extent of customization, specific configuration options selected and whether automated diagnostics are used. Therefore, the techniques will not necessarily include prescriptive lists of specific PeopleSoft menu paths, permission lists, or fields and values, but rather will provide a sample tool set for use or reference as appropriate in the reader's organizational environment.

Note that "customize" and "customization" in this guide are general terms that refer to the tailoring of a PeopleSoft environment to suit the customer's specific needs, either by way of configuration, modification or additional development of tables or programs.

Because there may be more than one control per risk, a numbering sequence for risks, controls and testing techniques has been adopted throughout each of the chapters dealing with the auditing of core business cycles or the application security infrastructure, as shown in **figure 4.15**.

In this way, the relationship among risks, controls and testing techniques for subprocesses (e.g., master data maintenance, purchasing, invoice process and payment) should be evident as the reader progresses through each of the chapters dealing with auditing the core business cycles and application security infrastructure.

Figure 4.15—Numbering Sequence for Risks, Controls and Testing Techniques

Number	Description
Risks	
1.1	Risk number 1 for the first subprocess
1.2	Risk number 2 for the first subprocess
2.1	Risk number 1 for the second subprocess
Controls	
1.1.1	Control number 1 for risk number 1 of the first subprocess
1.1.2	Control number 2 for risk number 1 of the first subprocess
1.2.1	Control number 1 for risk number 2 of the first subprocess
2.1.1	Control number 1 for risk number 1 of the second subprocess
Testing Techniques	
1.1.1	Testing technique for control number 1 for risk number 1 of the first subprocess
1.1.2	Testing technique for control number 2 for risk number 1 of the first subprocess
1.2.1	Testing technique for control number 1 for risk number 2 of the first subprocess
2.1.1	Testing technique for control number 1 for risk number 1 of the second subprocess

When control issues are identified, the auditor should attempt to uncover and report to management the causes of the problem and his/her recommendations. In this respect, COBIT helps meet the multiple needs of management by bridging the gaps among business risks, control needs and technical issues. It provides good practices across a domain and process framework and presents activities in a manageable and logical structure. COBIT's good practices provide a measure to judge against when things do go wrong and can assist in identifying problem causes.

The COBIT framework consists of the following four domains:
- Plan and Organize (PO)
- Acquire and Implement (AI)
- Deliver and Support (DS)
- Monitor and Evaluate (ME)

Some of the processes contained within these domains that are of particular relevance when assessing ERP systems include:
- AI6 Manage changes
- DS5 Ensure systems security
- DS9 Manage the configuration
- DS11 Manage data

Summary

This chapter looked at the audit impacts arising from the implementation of an ERP system (e.g., changes to audit methodologies) and recommended a PeopleSoft audit framework, including, for example, business processes and application security. It detailed the steps involved in taking a risk-based audit approach to ERP, including a description of key concepts (e.g., authorization and configuration), methods of testing configurable controls, access security and segregation of duties. Finally, the relationship between the recommended PeopleSoft audit framework and the COBIT framework was discussed, including COBIT's usefulness in identifying the causes of control breakdowns.

5. PeopleSoft HR Business Cycle

This chapter outlines the functionality of the PeopleSoft HR business cycle to provide the reader with a high-level understanding of the process. From a risk and controls perspective, the HR cycle has four main subprocesses, as shown in **figure 5.1**:

- Master Data Maintenance
- Commencements
- Personal Development
- Terminations

Figure 5.1—Human Resources Business Cycle

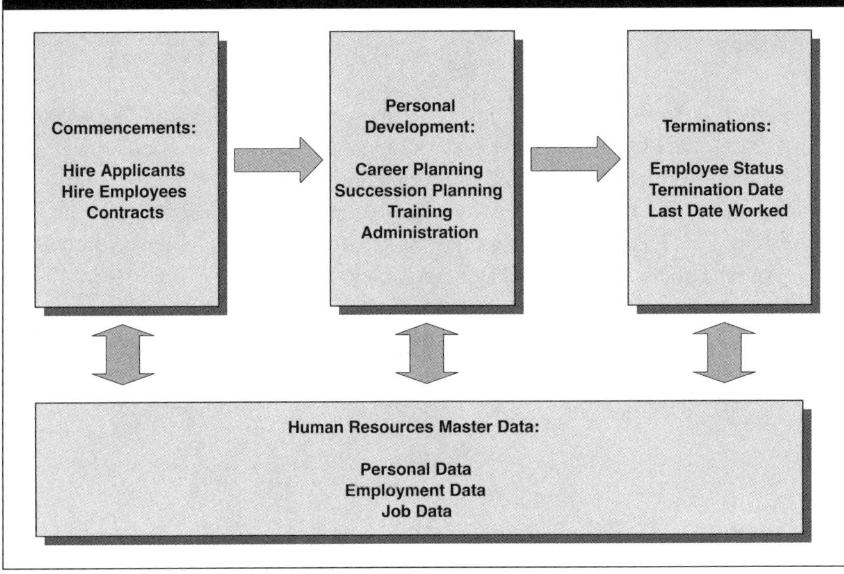

Master Data Maintenance

The HR master data stored within the PeopleSoft database form the basis of the HRMS processing functions. Payroll processing and the subsequent payments to employees and third-party recipients, in addition to the GL postings, are based on the information entered, validated and stored within the HR tables.

Three main types of master data are employed in the HR cycle and held in a number of base tables within the PeopleSoft database:

- Personal data
- Employment data
- Job data

Personal Data

Personal data refer to all the current and historical personal data about an employee. The associated database tables also contain the employee ID that is used as a unique identifier of the person within PeopleSoft. It should be noted that personal data might also be held on nonemployees, such as consultants or employees' dependents.

The distinction is recorded under the personal status field as either "e" for an employee or "n" for a nonemployee. The main data components and the corresponding tables in which the data are held are:

- Employee ID (PS_PERSON table)—This is the unique identifier within PeopleSoft for identifying the person. An employee may have more than one job in an organization but should only have one employee ID.
- Name (PS_NAMES table)—The name of the person. This should comply with strict naming conventions, e.g., last name suffix comma space first name space middle name.
- Home address (PS_ADDRESSES table)—The residential address of the person
- Mailing address (PS_ADDRESSSES table)—The address to be used for sending correspondence
- Home phone (PS_PERSONAL_PHONE table)—Home telephone number
- Citizenship status (PS_CITIZENSHIP table)—Indicates whether the person is a native or naturalized citizen of the installation country
- Original hire date (PS_PERSON table)—Indicates the date the employee was first hired
- Birth information (PS_PERSON table)—Stores the employee's birth date and country of birth

Employment Data

Employment data refer to information on an individual employee of the organization. Typically, this information is more static in nature and rarely changes during the course of an employee's career. Employment data are composed mainly of key dates such as:

- Hire/rehire date—The date of commencement of employment, which should not change
- Probation date—The start date of a probationary period for an employee
- Pay increases—The date of the most recent pay increase
- Length of service—A date that allows the length of actual service to be calculated, taking into account periods of leave, suspensions, etc.
- Termination date and last day worked—The date the individual ceases to be an employee and the last day for which the employee is to be paid

Employment data also include data on the position of the employee, such as business title, supervisor ID and work phone number. This is stored only if Position Management in PeopleSoft is enabled. Although most payroll settings are linked to specific jobs and stored as job data, such as compensation (salary) and salary plans (determining how a salary is calculated), there are certain payroll settings that are stored under employee data. These include details of payroll deductions and payment details (e.g., paycheck distribution and alternate pay name).

Employment data are stored in the PS_EMPLOYMENT table.

Job Data

All of the current and historical data related to an employee's job are stored in the PS_JOB table. These data form the core record in the HR database and hold information regarding:
- Employee status
- Salary/compensation
- Employee job/position
- Payroll settings
- Benefits status

The employee status indicates whether an employee is active (a), on leave (l), or terminated (t), etc. Job data also include the employee's business unit and department or location. In any organization, an employee may have more than one job. These may be represented by different job codes or employee record numbers. This increases the amount of data held for each employee and consequently increases the need for the integrity of the data to be maintained.

The milestones in an employee's career, such as hiring, leave of absence and pay rate changes, are indicated by actions and action reasons. The action specifies what event has taken place (e.g., leave of absence) and the action reason describes the reason for the event (e.g., maternity leave). In this way, the employee's career can be tracked. Job data also include payroll settings, which indicate the company (i.e., the legal entity for which the employee works); pay group, which determines how the employee is paid (e.g., hourly or salaried); and the basis upon which compensation is made and changed (e.g., standard hours and salary ranges).

Typical actions are:
- HIR—Hire
- LOA—Leave of absence
- PLA—Paid leave of absence
- JRC—Job reclassification
- PAY—Pay rate change
- BON—Bonus
- POS—Position change
- PRO—Promotion
- DEM—Demotion
- REH—Rehire
- RET—Retirement
- TER—Termination
- XFR—Transfer

Although the actual payments to individual employees are held within their payroll data, the compensation rates, frequencies and annual rates are linked to jobs and are held within the job data for an employee. The compensation rate is based on the compensation frequency and the annual rate. The annual rate is the annual salary for a particular job. The compensation frequency is the time period between pay days and can be:

- a—Annual
- m—Monthly
- s—Semimonthly
- b—Biweekly
- w—Weekly
- h—Hourly

For example, the monthly rate is the annual rate divided by 12, and the weekly rate is the annual rate divided by 52. The default compensation frequencies are determined at the implementation of the system.

Changes to Master Data

Throughout an employee's time with an organization, data change as a result of promotions, demotions, periods of absence, transferring jobs, etc. This should not require data to be amended directly in the payroll setup tables. Amendments should be made via Workforce Administration menus and pages. For example, changing an employee's job information is performed via Home→Workforce Administration→Job Information→Job Data, as shown in **figure 5.2**

Figure 5.2—Changing an Employee's Job Information

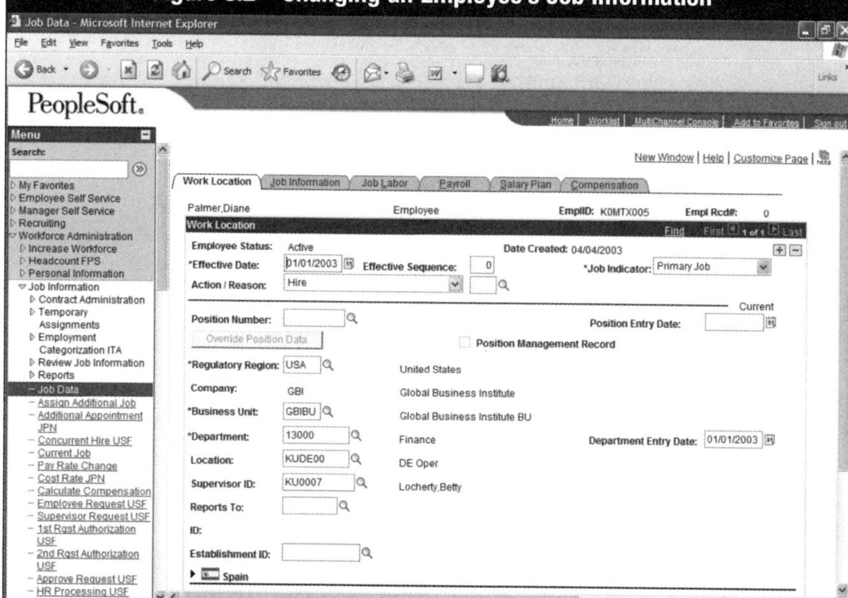

Commencements

When an applicant accepts an offer, the applicant is hired and employment commences. The personal status should be changed to "e," and employee status should be set to "a" to represent an active employee. Additional master data must be entered into the system as only some of the master data are collected during the recruitment process. Applicant records maintained during the recruitment process may be copied into employment records on hiring the applicant via Home →Recruiting →Hire Applicants→Copy Applicant to Employee (Country).

Every employee must be assigned an employee ID (EMPLID) that uniquely identifies the employee in the system. As shown in **figure 5.3**, this can be assigned automatically by the system or manually.

Figure 5.3—Employee ID

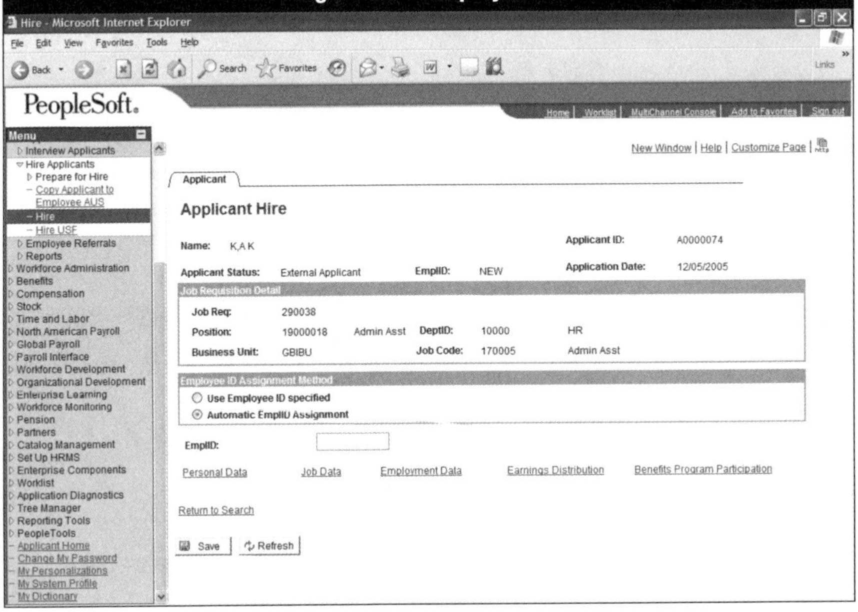

The following information must be entered, since these facts will have an impact on the payroll processing and/or reporting within the system:

- Employee ID
- National ID (or Social Security number)
- Job code (identifying the employee's job type within the organization)
- Employee record number
- Company
- Pay group
- Business unit
- Department ID
- Location (identifying the employee's physical location in the organization)

• Compensation (salary)
• Standard hours
• Deductions that the employee is allowed to receive and eligible benefits

It is important for all relevant data to be entered accurately upon hiring an employee, due to the dependency of the payroll processing functions. Organizations may adopt various data capture techniques, including résumé scanning or the use of add-on packages. If the employee self-service application has been implemented, employees may access personal information on the web site to perform self-service and administrative tasks, such as entering or changing personal information. In such cases, it is important to set up appropriate security to restrict access and to configure appropriate edit and validation controls.

Personal Development

Personal development encompasses a wide range of aspects of an employee's career, including:
• Career planning
• Succession planning
• Training administration

Career Planning

PeopleSoft's career planning functionality facilitates the development and tracking of employee career plans. This functionality takes into consideration information on employee competencies and accomplishments (e.g., education, qualifications and training), and the information is maintained in the PeopleSoft database. By formalizing and automating employee career plan administration, an organization is in a better position to manage and develop employee skills to meet its associated operational requirements.

An overview of the creation, submission and approval of career plans using the Plan Careers business process is illustrated in **figure 5.4**.

Figure 5.4—Career Planning Process

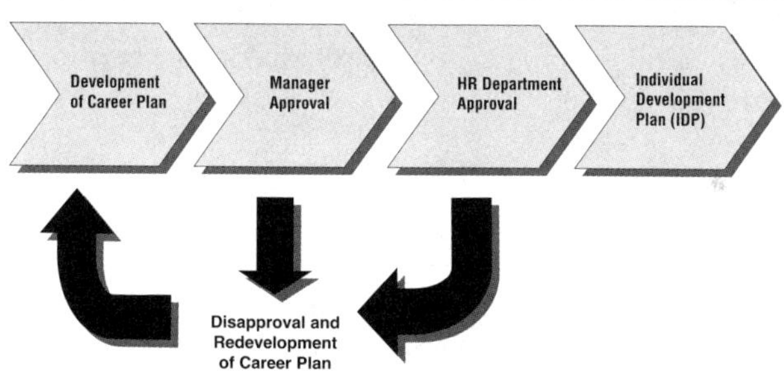

Generally, the development of a career plan requires employees to:

- Specify their job and location preferences
- Determine their preferred career paths for job progression
- Set career goals
- Evaluate strengths and development areas
- Agree to a training plan

With this information held in the database, it is possible to compare employees and rank their potential for movement into other jobs, as shown in **figure 5.5**.

Figure 5.5—Employee Comparison

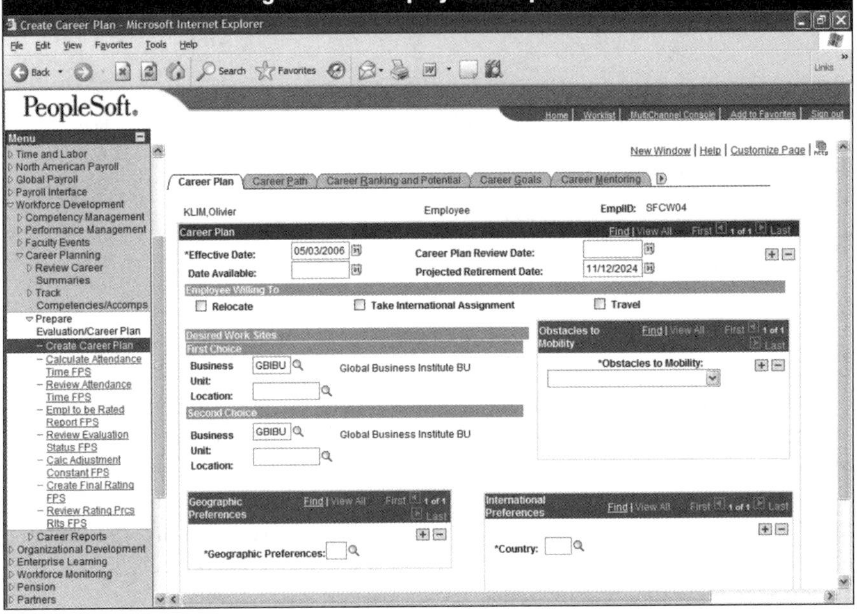

The first step is to record the employee's current job details and his/her aspirations in terms of job progression and availability to relocate to other departments or geographical areas. This helps define a career path for the individual. Career paths outline the logical progression of employees within an organization and help illustrate the hierarchical relationship among jobs. The stages along the logical job progression are referred to as career move levels, as shown in **figures 5.6** and **5.7**.

An employee's preferred career path may be a variation of the default career paths configured in PeopleSoft. The career path should contain information regarding the career move options available at the various career move levels and an estimation of the employee's readiness for a move to the next level. For instance, an employee may not have the required skills currently but may be able to develop them within the next two years. This can be stored in the career path data. An important aspect of the career planning process is to identify and evaluate employee strengths and areas for development based on competencies (e.g., abstract thinking, stress control, expertise) set up in the system, as shown in **figure 5.8**. Training plans can then be set up to identify courses that need to be attended, along with the location and timing of the courses, as shown in **figure 5.9**.

Figure 5.6—Career Path

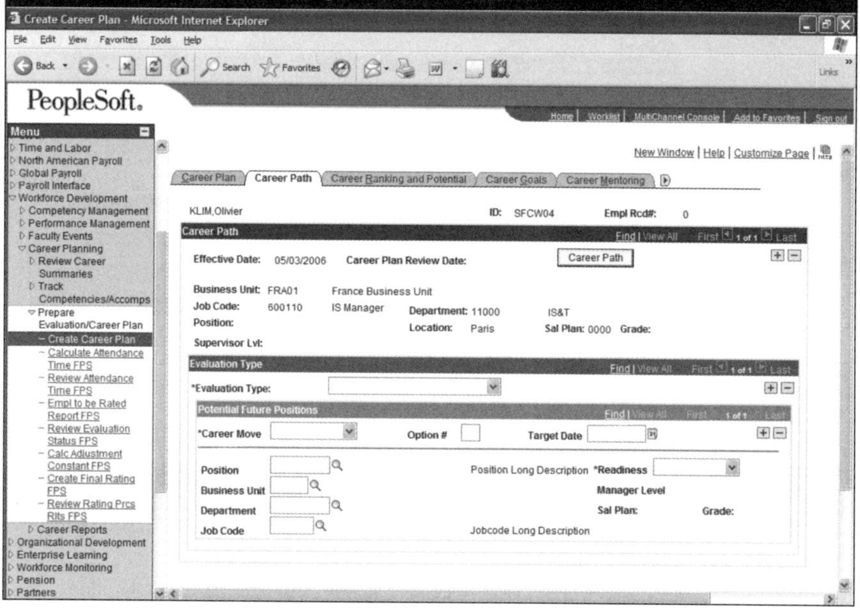

Figure 5.7—Career Move Levels

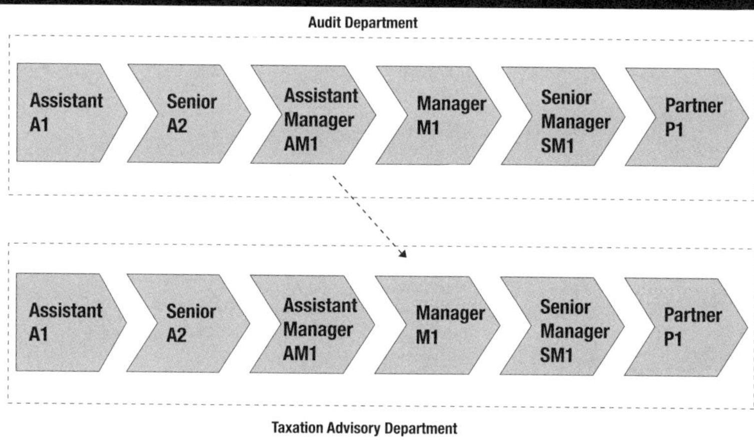

Employees progress through their careers through career move levels.

- - - - - - - -→ Optional career move level

Figure 5.8—Competencies

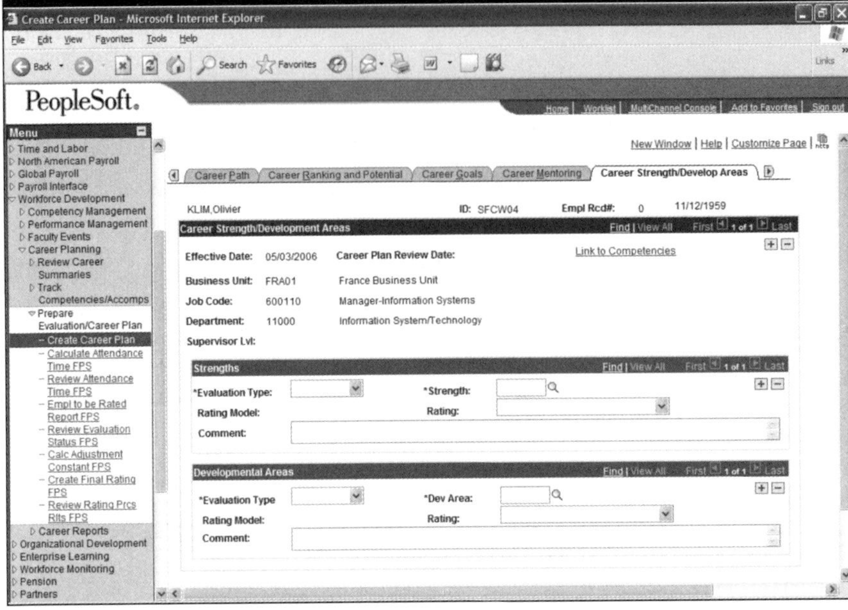

Figure 5.9—Training Plan

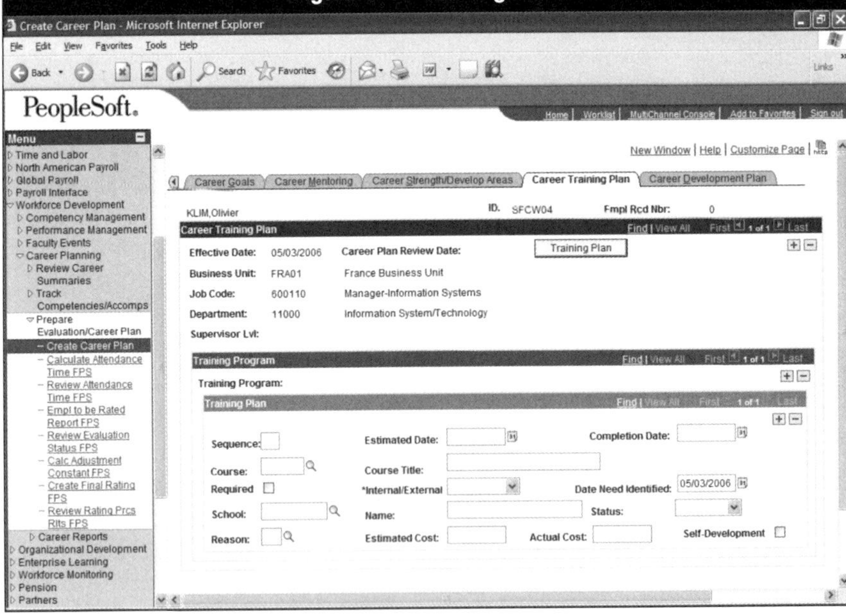

On the basis of employee strengths and development areas, it is possible for management to rank employees in the same job (i.e., with the same job code), thereby making the decision for promotion potentially more objective.

Succession Planning

Succession planning is an optional component within PeopleSoft used to identify potential candidates with the required competencies to move into particular jobs or positions. It may be used in conjunction with career planning where career paths, employee readiness and retirement information signify the estimated vacancy dates of jobs. This includes existing employees and nonemployees, such as third-party consultants, who may have data held on them within the HR databases.

The people who currently occupy a position are known as incumbents. An organization may choose to set up succession plans for only a number of key positions. This is accessible via Home→Organizational Development→ Succession Planning→Create Succession Plan, as shown in **figure 5.10.**

Figure 5.10—Succession Plans

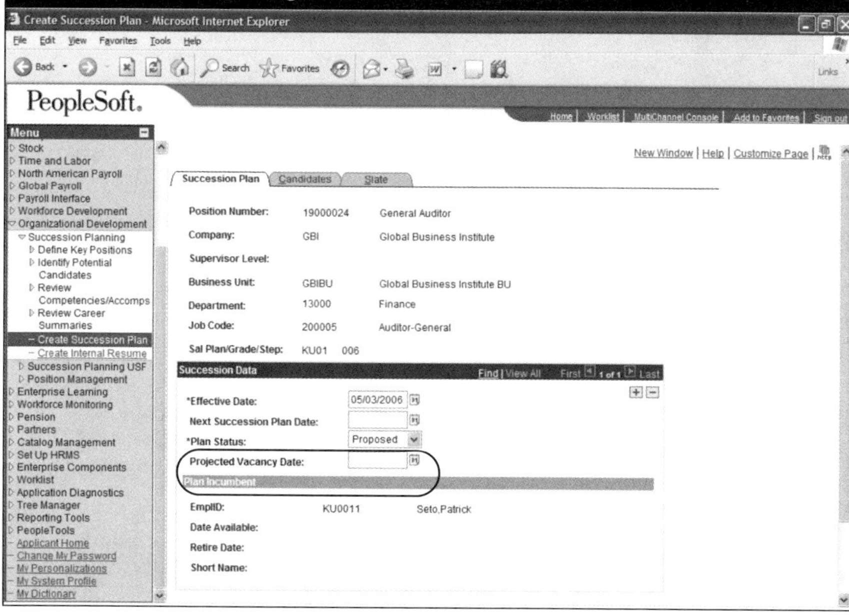

The main stages in succession planning include:

- Projected vacancy date identification—This is the date of the expected movement of the current incumbent (e.g., through retirement), as shown in **figure 5.10**.
- Appropriate candidate identification and selection—The system will identify succession candidates and their ranking in terms of the most appropriate person to move into the position and replace the outgoing incumbent, as shown in **figure 5.11**. The succession candidate's readiness to move into the position is derived from his/her career plan (discussed earlier), which in turn is determined by his/her competencies and accomplishments.

Figure 5.11—Candidate Identification

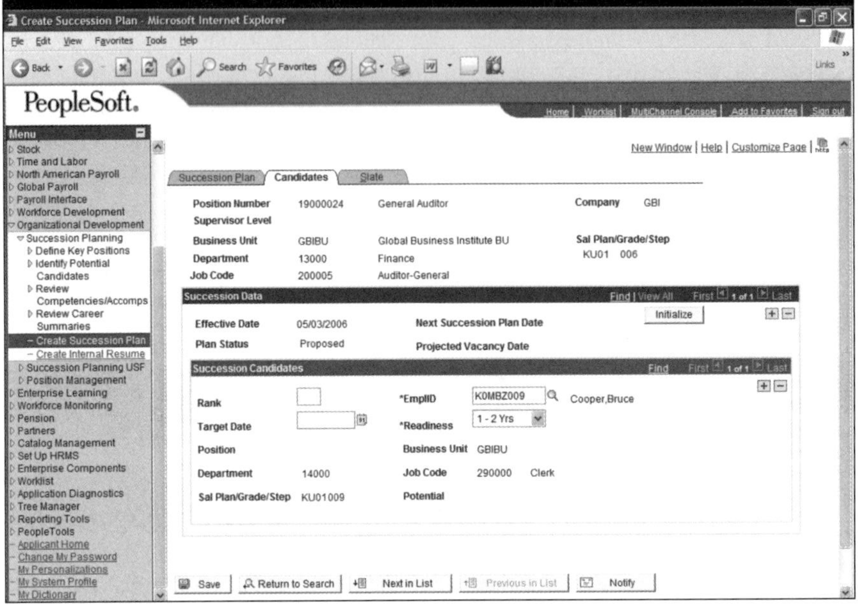

Training Administration

Personal development may be achieved through attendance at formal courses. An organization must define courses, as shown in **figure 5.12**, via Home→Enterprise Learning→Define Course/Cost Details→Courses. Courses are then linked to training programs, as shown in **figure 5.13**, via the menu navigation path Home→ Enterprise Learning→Define Course/Cost Details→Program Information.

Each course can have training budgets defined and standard materials required to teach that particular course. In addition, courses can have competencies and accomplishments attached to them to act as either prerequisites to attend a course or designated achievements following completion of the course, as shown in **figure 5.14**.

The following competencies and accomplishments have to be set up in the system:

- Organization-defined competencies (abstract thinking, leadership, motivation, etc.)
- Certifications and professional qualifications, e.g., Certified Information Systems Auditor (CISA), Certified Public Accountant (CPA) and Chartered Accountant (CA)
- Professional memberships (e.g., ISACA)
- Degrees and education

Figure 5.12—Course Definitions

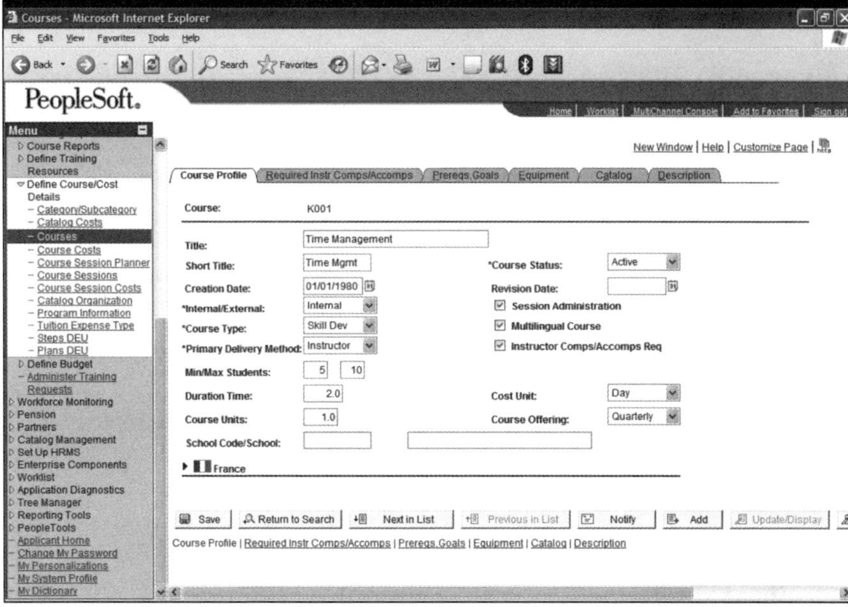

Figure 5.13—Course Link to Training Program

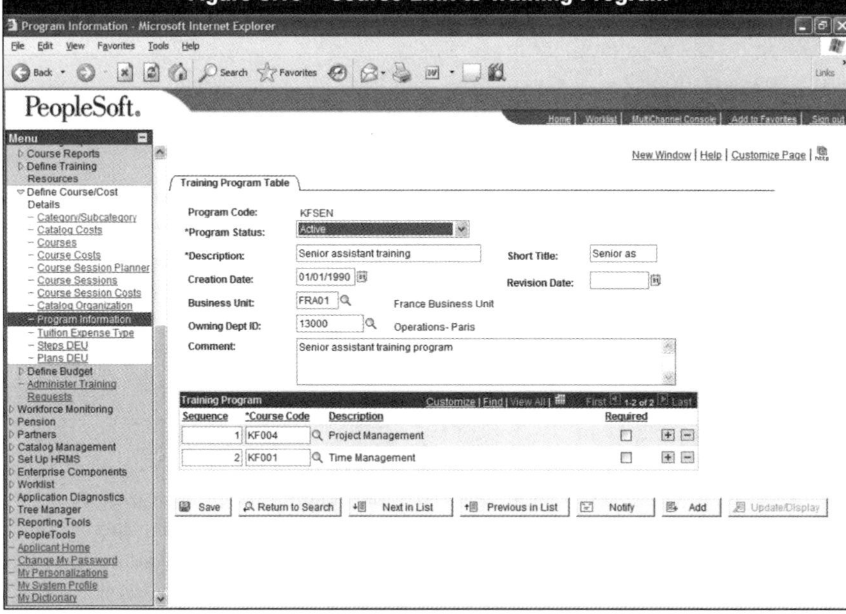

Figure 5.14—Course Prerequisites/Goals

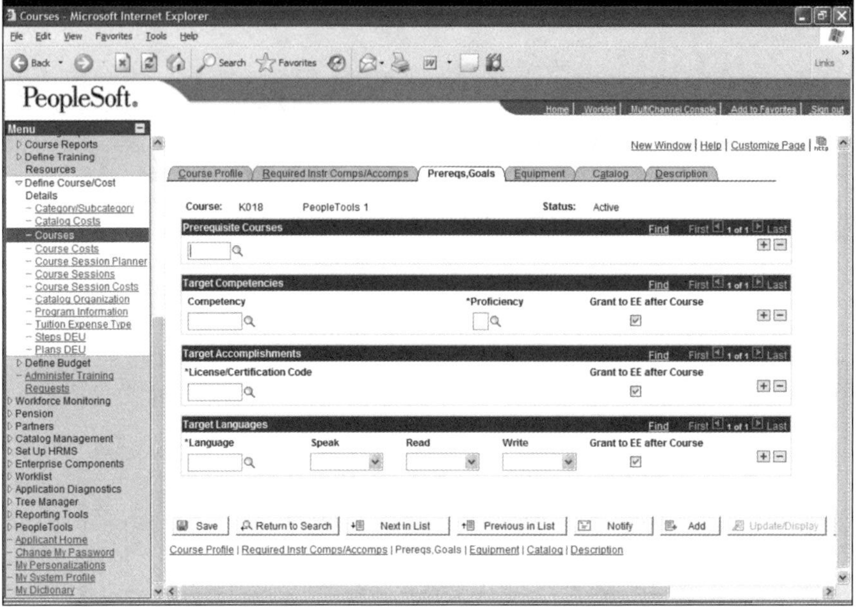

Personal development courses may be run in-house or by an external organization. If run externally, training vendors may be set up in the system (Home→Enterprise Learning→Define Training Resources→ Vendors). For each training vendor, the following details are stored in the system:

- Key contacts
- Address
- Certifications held
- Areas of expertise

Additionally, details may be stored in the system regarding:

- Training materials and equipment required for the courses
- Training facilities available (either internal training rooms or external training vendor facilities) including:
  - Room sizes
  - Existence of equipment, such as overhead projectors
  - Cost of hiring the room

Courses cannot take place without qualified instructors; therefore, it may be necessary to formally define instructors in the system. By identifying the competencies and accomplishments of the instructors stored in the database, it is possible to match up those skills with those required to teach the relevant courses to identify the most appropriate person to teach the course.

Once personal development courses, instructors and training facilities have been established in the system, employees must enroll for the relevant courses. Each course the employee completes should update his/her competency and accomplishments profile in line with the employee's desired career progression defined in his/her career plan.

Terminations

The termination of an employee's employment results in a change to his/her status in the system. The employee status is changed as a result of an action and action reason in the system, as previously discussed in the Job Data section of this chapter. Since each job that an employee has within an organization (noting that an employee may have multiple jobs) has an employee status attached to it, the employee status for every job should be changed accordingly. The relevant action options could be:

- ret—Retirement
- t—Termination
- twb—Terminated with benefits
- twp—Termination with pay

All these actions are status-related and would result in status changes in the system, such as:

- q—Retired with pay
- r—Retired
- t—Terminated
- u—Terminated with pay
- v—Termination pension payout

Terminations or retirements are processed, as shown in **figure 5.2**, via Home→Workforce Administration→Job Information→Job Data. An additional work location record must be created with the effective date of the termination or retirement, which is entered as an action and reason. **Figure 5.15** shows a termination with a reason of terminated with pay. The employment data automatically populate with the termination date and last day worked, as shown in **figure 5.16**.

Termination Date and Last Day Worked

As mentioned previously, the termination date represents the date on which employment ceased, and the last day worked represents the last day for which an employee is to be paid. Normally, these two dates are the same. However, if an employee happened to be on a leave of absence when terminated, the last day worked (i.e., the last day to be paid) is the last day of the leave of absence. Due to the impact on the payroll processing, it is important for such information to be accurately reflected in the system.

Figure 5.15—Terminated With Pay

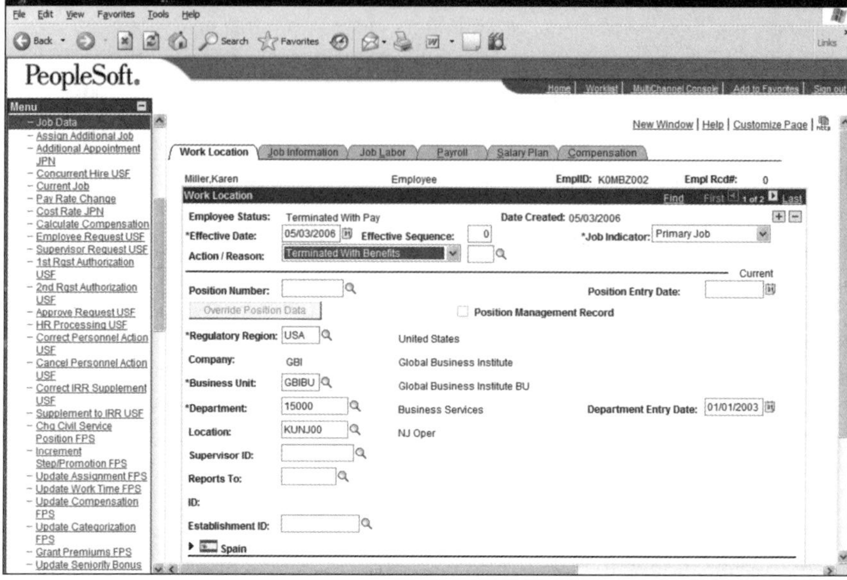

Figure 5.16—Employment Termination Date

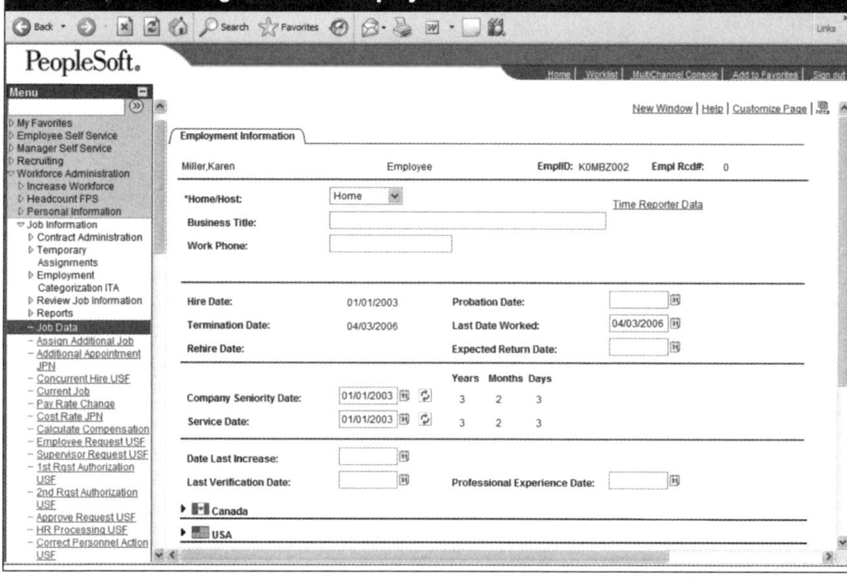

Summary

The HR module underpins all the processing in the HRMS application and contains all the basic information and functions to administer and manage employees in the system. The main business process components are composed of:

- Commencements—Involving the hiring of applicants (new employees) and employees (transfer or new role for current employees) as a result of the recruitment process. It is here that the basic employee information is set up regarding personal details, job details and contracts details.
- Personal Development—Here an employee's career progression can be planned, and his/her competencies to perform the jobs can be tracked. This enables performance evaluation and aids the promotion process. Training plans and courses can be set up in line with career plans to help an employee develop the skills required to progress.
- Terminations—Employees may leave an organization for many reasons, and the system facilitates the recording and processing of these events.
- Master Data Maintenance—Each of these subprocesses relies on the standing data held within the underlying databases, and the maintenance of master data is pervasive throughout the HR business process.

6. Auditing PeopleSoft HR Business Cycle

Chapter 5 outlined the four main subprocesses of the HR business cycle. This chapter looks at the significant risks, key controls and techniques to test the controls for each of the four main subprocesses:
- Maintaining Master Data
- Commencements
- Personal Development
- Terminations

Figure 4.15 lists the numbering sequence for the risks, controls and testing techniques.

The main security risk control considerations surrounding these business cycle components can be broadly categorized into the following:
- Access (user security)—The application security design should be implemented to support the operational access requirements of users and at the same time act as the primary preventive control to maintain adequate segregation of duties. User security can be used to define segregation of duties, while row-level security is used to prevent users from accessing data from business units outside of their own.
- Integrity checking (edit and validation)—The integrity of the data held in the system is also reliant on the configurable controls implemented. These controls may be preventive in nature in terms of up-front, online edit and validation checks; detective, such as the retrospective review of system exception reports generated; or a combination of both types.

For each of the business cycle components, the associated risks, controls and testing techniques will be separated into the two categories.

Master Data Maintenance

Master Data Maintenance: Risks

Master data affect the efficient flow of documents and transactions through the system. The inaccurate, incomplete, invalid or untimely creation or maintenance of master data can affect multiple areas within the organization, as a transaction progresses through to the payroll cycle. Significant risks associated with the maintenance of HR master data include:

1.1 **Access to HR setup tables and master file transaction**—The HR business cycle is reliant on a number of key tables in the database, and the data held in these tables are used throughout the HR and Payroll applications. There are a number of table types (and associated data) that should be considered, such as the personal data tables (PS_PERSON,

PS_NAMES, PS_ADDRESSES and PS_CITIZENSHIP tables), job (PS_JOB table) and employment (PS_EMPLOYMENT table) data. In addition, there are a number of configurable tables, including:

- Business Unit—Represents an organization or subset of an organization and is used to categorize transactions into logical groupings
- Set ID—Used to gather control data into logical groupings
- Job Code—Identifies a specific type of job in the organization
- Pay Group—Used to organize employees in groups for HR, e.g., employees of the same pay frequency or pay type (salaried, etc.)
- Competency—Used to organize and group competencies in relation to jobs

The most extensive of these nonemployee-specific foundation tables is the Installation table (PS_INSTALLATION). The Installation table contains many of the default settings, including the minimum and maximum standard hours, compensation rate codes, and default compensation frequency. Many of the other tables use the Installation table to edit against during the day-to-day HR processing activities.

If access to these HR setup tables is not restricted, inappropriate and unauthorized modifications may be made to HR master data, impacting the payroll processing, subsequent payment to employees and reporting to internal management. In addition, the data held in the database may not accurately reflect the employee's conditions, employment or personal details.

HR staff will access HR functions on a day-to-day basis via the PeopleSoft application. While these activities may not require direct access to the underlying HR setup tables, the transactional data may have an impact on the HR processing and, subsequently, the payments made to employees, e.g., changes to pay rates or changes to an employee's job. Such changes are performed via the Workforce Administration menus (Home→Workforce Administration). If access to these functions is not restricted, unauthorized changes to the components (earnings, allowances, deductions, taxes, etc.) that make up an employee's HR calculation may be made.

In addition, both HR and payroll users might access the same menus as part of their responsibilities; if access is not restricted appropriately at the row (or even field) level, segregation of duties may be compromised. For example, if a single user has access to hire a new employee and process the payroll, it would be easy for someone to create a fictitious employee and process a fraudulent paycheck.

PeopleSoft prevents users from updating their own data, by querying the employee ID of the user logged into the program. If the employee ID of the user logged in equals the employee ID of the current row, an error message will be displayed and the user will not be allowed to save the data.

1.2 **Changes to employee HR master data**—The accuracy, completeness and validity of employee HR master data changes are critical. If improper updates are made to the employee HR master file, HR payments and deductions may be negatively impacted or may result in out-of-date or incorrect master data. For instance, it is important for changes to be made using valid codes, e.g., Empl ID, job codes, competencies and accomplishments. Any invalid or incorrect information could be used for payment details, compensation rates and deductions.

Master Data Maintenance: Key Controls

Key controls over the maintenance of HR master data include:

1.1.1 Access security matrices and documentation should be in place, defining the roles, permission lists, menus and pages required for different job functions within the HR department. This documentation should have been reviewed and approved by management prior to implementation.

Access to define the HRMS business rules (via Home→Set Up HRMS) and the administration of employee HR data (via Home→Workforce Administration) should be restricted to authorized personnel and the access established to support segregation of duties. Add/Correction/Update access to Set Up HRMS should be restricted to the HR administrator only. Row-level security should be set to restrict HR and HR users from having access to update their own HR data. An error message should be displayed informing users that they do not have access to make such changes. The main tables to be restricted are:

- PS_JOB
- PS_EMPLOYMENT
- PS_PAYGROUP_TBL
- PS_DEPT_TBL
- PS_COMPANY_TBL
- PS_LOCATION_TBL
- PS_INSTALLATION
- PS_JOBCODE_TBL

1.2.1 Edit and validation checks have been implemented. For example, changes to job codes are validated against the Job Code table to ensure that the code exists, and the system issues a warning to the user if an invalid code is chosen. It should be noted that many of the data entry fields in PeopleSoft are populated via drop-down boxes or have look-up tables or prompt lists that detail all possible values.

1.2.2 Audit logs should be kept of changes to employee master data and should be reviewed by management on a periodic basis.

Master Data Maintenance: Testing Techniques

Testing techniques for HR master data controls include:

1.1.1 Review access security matrices and access assignment documentation to gain an understanding of the security design. Corroborate this understanding by generating lists of users with access to the Workforce Administration, Compensation, Set Up HRMS and Global Human Resources Rules menus, and review their level of access by writing the following query in PeopleSoft Query Manager:

```
SELECT A.OPRID, A.OPRDEFNDESC, A.ACCTLOCK,
B.ROLENAME, C.CLASSID, D.MENUNAME, D.BARNAME,
D.BARITEMNAME, D.PNLITEMNAME, D.DISPLAYONLY,
D.AUTHORIZEDACTIONS

FROM PSOPRDEFN A, PSROLEUSER B, PSROLECLASS C,
PSAUTHITEM D

WHERE A.OPRID = B.ROLEUSER AND B.ROLENAME =
C.ROLENAME AND C.CLASSID = D.CLASSID
```

Order by A.OPRID, B.ROLENAME, C.CLASSID, D.MENUNAME to ensure that the user IDs (OPRID), role (ROLENAME), permission lists (CLASSID) and components (MENUNAME) are listed in alphabetical order.

The above query may be appended in Query Manager due to the large amount of data returned. Alternate options include extracting the tables in a Microsoft Access database or ACL and performing the query offline.

Also, generate a list of users with access to the setup pages within PeopleSoft menus, and review their level of access by writing the following query in PeopleSoft Query Manager:

```
SELECT A.OPRID, A.OPRDEFNDESC, A.ACCTLOCK,
B.ROLENAME, C.CLASSID, D.MENUNAME, D.BARNAME,
D.BARITEMNAME, D.PNLITEMNAME, D.DISPLAYONLY,
D.AUTHORIZEDACTIONS

FROM PSOPRDEFN A, PSROLEUSER B, PSROLECLASS C,
PSAUTHITEM D

WHERE A.OPRID = B.ROLEUSER
AND B.ROLENAME = C.ROLENAME
AND C.CLASSID = D.CLASSID
AND D.BARNAME LIKE 'SETUP%
```

Order by A.OPRID to ensure that the user IDs (OPRID) are listed in alphabetical order.

The D.AUTHORIZEDACTIONS column will contain values that represent the action types that the user is authorized to perform, where high-risk values are:
- 8—Correction
- 9—Add Correction
- 10—Update/Display Correction
- 11—Add Update/Display Correction
- 12—Update/Display All Correction
- 13—Add Update/Display All Correction
- 14—Update/Display Update/Display All Correction
- 15—Add Update/Display Update/Display All Correction
- 136—Correction Data Entry

Note :
- The values found above can be obtained from the PSPGEACCESSDESC table.
- The D.DISPLAYONLY column will have a value of 0 or 1:
  - 1 means all fields in the page are "display only" to the user.
  - 0 means this setting is turned off, and the action type codes indicate the level of access granted.

Generate a list of users and the row-level security defined by writing the following query in PeopleSoft Query Manager:

```
SELECT A.OPRID, A.OPRDEFNDESC, A.ACCTLOCK, B.SETID,
B.DEPTID, C.DESCR, B.ACCESS_CD,
TO_CHAR(B.TREE_EFFDT,'YYYY-MM-DD'),
B.TREE_NODE_NUM,
B.TREE_NODE_NUM_END,C.SETID,C.DEPTID,TO_CHAR(C.EFFD
T,'YYYY-MM-DD')

FROM PSOPRDEFN A, PS_SCRTY_TBL_DEPT B, PS_DEPT_TBL C
WHERE A.ROWSECCLASS = B.ROWSECCLASS
AND B.SETID = C.SETID
AND B.DEPTID = C.DEPTID
AND C.EFFDT = (SELECT MAX(C_ED.EFFDT) FROM
PS_DEPT_TBL C_ED
WHERE C.SETID = C_ED.SETID
AND C.DEPTID = C_ED.DEPTID
AND C_ED.EFFDT <= SYSDATE)
```

Order by A.OPRID, C.DESCR to ensure that the user IDs (OPRID) and department descriptions (DESCR) are listed in alphabetical order.

Select a sample of HR users and assess whether they have access to update their own HR data (i.e., job) by observing them attempting to make such changes.

1.2.1 Review security design documentation detailing the configured controls implemented in the system and approved by management. In particular, review the online edit and validation checks, range checks, etc.

For either a sample of the edit and validation checks or for the entire population, enter changes to employee data and observe the success or failure of these attempts. Organizations may be reluctant to allow auditors to have access to make test changes in the production environment. Consequently, the following audit tests should be performed in the Test or Quality Assurance (QA) environment. It is important to corroborate that the configuration of controls in the Test/QA environment is the same as that in the production environment. Alternatively, the tables could be extracted to a Microsoft Access database or ACL and queried offline.

For example, attempt to change the bank ID and branch ID of an employee's bank information via Home→Workforce Administration→Personal Information→Biographical→Bank Accounts. Change the bank ID and/or branch ID to an erroneous value and observe whether a warning message is displayed.

Attempt to change the employee's pay group via Home→Workforce Administration→Job Information→Job Data→Payroll. Change the pay group field to an erroneous value and observe whether a warning message is issued.

Review the DATE LAST INCREASE field via Home→Workforce Administration→Personal Information→Job Data→Employment Data (at the bottom of the page), and determine whether this corresponds to the last authorized pay increase. It should be noted that not all potential pay increase scenarios impact this date change. Consequently, this testing technique on its own may not be considered an effective audit technique to identify potential unauthorized changes and should be supplemented by other testing techniques.

For example, to generate a sample of employees, generate a compensation history by writing the following query in query master:

```
SELECT JO.EFFDT, JO.ACTION, JO.ACTION_REASON,
JO.ANNUAL_RT, JO.EMPLID
FROM PS_JOB J
WHERE JO.CHANGE_AMT <> 0
AND JO.EMPLID = 'specific EmplID'
```

Order by JO.EFFDT to ensure that the output is in effective date (EFFDT) order.

Review the compensation history and investigate the validity of the changes.

1.2.2 Review security design documentation detailing the configured controls implemented in the system and approved by management, particularly the audit trails setup. Determine with relevant management the procedures in place for generating, reviewing and investigating audit reports showing changes to employee master data. Inspect a sample of audit trail reports for evidence of review and rectification of exception items identified.

Commencements

Commencements: Risks

Significant risks associated with processing commencements include:

2.1 **Access to the hiring process**—Information regarding an applicant may already exist as master data following the recruitment process. Once an applicant is hired, additional master data, such as contract information, may be entered into the system. Contract data can be set up in the system via Home→Recruiting→Hire Applicants→Prepare for Hire→Create Employment Contracts. If access to hire employees and maintain contract information, such as compensation (salary), standard hours, deductions and eligible benefits, is not restricted, employees may be inappropriately hired, phantom employees may be created, or inappropriate/unauthorized changes may be made to contract information. Consequently, data held in the database may not accurately reflect employee information or conditions of employment for specific employees.

2.2 **Changes to employee contract data**—All relevant data should be entered accurately on hiring an employee due to the dependency of the payroll processing functions. If incorrect employee data are held in the database, subsequent payroll processing and/or payroll reporting may be inaccurate, leading to inappropriate or inaccurate payments to employees.

Commencements Key Controls

Key controls over the processing of commencements include:

2.1.1 Access security matrices and documentation should be in place and maintained defining the roles, permission lists, menus and pages required for different job functions within the HR department. This documentation should have been reviewed and approved by management prior to implementation.

2.1.2 Access to hire employees functions (via Home→Recruiting→Hire Applicants→Hire) and maintain employee contract information (via Home→Recruiting→Hire Applicants→Prepare for Hire→Create Employment Contracts) should be restricted to authorized personnel and established to support segregation of duties.

2.2.1 Edit and validation checks have been implemented. For example, changes to job codes are validated against the Job Code table to ensure that the code exists and the system issues a warning to the user if an invalid code is chosen. Business units and department IDs entered are validated against a list of valid business units and department IDs. It should be noted that many of the data entry fields in PeopleSoft are populated via drop-down boxes or have look-up tables or prompt lists that detail all possible values.

Commencements: Testing Techniques

Testing techniques for commencement processing include:

2.1.1 Review access security matrices and access assignment documentation to gain an understanding of the security design. Determine if such documentation was authorized by management prior to implementation.

2.1.2 Generate lists of users with access to the Workforce Administration, Workforce Development, Recruiting and Applicant Contract Data menus and review their level of access by writing the SQL query detailed previously in the Master Data Maintenance: Testing Techniques section 1.1.1, in PeopleSoft Query Manager.

Select a sample of HR users and assess whether they have access to update their own HR data (i.e., job) by observing them attempting to make such changes.

2.2.1 Review security design documentation detailing the configured controls implemented in the system and approved by management, particularly the online edit and validation checks, range checks, etc. For either a sample of the edit and validation checks or for the entire population, enter changes to employee contract data (via Home→Workforce Administration→Job Information→Contract Administration→Update Contracts), and observe the success or failure of these attempts and whether a warning message is displayed. [Note that the above menu navigation path is different from Home→Recruiting→Hire Applicants→Prepare for Hire→Create Employment Contracts, which is for creating *applicant* contracts. The first menu path described is for access to *employee* contracts.]

Organizations may be reluctant to allow auditors to have the ability to make test changes in the production environment. Consequently, the following audit tests should be performed in the Test or QA environment. It is important to corroborate that the configuration of controls in the Test/QA environment is the same as that in the production environment.

Personal Development

Personal Development: Risks

Significant risks associated with processing personal development include:

3.1 **Access to career planning**—As discussed in chapter 5, the career planning functionality of PeopleSoft tracks employee career plans, and competency and accomplishment information held in the databases. Career planning information is used in succession planning to assist management in identifying potential succession candidates. If access to career planning is not restricted, unauthorized or inappropriate changes may be made to employee competency and accomplishment data. Consequently, inaccurate information regarding employee skill sets may lead to incorrect promotion decisions.

3.2 **Access to succession planning**—Access to succession planning should be restricted to ensure that succession plans adequately reflect the needs of the organization by identifying key positions, current incumbents and potential succession candidates. If such access is not restricted, information regarding incumbents and potential succession candidates may not be accurately reflected in the system. Consequently, the identification of the resource requirements of the organization may not be adequate.

3.3 **Access to training administration**—Employee competencies and accomplishments may be achieved through the attendance of formal training courses. Such training courses and the associated training programs should be designed to develop employee skills in line with the needs of the organization. If access to the course tables and training program tables is not restricted, the training courses available may not be relevant. In addition, the associated course budgets, prerequisite courses, and target competencies and accomplishments may not be accurately reflected in the system.

Personal Development: Key Controls

Key controls over the processing of personal development include:

3.1.1 Access security matrices and documentation should be in place, defining the roles, permission lists, menus and pages required for different job functions within the HR department. This documentation should have been reviewed and approved by management prior to implementation.

3.1.2 Access to maintain employee strengths and development areas as part of an employee's career plan (via Home→Workforce Development→Career Planning→Prepare→Create Career Plan) should be restricted to authorized HR personnel.

3.2.1 Access to succession planning (via Home→Organizational Development→Succession Planning→Create Succession Plan) should be restricted to authorized HR personnel.

3.3.1 Only authorized HR personnel should have access to:

- Define courses (via Home→Enterprise Learning→Define Course/Cost Details→Courses)

- Maintain training program tables (via Home→Enterprise Learning→Define Course/Cost Details→Program Information)

Personal Development: Testing Techniques

Testing techniques for personal development include:

3.1.1 Review access security matrices and access assignment documentation to gain an understanding of the security design. Determine if the documentation was authorized by management prior to implementation.

3.1.2 Generate lists of users with access to:

3.2.1 • Career Planning—Home→Workforce Development→Career Planning→Prepare→Create Career Plan

3.3.1 • Succession Planning—Home→Organizational Development→Succession Planning→Create Succession Plan

- Training Administration (Course Tables)—Home→Organizational Development→Succession Planning→Create Succession Plan
- Training Administration (Training Program Tables)—Home→Enterprise Learning→Define Course/Cost Details→Program Information

Review their level of access by writing the SQL query detailed in Master Data Maintenance Testing Technique 1.1.1 in PeopleSoft Query Manager. Select a sample of HR users, and assess whether they have access to update the strengths and development area pages of their own career plans by observing them attempting to make such changes.

Terminations

Terminations: Risks

Significant risks associated with processing terminations include:

4.1 **Access to process terminations**—If access to terminate employees is not restricted, there is an increased risk that employees may be inappropriately or incorrectly terminated in the system.

Terminations: Key Controls

Key controls over processing terminations include:

4.1.1 Access security matrices and documentation should be in place, defining the roles, permission lists, menus and pages required for different job functions within the HR department. This documentation should have been reviewed and approved by management prior to implementation.

4.1.2 Access to terminations (via Home→Workforce Administration→Job Information→Job Data) should be restricted to authorized HR personnel.

Terminations: Testing Techniques

Testing techniques for the processing of terminations include:

4.1.1 Review access security matrices and access assignment documentation to gain an understanding of the security design. Determine if the documentation was authorized by management prior to implementation.

4.1.2 Generate lists of users with access to terminate employees on the system (via Home→Workforce Administration→Job Information→Job Data), and review their level of access by writing the SQL query detailed in Master Data Maintenance Testing Techniques 1.1.1 in PeopleSoft Query Manager.

4.1.3 Evaluate the current process for removing terminated employee access to PeopleSoft to ensure efficient and timely removal of user access.

Summary

This chapter outlined the risks, key controls and testing techniques surrounding the PeopleSoft HR business cycle. Among the key risks are unrestricted access to HR setup tables and commencement and termination processing, leading to inappropriate and/or unauthorized modifications made to HR data.

7. PeopleSoft Payroll Business Cycle

This chapter outlines the functionality of the PeopleSoft Payroll business cycle and provides a high-level understanding of the process. From a risk and controls perspective, the Payroll cycle has four main subprocesses as shown in **figure 7.1**:

- Master Data Maintenance
- Recording Attendance and Leave Processing
- Calculating and Disbursing Payroll
- Reporting and Reconciliation

Figure 7.1—Payroll Business Cycle Subprocesses

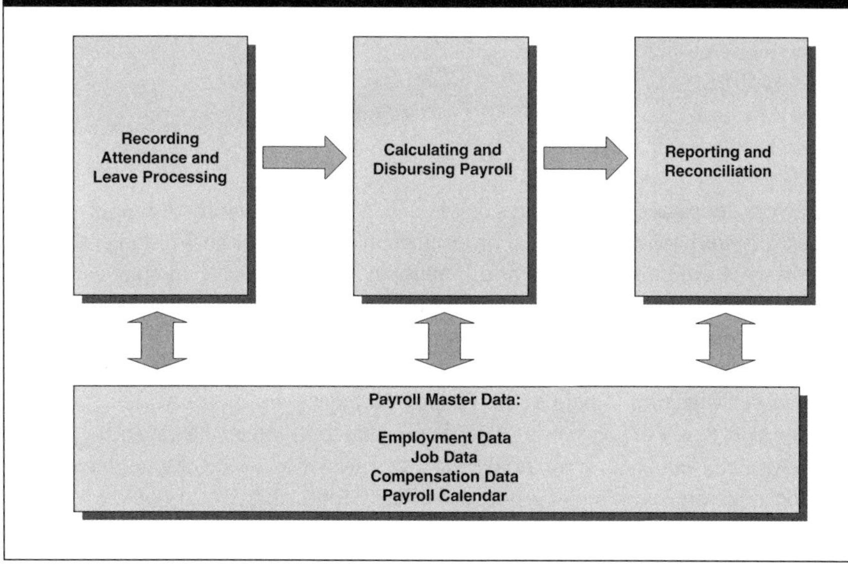

Master Data Maintenance

Payroll master data are used to calculate an employee's paycheck during the payroll process. The payroll master data make use of the basic information accumulated through the HR module. Some payroll settings are defined within the HR master data, for example:

- Employment master data hold information regarding deductions and pay groups.
- Job master data hold information about compensation and salaries, pay frequency, and standard hours.

The main types of payroll master data used to calculate a paycheck are:

- Earnings
- Deductions
- Garnishments
- Taxation

The data in the previous paragraph are in addition to the HR master data utilized, such as personal details, employment details and job information. (HR master data are discussed in detail in chapter 5.)

Earnings

Earnings are the positive payments made to employees and are driven by a number of different components, including the compensation rate, or salary, and the pay frequency (i.e., how often employees are paid). There are many different types of earnings, and each of these is defined by an earnings code in the system, for example:

- reg—Regular pay
- bns—Bonus
- adv—Advance
- com—Commission
- otp—Overtime
- vac—Vacation
- exp—Expense reimbursement

Employees are placed in a pay group, which is a logical grouping of employees specifically for payroll purposes. For instance, pay groups may distinguish the employees of different countries or different pay frequencies (i.e., employees paid weekly, biweekly and monthly form three different pay groups). The assignment of employees to pay groups not only determines their pay frequency, but also, depending on the implementation, defines other default payroll parameters, such as minimum and maximum net pay (in PeopleSoft Payroll for North America). Each pay group has a set of earn codes that are relevant to it, referred to as earning plans. As a consequence, when new earn codes are set up in the earning table, they must be associated with a pay group in the Pay Group table.

Earnings are set up via one of two paths:

- Home→Setup HRMS→Product Related→North American Payroll→Compensation and Earnings→Earnings Table
- Home→Setup HRMS→Product Related→Global Payroll→Elements→Payroll Elements→Earnings

Deductions

Deductions are the amount subtracted from the earnings in the payroll calculation normally payable to external parties (e.g., union dues, medical insurance, loan payback). As with earnings, there are a significant number of deduction types, for example:

- loan—Load payback
- union—Union dues
- unionc—Union dues—Canada
- usbond—US savings bond deduction
- life—Life insurance plan

- basmed—Basic medical
- dental—Dental plan

The following parameters can be defined for deductions:

- Before or after tax—This defines whether deductions are applied before or after the tax has been calculated.
- Priority—This defines the order in which deductions are taken from an employee's earnings.
- Deduction table schedule—This defines when a deduction is scheduled to occur. That is, if a weekly paid employee has monthly deductions, the amounts are to be deducted only once a month and not from every weekly paycheck.

Deductions are set up via either of two paths:

- Home→Setup HRMS→Product Related→North American Payroll→Deductions→Deductions Table.
- Home→Setup HRMS→Product Related→Global Payroll→Elements→Payroll Elements→Deductions

Garnishments

Garnishments are another form of deduction from an employee's earnings and are set up at the employee level. These are deductions that usually occur when an employee owes money to external third parties (e.g., court orders). Even if an employee owes money to external parties and garnishments have been set up, it is possible to have a certain amount of the employee's net pay "protected." Protected net pay is an amount defined in the system that represents the minimum net pay that must be paid to an employee irrespective of garnishment to be deducted. Garnishments are deducted only to the extent that the protected net pay amount is maintained. Garnishments are set up via one of two paths:

- Home→Global Payroll→Payee Data (Country)→Garnishments→Assign Garnishments (Country)
- Home→North American Payroll→Employee Pay Data→Deductions→Create Garnishments

Taxes

Taxes differ depending on the country of implementation. Tax rules and rates are held in the system for local (e.g., municipal), state and federal taxes. The calculation of tax is dependent on the tax type and can be a percentage of taxable gross earnings or based on a graduated scale that is dependent on the marital status or income of the employee. In addition to these rules, employee-specific tax data are also held in the system. Employee tax data can be maintained manually via either of two paths:

- Home→Global Payroll→Payee Data→Taxes→Maintain Tax Data (Country)
- Home→North American Payroll→Employee Pay Data→Tax Information→ Update Employee Tax Data

Other Pertinent Master Data

Banking details are maintained for the source bank (i.e., the bank and branch from which funds are transferred) and disbursement banks (i.e., the bank and branch to which funds are transferred). It is important to remember that disbursement banks not only include employee bank details for their net pay, but also for third-party recipients, such as healthcare providers. This information is held in the Bank table and Bank Branch table (Home→Set Up HRMS →Common Definitions→Banking→Banks). The employee's individual banking information is maintained within Home→Workforce Administration→Personnel Information→Biographical→Bank Accounts.

In addition to defining the destination bank and account, an employee may require certain percentages or amounts of their net pay to be paid into different bank accounts. This is referred to as net distribution and is accessed via either of two paths:

- Home→Global Payroll→Payee Data→Net Pay/Recipient Elections→Specify Net Pay Elections
- Home→North American Payroll→Employee Pay Data→Record Direct Deposit

If the Employee Self Service component is configured, employees can update their own net distribution via Home→Employee Self Service→Payroll and Compensation→Payroll Payment Instructions.

Employees are not the only entities to receive payments from an organization during the payroll process. Third-party providers, such as health insurance companies and government bodies, also receive payments in the form of deductions from an employee's earnings. These third-party entities are referred to as recipients. For recipients to receive the employee deductions, it is necessary to store their bank details in the system along with the frequency of payment. Even if an employee is paid weekly, their deductions may be paid to a recipient only on a monthly, quarterly or annual basis.

It is relevant at this stage to revisit some of the master data components introduced in chapter 5 for the HR business process, which is particularly applicable to payroll processing. Job data contain all the current and historical data related to an employee's job and hold certain payroll settings, such as the company name (i.e., the legal entity that the employee works for); pay group, which determines how the employee is paid (e.g., hourly, salaried) and the basis upon which compensation is made and changed (e.g., standard hours, salary ranges); and compensation rates and frequencies.

Recording Attendance and Leave Processing

This subsection provides an overview of the functionality of the time and labor system. An employee (or even a nonemployee) may have been set up in the HR system, but he/she is not automatically set up in the Time and Labor system. Not all people within an organization report or account for their time in the same way; some employees are not required to report their time at all (e.g., senior management). If an employee is required to account for his/her time as part of the job, he/she must be enrolled as a time reporter. Time reporters must be assigned to a work group, which defines the type of time reporting. There are two types of time reporting—positive and exception—as shown in **figure 7.2**.

Figure 7.2—Types of Time Reporting

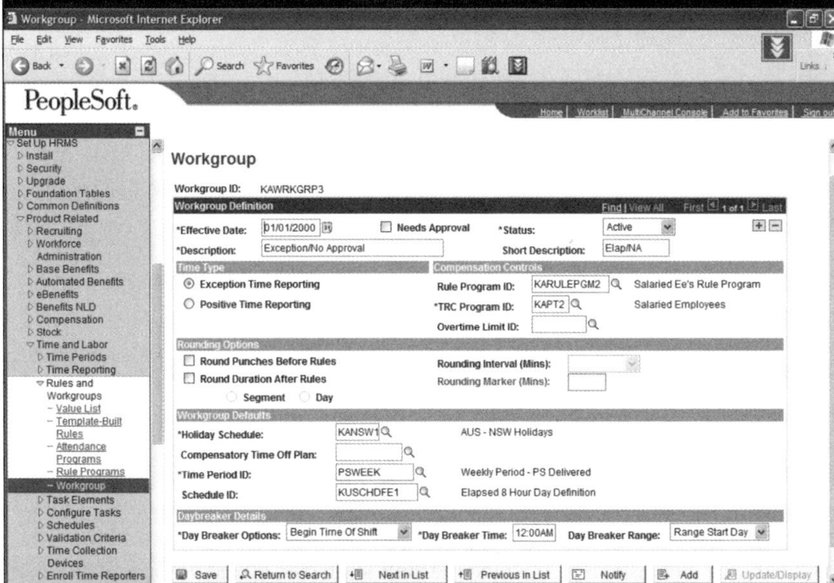

Positive Time Reporting

Time reporters are required to report the time they work in any given period before they are paid for it. This is similar to submitting a time sheet and being paid only for the time worked and is common for time reporters who are normally paid on an hourly basis.

Exception Time Reporting

Many employees may have standard hours defined in their contract and under their master data in the system. Consequently, it is assumed that they have worked these hours and, thus, are compensated for them. Instances where they are not paid are the "exceptions" (hence the term exception time reporting), e.g., when leave without pay is requested or unpaid sick leave is taken.

Employees within PeopleSoft are paid on the basis of payable time. Payable time is the time an employee has worked and for which he/she is entitled to compensation or pay. Consequently, payable time for positive time reporters is directly represented by the time that is entered into the system indicating the hours they have actually worked in a given period. Payable time for an exception time reporter is based on default standard hours unless adjusted for an exception.

It should be noted that when the time is submitted to the system, it is classified as reported time. It becomes payable time when it has been validated as part of the time administration process. Time is reported within PeopleSoft against time reporting codes (TRCs) that describe the activity that has occurred during the time being reported. TRCs are set up within the Time and Labor application and are analogous with earnings codes. It is at this level that overtime compensation differentials can be defined. For example, if a time worker works on weekends, he/she is paid two times his/her hourly rate.

Time recording in the system may be performed either by the employee via the self-service functionality or by payroll staff on the basis of approved manual time sheets submitted. In some cases, online approval may be required before a time reporter is paid for his/her time submitted. The time entry must be set to Needs Approval for this to occur.

It is important for payroll processing purposes to define when a period for pay begins and ends. For normal day-to-day jobs (e.g., 9 a.m. to 5 p.m. jobs), this is easy. However, time reporters may work shifts that span calendar days; therefore, it is necessary to determine how their time will be attributed across the days worked. The point where one working day crosses over to the next working day is referred to as a day breaker; this can be midnight, in line with the normal calendar day, or any point in time that is appropriate. For instance, if a shift worker works overnight, his/her effective working day does not coincide with the calendar day so the day breaker is different. The system provides options to assign all the time worked to the calendar day on which the shift started or ended or the day on which the majority of the time was worked. It even allows apportionment of the time across calendar days.

Time can be entered in the system via what is referred to as rapid time entry. This is accessed via Home→Time and Labor→Report Time→ Report Rapid Time. Once the time has been reported, it must be submitted for validation by the system. This includes verification that the employee is an active employee on the system. Any errors identified are stored for review via the Manage Group Exceptions page, as shown in **figure 7.3**. This reported time is converted to payable time within the system and is subsequently paid through the banking process discussed later in this chapter.

Figure 7.3—Exceptions Report

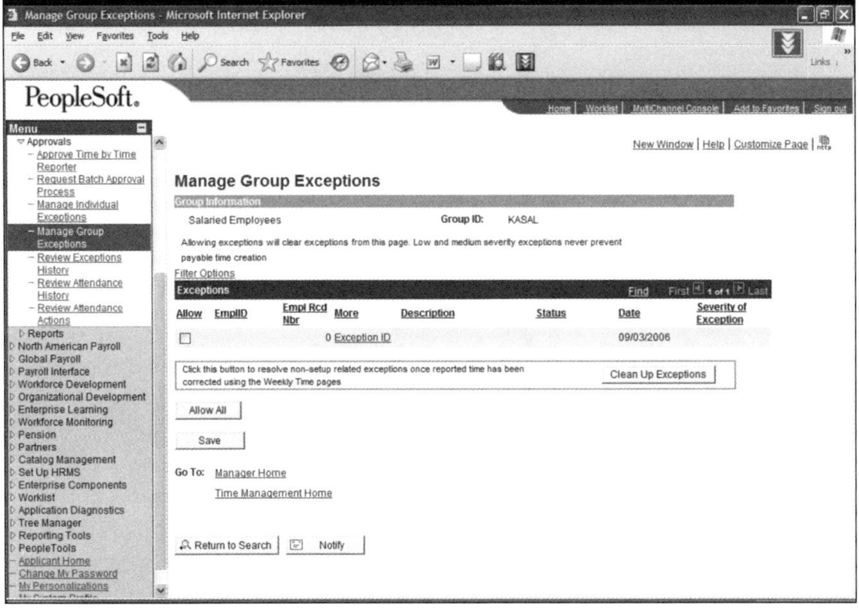

Tracking Time and Attendance

It is possible to track time, attendance and a time reporter's attendance habits. For instance, it is possible to monitor if an employee is continually late for work or leaves early and to specify violation actions. Violation actions can be based on points accumulated for violations (e.g., late for work or long lunches). Based on the points built up, actions can be specified (e.g., issue a verbal or written warning). Violation history can also be monitored for a specified period of time.

Leave and Absence Processing

Employees may take a leave of absence for a number of reasons (e.g., annual leave, sick leave, study leave). Within PeopleSoft, absences are described by absence types (e.g., sickness). Absence types are associated with one or more absence codes, which provide detailed descriptions for a specific type of absence. For example, a number of illnesses (general sickness, surgery, etc.) may be tracked as absence codes under the absence type of sickness, as shown in **figures 7.4** and **7.5**.

Absence classes are logical groupings of absence types that are established in the system for reporting purposes, dependent on the country or region of implementation. Absence classes are identified within PeopleSoft by the set ID.

Whether an employee is paid during his/her period of absence is defined in the Absence Type table.

Figure 7.4—Absence Type Table

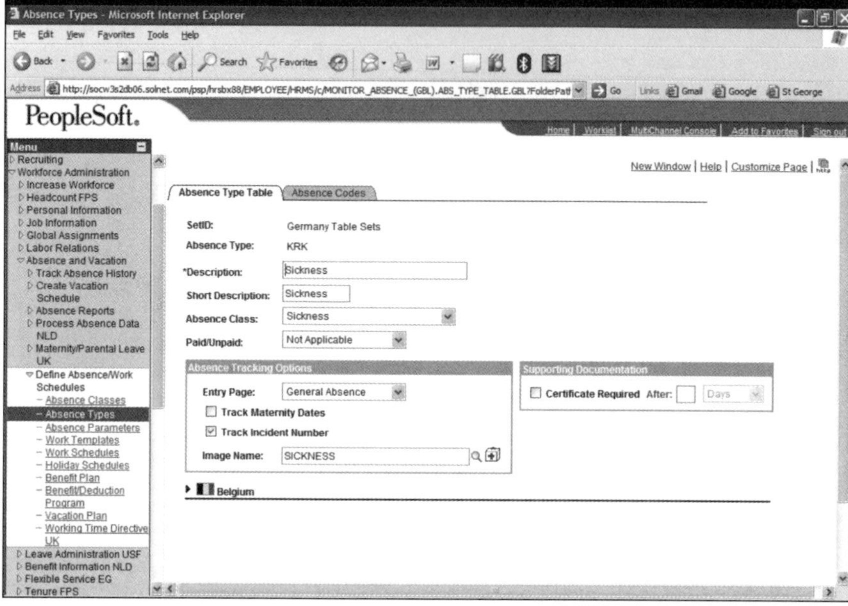

Figure 7.5—Absence Codes

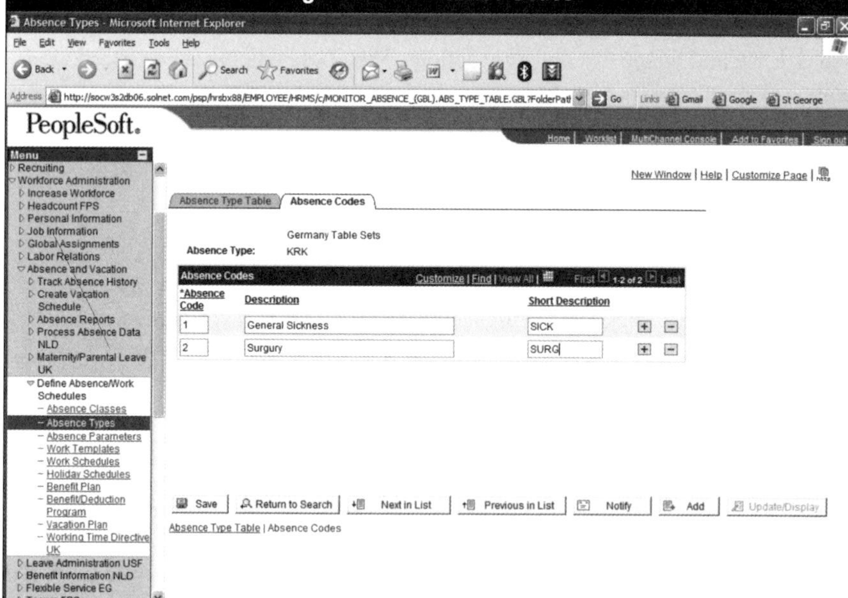

Setting up the types of absences in the system facilitates the monitoring of absences. Unplanned absences are referred to as general absences; these are entered into the system together with follow-up actions taken and comments, if necessary, as shown in **figures 7.6**, **7.7** and **7.8**.

Figure 7.6—Absence Data

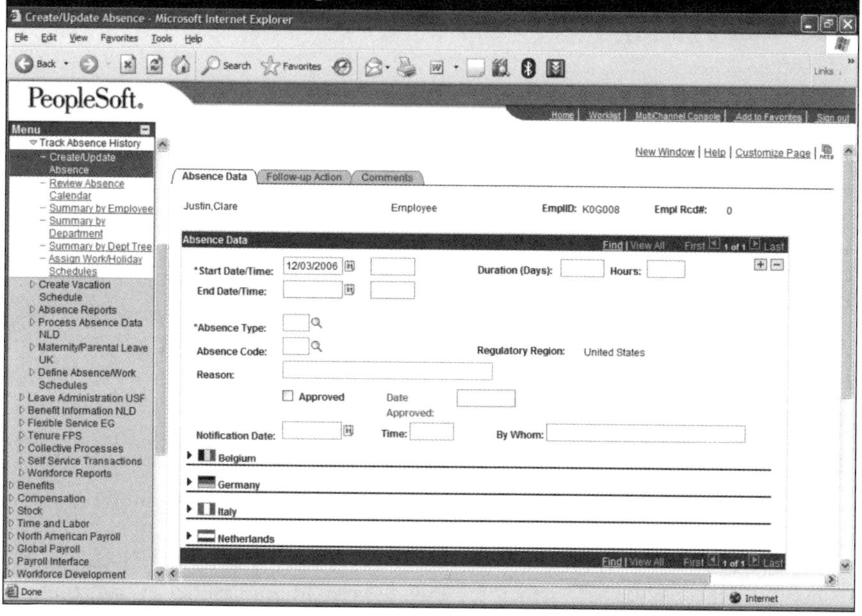

Figure 7.7—Absence Follow-up Action

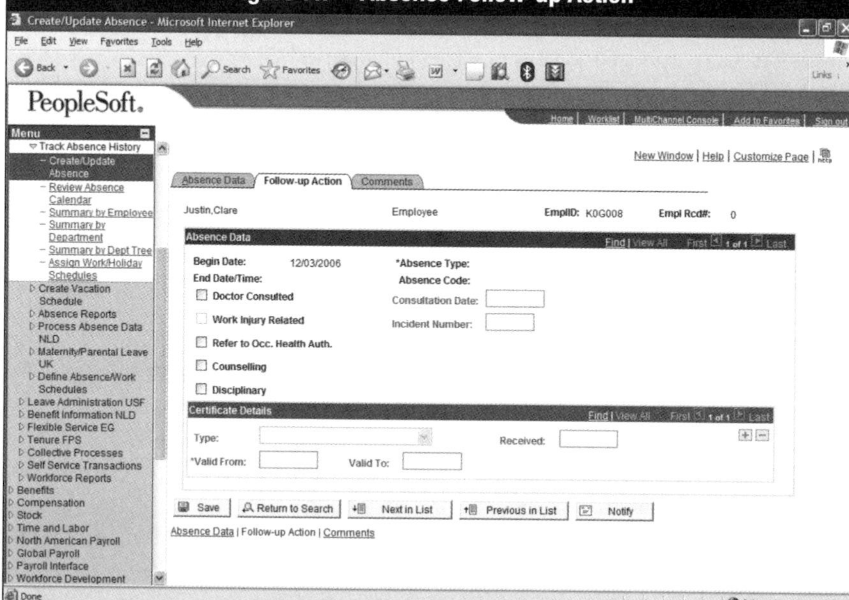

Figure 7.8—Absence Comments

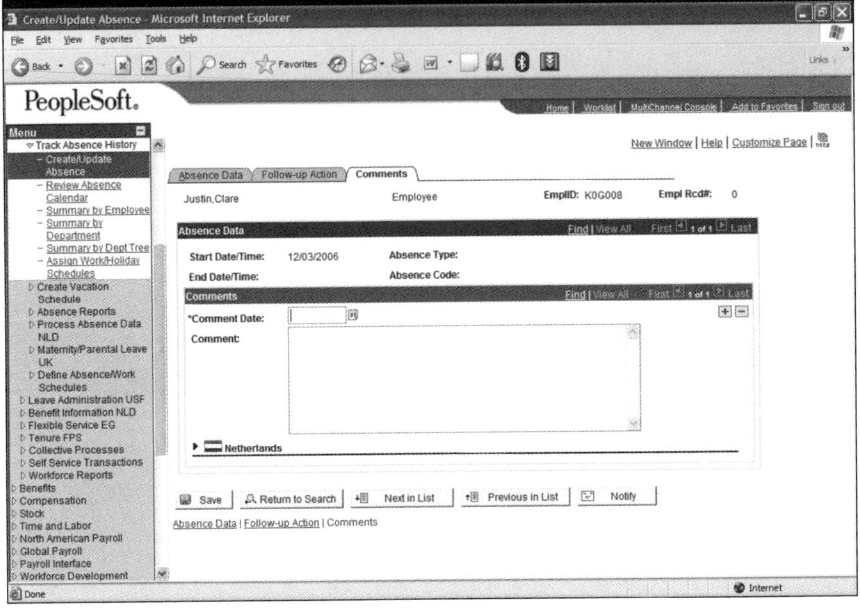

Annual leave or vacation absences must be set up as vacation plans in the system. An organization may wish to set up different vacation plans for different countries or regions, but each vacation plan must have the following criteria defined:

- Maximum leave balance—This represents the maximum number of days that an employee may hold as an annual leave entitlement.
- Maximum leave carryover—This represents the maximum number of days that an employee may carry over into the next period if he/she does not use up his/her annual leave entitlement in a particular period.
- Accrual frequency—This represents the period over which an employee builds up or accrues his/her annual leave entitlement.
- Entitlement rate value—This allows an organization to vary an employee's annual leave entitlement based on his/her length of service or age.

Vacation plans are normally included in benefits programs, which are then assigned to employees. Benefits administration is not included for the purposes of this guide.

Employee leave or vacation accruals are updated by running the PeopleSoft Vacation Accrual process. This is done via Home→Workforce Administration→Absence and Vacation→Create Vacation Schedule→Accrue Vacation. This process should be run prior to submitting vacation requests to the system, to ensure that the employee's leave accrual is up to date.

Vacation requests are entered and approved in the system via Home→Workforce Administration→Create Vacation Schedule→Request/Approve Vacation, as shown in **figure 7.9**.

Figure 7.9—Vacation Request

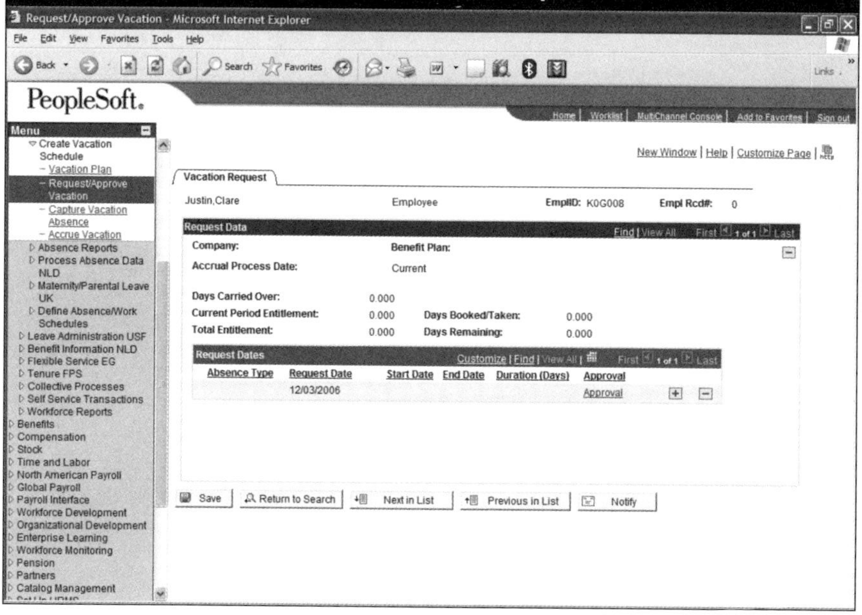

Self-service Components

The introduction of self-service functionality allows users (employees, applicants, etc.) to access the system and administer various elements of their own information. Employees are able to enter time worked and request a leave of absence, among other functions. Payees can use the self-service features of PeopleSoft Global Payroll to review absence balances through a web browser, enter requests for absences and forecast absence balances as of a particular date. Managers can use the self-service features to enter and approve requests for absences. In addition, employees can use the self-service features to enter time worked, and managers can approve time worked via the self-service features.

Time

A time reporter can enter his/her time via Home→Employee Self Service→Time Reporting→ Record Time→Report Weekly Punch Time. As shown in **figure 7.10**, the Date, Time and Type (e.g., in, out, meal, break) are required fields within the Punch Time entry.

Absence Request

An employee can review his/her vacation accrual balance or request a leave of absence via Home→Employee Self Service→Time Reporting→Record

Figure 7.10—Weekly Punch Time

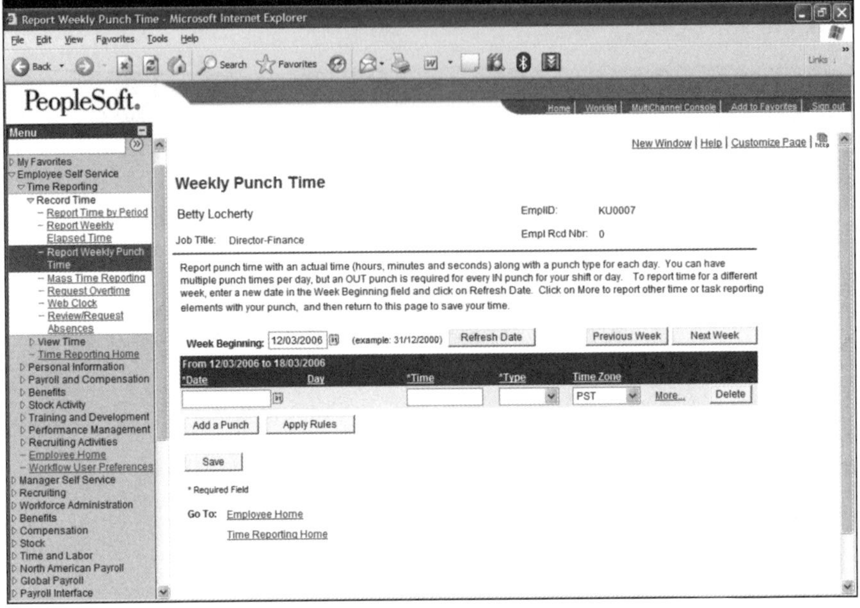

Time→Request/Review Absences, as shown in **figures 7.11** and **7.12**. A manager can approve an absence request via Home→Manager Self Service→Time Management→Approvals→Approve Absence Requests.

Figure 7.11—Absence History

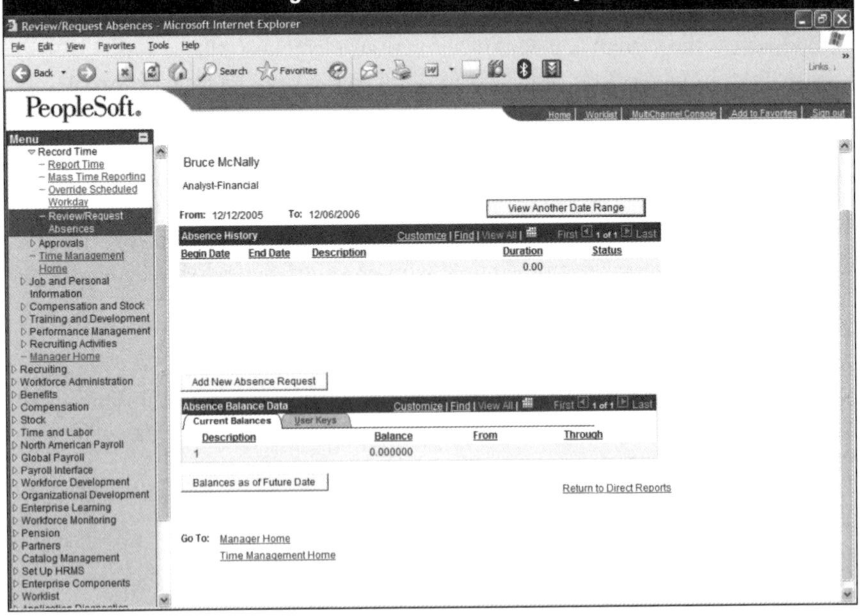

Figure 7.12—Absence Detail

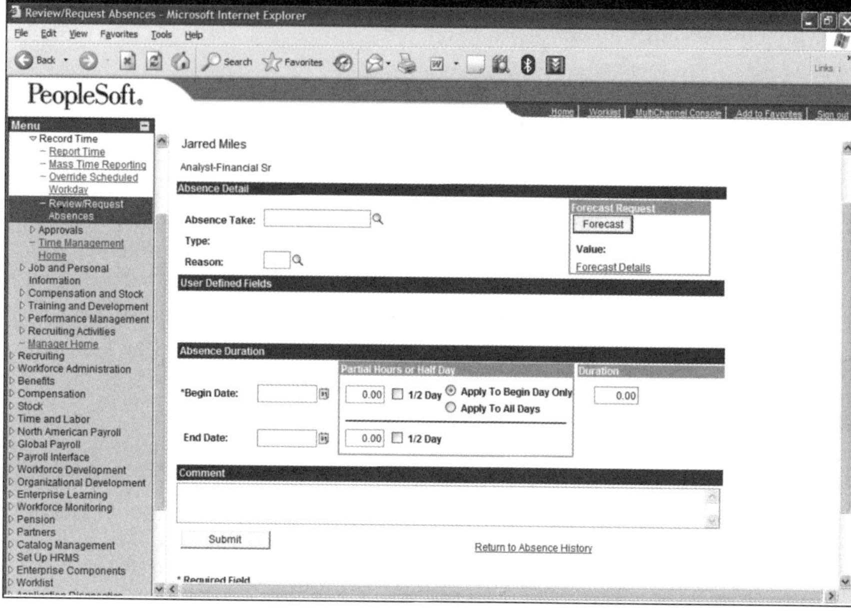

Calculating and Disbursing Payroll

The payroll process takes the master data related to employees, job data, time and attendance data, and deduction and taxation data to calculate the net pay for employees within an organization. **Figure 7.13** illustrates a simplified version of a payroll process. The payroll process within PeopleSoft can be divided into three subprocesses:

- Payee Identification/Payee Selection
- Payroll Calculation
- Payroll Confirmation (finalization)

Figure 7.13—Simplified Payroll Process

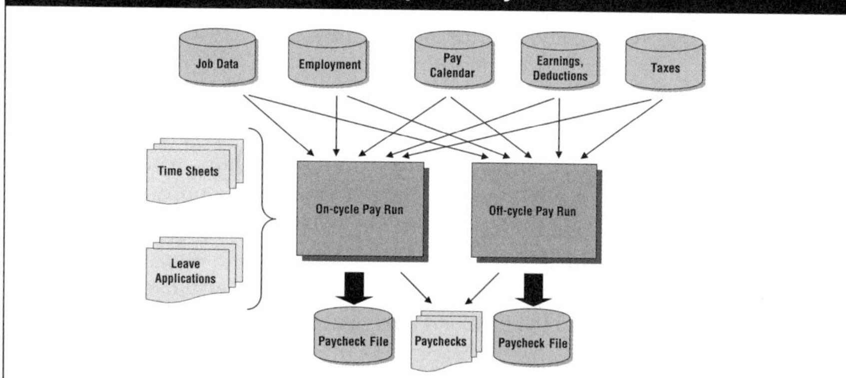

PeopleSoft delivers two payroll processing applications within PeopleSoft HRMS: PeopleSoft Global Payroll and PeopleSoft North American Payroll. They are described in the following sections.

Before a payroll run can be processed, a pay calendar must be established in the system. The pay calendar defines all the pay periods (i.e., pay dates) for each company and a pay group is set up. The pay period dates of a particular payroll period determine the earnings, deductions and absences that are to be included in a specific pay run calculation. There are two types of pay runs: on cycle and off cycle.

The on-cycle pay run represents the automatic, normal payroll processing run, which corresponds to the planned pay runs defined in the pay calendar. Off-cycle pay runs involve the processing of *ad hoc* pay (e.g., for mistakes made in the original on-cycle pay run or for emergency payments to employees).

PeopleSoft Global Payroll

The Payroll Run process is an iterative process in the Global Payroll component; each phase of the Payroll process is initiated from the Calculate Absence and Payroll Process page (Home→Global Payroll→Absence and Payroll Processing→Calculate Absence and Payroll).

The phases of the Payroll process include:
- Payee Identification
- Payroll Calculation
- Payroll Finalization

In the first phase (Payee Identification), PeopleSoft iterates through each of the pay calendars for the selected calendar group and identifies the payees associated with each particular calendar. Payees are associated with a calendar during calendar setup.

The Payee Identification process is initiated by selecting the Identify option in the Calculate Absence and Payroll page (Home→Global Payroll→Absence and Payroll Processing→Calculate Absence and Payroll).

At this stage, it is possible to make further manual adjustments to take into account last-minute changes, such as additional hours not already recorded, bonus or commission adjustments, a recent termination, or a new hire. While the Payee Identification phase can be run only once per pay calendar group, any changes, such as those mentioned, will be included in the pay run during the Payroll Calculation phase. Predefined "trigger definitions" generate a trigger for a specified data change. Triggers are then identified during the Payroll Calculation phase of the Payroll run, and the changed data are included.

Once payees have been identified, the Payroll Calculation phase can begin. During this phase, the net and gross pay for each employee are calculated by identifying the employee's salary and standard hours, or hourly rates and hours worked. This is adjusted by the system for any leave taken, which may be paid or unpaid, or changes to circumstances that can have an impact on earnings (e.g., job changes or pay rate changes during the period).

The individual deductions, taxes and garnishments relevant for each employee are also applied to arrive at a net pay amount. From the setup of the deductions (whether defined as before- or after-tax deductions) in the system, PeopleSoft applies the deductions and taxes accordingly and determines the net pay amount. The Payroll Calculation phase is an iterative process; after each calculation run, the results can be viewed and verified. Changes can then be made to data before the calculation process is run again. A calculation run can be set either to Recalculate All, which recalculates the net pay for all payees, or Calculate, which calculates the net pay only for changed payees.

The results from the Payroll Calculation phase can be viewed after each phase using a number of pages, including:

- Processing Statistics—Shows the processing results by the number of payees who are in error, calculated, finalized, active, inactive, cancelled and suspended. Process statistics are accessed via Home→Global Payroll→Absence and Payroll Processing, Review Absence/Payroll Info→Processing Statistics.
- Payee Status—Shows the current status of payees for a calendar group. This page can be used to drill down on payees identified in the processing statistics. It is also possible to enter processing instructions for each payee. The payee status is accessed via Home→Global Payroll→Absence and Payroll Processing, Review Absence/Payroll Info→Payee Status.
- Payee Iterative Lists—Shows all payees processed during the last iteration/batch process. Iterative lists are accessed via Home→Global Payroll→Absence and Payroll Processing, Review Absence/Payroll Info→Payee Iterative List.
- Results by Calendar—Displays payee data regarding earnings, deductions and adjustments. This page can be accessed via Home→Global Payroll→Absence and Payroll Processing, Review Absence/Payroll Info→Results by Calendar.

The final stage of the Payroll process is the Payroll Confirmation or Payroll Finalization. This is performed once all processing errors have been resolved. In addition to confirming the Payroll Calculation stage, the Payroll Confirmation stage updates all balances in the system (e.g., employee year-to-date pay amounts, deductions taken, taxes paid year to date), updates deduction arrears and leave accruals, and assigns check/advice numbers.

PeopleSoft North American Payroll

The North American Payroll component of PeopleSoft is also a three-stage process:
- Paysheet Creation
- Payroll Confirmation
- Payroll Finalization

The first step in the North American Payroll process is the creation of paysheets. This step opens the payroll period. Paysheets are composed of paylines, and each payline represents a paycheck. The paysheet summarizes the employee's total gross earnings by identifying his/her salary and standard hours, or hourly rates and hours worked. This is adjusted by the system for any leave taken, which may be paid or unpaid, or changes to circumstances (e.g., job changes or pay rate changes during the period) that have an impact on the earnings. It is possible to make further manual adjustments to take into account last-minute changes, such as additional hours not already recorded, bonus or commission adjustments, or a recent termination. PeopleSoft delivers an SQR program (Precalculation Report or PAY035) that can be run prior to the next stage (Payroll Confirmation) to identify any possible errors due to a lack of data integrity. For example, this precalculation audit can identify invalid pay rate codes in the pay earnings or find that an earning has missing or invalid state tax data. The payee identification phase is initiated via the menu path Home→North American Payroll→Payroll Processing→Create Initial Paysheets.

The payroll calculation takes the paysheet earnings calculation derived in the Paysheet Creation stage and applies the individual deductions, taxes and garnishments relevant for each employee to arrive at a net pay amount. From the setup of the deductions (whether they are set up as before- or after-tax deductions) in the system, PeopleSoft applies the deductions and taxes accordingly and determines the net pay amount. Payroll calculation can be run in two modes: as a preliminary calculation allowing further adjustments to be made or errors to be fixed, or as a final pay calculation ready for the payroll to be confirmed. It is possible to avoid certain checks in the system by setting the OK to Pay flag of a payline to No. If this is the case, the Payroll Confirmation stage will remove these paylines, which will have to be regenerated with new paysheets. This function is sometimes used for nonstandard paid employees, such as employees paid hourly, to ensure an element of manual intervention to review the calculation for these employees.

Results from the payroll calculation can be viewed on the:
- Review PayCheck page—Provides detailed earnings, deductions and calculations for net pay. Access via Home→North American Payroll→Payroll Processing→Run Payroll→Review PayCheck.
- Error Messages page—Provides details of any errors that occurred during calculation. These can be corrected before the pay confirmation phase. Access via Home→North American Payroll→Payroll Processing→Review Processing Messages→Error Messages.

The preliminary pay calculation and the final pay calculation perform the same checks and processing; however, running the pay calculation under preliminary mode will not allow the payroll confirmation process to proceed. The pay calculation phase is initiated via the menu path Home→North American Payroll→Payroll Processing→Calculate Pay.

The final stages of the payroll process are Payroll Confirmation and Payroll Finalization. These are performed once all processing errors have been resolved and paychecks have been produced. In addition to confirming the payroll calculation stage, Payroll Confirmation updates all balances in the system (e.g., employee year-to-date pay amounts, deductions taken, taxes paid year to date), updates deduction arrears and leave accruals, and assigns check/advice numbers. Payroll Finalization is initiated via Home→North American Payroll→Payment Processing→Confirm Pay.

Pay Distribution

Pay can be distributed in one of two ways: via checks or direct deposit into a bank account. PeopleSoft provides mechanisms for both.

Checks are generated and can be printed via Home→North American Payroll→Payroll Processing→Create Checks→Print Checks.

There are two additional check types that should be mentioned at this stage:

- Online check—These are single checks that can be written online instantly if required (e.g., for emergency payments).
- Final check—This relates to the final check that an employee receives upon termination or retirement. This is processed via the Final Check Request menu in the system.

Direct deposit generates an electronically transmittable file that specifies payees, their bank accounts and the amounts they are to be paid. This file is then uploaded to the bank, and the funds are transferred directly into the payee's accounts.

The system will store the bank details of all employees and third-party recipients, such as health insurance providers and government bodies. The direct deposit or banking process for North American Payroll is initiated via Home→North American Payroll→Payroll Processing→Create Direct Deposit→Direct Deposit File.

For Global Payroll, the menu path is Home→Global Payroll→Payment Processing→Create EFT Payment File (Country).

It is possible to group payees into streams based on employee IDs. This is an optional function and allows different payment files to be processed by stream. Whether or not streams are used in the implementation, the payment file is created based on the confirmed pay run produced as a result of the Payroll process and is finalized for payment. The calculation and finalization phases can be split, and a payroll administrator can view the base payment data before they are processed for final payment. A payroll administrator or payroll manager using Home→Global Payroll→Payment Processing→Review Payments by CAL Group can view, as a minimum, the payments, deductions and net pay, as shown in **figure 7.14**.

Figure 7.14—View Net Pay or Deductions

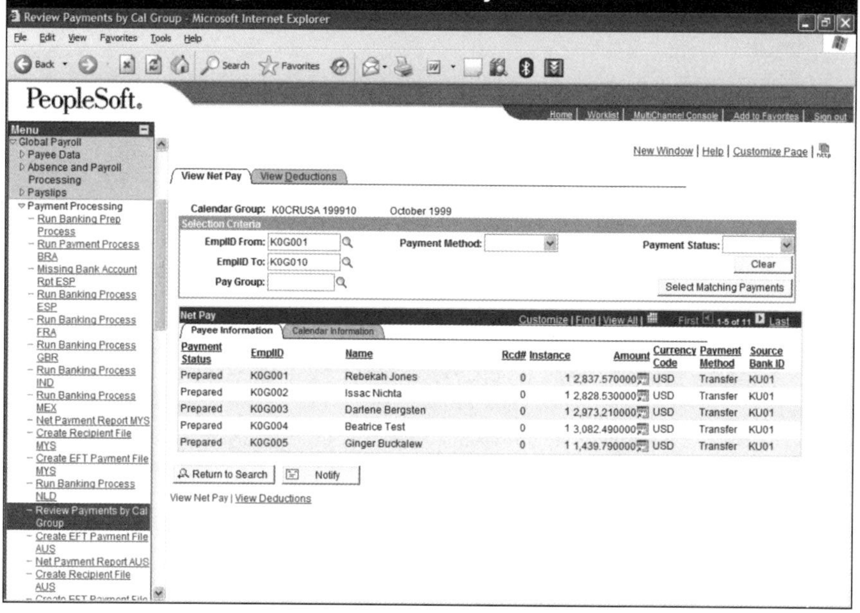

The transfer of the EFT file to banks is dependent on the organization. Some utilize a bank's own EFT transfer software, which may reside as a stand-alone system, and the payment file physically transferred to the EFT machine. Alternatively, an EFT file may be transferred via the internal network to the bank transfer system. Whichever mechanism is used, it is important for the EFT file to remain secure when it is in transit between PeopleSoft and the banking system.

In addition to the payment being processed, pay slips are distributed to the payees. The destination (e.g., home address or office location) of the pay slips is held within the payee's personal master data. Pay slips can also be delivered electronically and accessed through the Employee Self Service component.

Reporting and Reconciliation

A number of reports are available within PeopleSoft at various stages of the payroll process to identify exceptions and validate data before the next stage of the process. For instance, a list of the employees not processed in the current payroll on the Payroll Error Message for Employees report (i.e., employees with OK to Pay set to No) can be run at the paysheet creation (or payee identification) stage to identify errors.

The Payroll Error Message for Employees report can also be run at the pay calculation stage to identify any further exceptions. If the payroll calculation is run in preliminary mode, it may also be appropriate to generate a payroll summary for review prior to running the final payroll calculation. The payroll confirmation stage completes the payroll process. At this point, the following reports may be generated for review by the payroll administrator:

- Payroll Summary
- Payroll Register
- Deductions Register
- Other Earnings Register
- Leave Accruals

Although it is important that the payroll be calculated accurately, completely and on a timely basis, the interface with the GL is also important from a management reporting point of view. For the GL to be updated with the results of the confirmation (or finalization) of the payroll process, the GL process must be finalized. This is sometimes referred to as publishing the payroll data to the GL. When PeopleSoft Global Payroll or PeopleSoft North American Payroll components are integrated with PeopleSoft General Ledger components, the GL can be published automatically from within PeopleSoft Global Payroll.

The process is similar to running the banking (or payment) process. As shown in **figure 7.15**, the GL run control process is accessed for Global Payroll via Home→Global Payroll→Time & Labor/GL Costs→Send Costs to GL→General Ledger Run Control.

The GL run is performed by calendar group (i.e., payroll calendar group) and, if applicable, by stream. The Calculate option generates the GL transactions before actually making the GL postings. This allows the user to review the transactions and correct any errors if necessary. It is possible to generate GL transactions only for payroll runs that have been confirmed in the payroll process.

Figure 7.15—GL Run Control

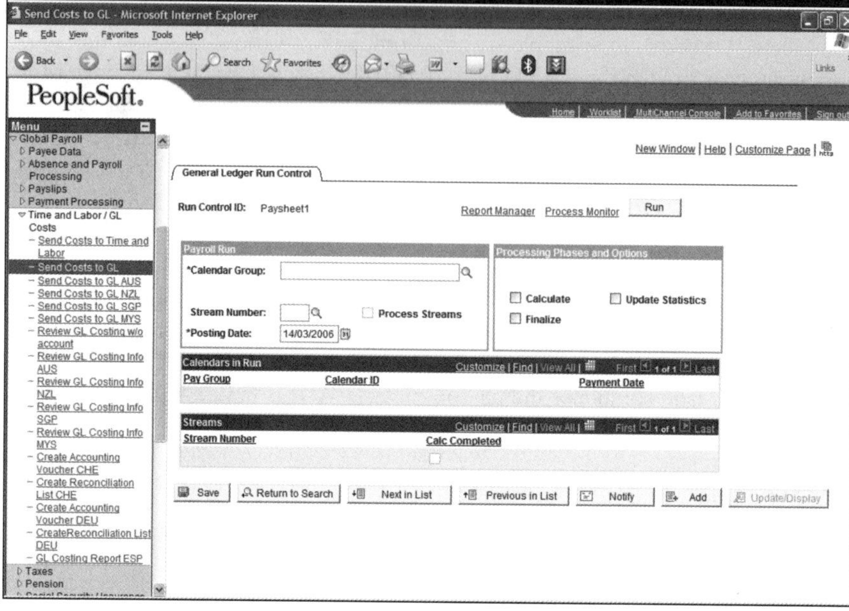

It is possible to select a posting date that is not the current date; this date can be an earlier day, as long as it adheres to the GL period end closing dates. Once all of the errors are rectified, the GL run control process can be finalized and completed. This results in the corresponding GL accounts being updated with earnings, deductions, taxes and cumulative balances, which are a direct reflection of the figures generated in the payroll module.

Summary

The PeopleSoft Payroll cycle is highly integrated with the HR cycle discussed in chapters 5 and 6, as data shared with the HR cycle directly impacts the payroll processing. Profiles of employees (as well as nonemployees), including their compensation details, must be defined in the system. They must perform their duties to be compensated, and this must be captured in the system. Based on their work, the amount of compensation is calculated (taking into account deductions and taxes), and this financial information must be reflected in the financial statements and management reporting. Hence, the Payroll business process can be divided into four components covering all these aspects:

- Master Data Maintenance—Master data encompass personal data, job data, earnings, deductions and taxes, which are required to calculate a worker's net pay.
- Recording Attendance and Leave Processing—Time worked (or attendance) can be based on positive time submitted to the system or on standard hours, which are reduced on an exceptions basis by many different types of leave.

- Calculating and Disbursing Payroll—The payroll process consists of three stages: payee identification, payroll calculation and Payroll Confirmation (or Finalization). The banking process is initiated to physically pay the workers.
- Reporting and Reconciliation—The results of the payroll process must be transferred to the GL through the GL run control process, which automatically updates the predefined GL account codes with earnings, deductions, taxes and cumulative balances.

8. Auditing PeopleSoft Payroll Business Cycle

Chapter 7 outlined the four main subprocesses of the Payroll business cycle. This chapter looks at the significant risks, key controls and techniques to test the controls for each of the four main subprocesses, as shown in **figure 8.1**:

- Maintaining Master Data
- Recording Attendance and Leave Processing
- Calculating and Disbursing Payroll
- Reporting and Reconciliation

Figure 8.1—Payroll Business Cycle Subprocesses

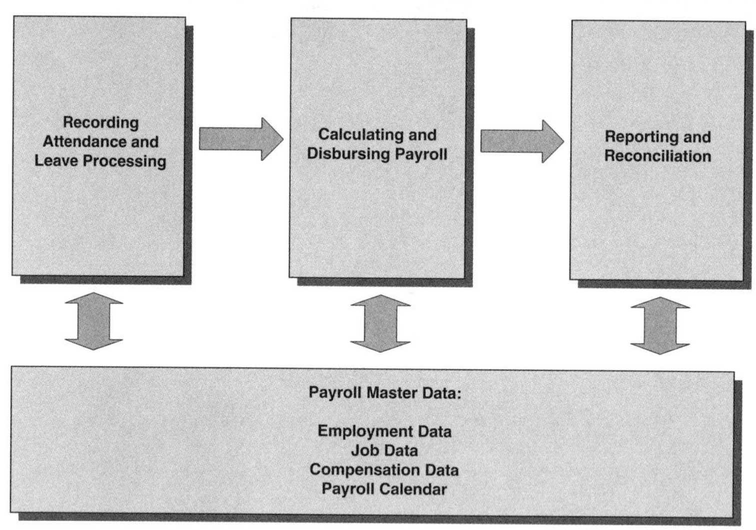

The main process risk control considerations surrounding these business cycle components may be broadly categorized into the following:

- Access—User security
- Integrity checking—Edit and validation

Refer to chapter 6 for their definitions.

For each of the business cycle components, the associated risks, controls and testing techniques are separated into the two categories.

Master Data Maintenance

Master Data Maintenance: Risks

Master data affect the efficient flow of documents and transactions through the system. The inaccurate, incomplete, invalid or untimely creation or maintenance of master data can affect multiple areas within the organization as a transaction progresses through the Payroll cycle. Significant risks associated with the maintenance of payroll master data include:

1.1 **Access to Payroll Setup tables and Master File transaction**—The Payroll business cycle is reliant on a number of key tables in the database, and the data held in these tables are used throughout the HR and payroll applications. There are a number of types of tables (and associated data) that should be considered. Prepayroll process tables and data that drive the payroll calculation may be employee-specific, such as the job (PS_JOB table) and employment (PS_EMPLOYMENT table) data. As discussed in previous chapters, these hold some of the employee's payment settings (e.g., compensation, deductions and employee's pay group). Other prepayroll process control tables are not employee-specific. These configuration-type control tables include:

- Business Unit—Represents an organization or subset of an organization and is used to categorize transactions into logical groupings
- Set ID—Used to gather control data into logical groupings
- Job Code—Identifies a specific type of job in the organization
- Pay Group—Used to organize employees in groups for payroll, e.g., employees of the same pay frequency or pay type (salaried, etc.)
- Earnings—Defines the different earning types (e.g., regular pay, sick pay, overtime, advance) that exist. Earning types are identified in the system by earnings codes. The earnings table also contains a description and calculation rules for each earnings code.
- General Deductions—Defines the different deduction types (e.g., loan payback, union dues, basic medical) that exist. Deductions are identified by deduction codes. The deductions table also contains a description, priority (order in which deductions are taken) and maximum arrears (maximum amount that can be deducted at once if in arrears).
- Federal, State and Local Taxes and Rates—These tables contain the employee taxation elections, tax status (the type of tax calculation, e.g., single or married) and tax rules. These are used to calculate the tax deductions as part of the payroll processing.

The most extensive of these nonemployee-specific foundation tables is the Installation table. The Installation table contains many of the default settings, such as the minimum and maximum standard hours, compensation rate codes and default compensation frequency. Many of the other tables use the Installation table to edit against during the day-to-day payroll processing activities.

If access to these payroll setup tables is not restricted, inappropriate and unauthorized modifications may be made to payroll master data, impacting payroll processing, subsequent payment to employees, and reporting to internal management and external third parties (e.g., for tax purposes). In addition, the data held in the database may not accurately reflect the employee's conditions of employment or his/her personal details. Payroll staff access payroll functions on a day-to-day basis via the PeopleSoft application. While these activities may not require direct access to the underlying payroll setup tables, the transactional data, e.g., changes to pay rates or changes to an employee's job, may have an impact on the payroll processing and, subsequently, the payments made to employees. Such changes are performed via the Administer Workforce menus (Home→Workforce Administration→Job Information). If access to these functions is not restricted, unauthorized changes to the components (earnings, allowances, deductions, taxes, etc.) that make up an employee's payroll calculation may be made.

Earnings are set up via one of two paths:
- Home→Setup HRMS→Product Related→North American Payroll→Compensation and Earnings→Earnings Table
- Home→Setup HRMS→Product Related→Global Payroll→Elements→Payroll Elements→Earnings

Deductions are set up via one of two paths:
- Home→Setup HRMS→Product Related→North American Payroll→Deductions→Deductions Table
- Home→Setup HRMS→Product Related→Global Payroll→Elements→Payroll Elements→Deductions

Garnishments are assigned via one of two paths:
- Home→Global Payroll→Payee Data (Country)→Garnishments→Assign Garnishments (Country)
- Home→North American Payroll→Employee Pay Data→Deductions→Create Garnishments

Employee tax data can be maintained manually via one of two paths:
- Home→Global Payroll→Payee Data→Taxes→Maintain Tax Data (Country)
- Home→North American Payroll→Employee Pay Data→Tax Information →Update Employee Tax Data

In addition, both HR users and payroll users might access the same menus as part of their responsibilities. If access is not restricted appropriately at the row (or even field) level, segregation of duties may be compromised, enabling users to access their own records.

1.2 **Changes to Payroll Setup tables**—If changes made in the payroll setup tables are not made completely and accurately, such changes may not have the desired impact on other tables in the system, leading to a degradation of the data integrity.

1.3 **Changes to Employee Payroll Master Data**—The accuracy, completeness and validity of employee payroll master data changes are critical. If improper updates are made to the employee payroll master file, payroll payments and deductions may be negatively impacted or may result in out-of-date or incorrect master data. For instance, it is important that changes be made using valid codes (e.g., emplID, job codes, earnings and deduction codes). Any invalid or incorrect information could be used for payment details, compensation rates and deductions.

1.4 **Excessive payments**—While the integrity of compensation rates is important in maintaining the accuracy and integrity of the payroll calculation and reducing the risk of overpaying employees, the payment of excessive earnings through multiple earning codes should also be controlled to mitigate the risk of overpayment.

1.5 **Excessive salary increases**—Employees receive salary increases during their tenure with an organization. This occurs through a promotion with a set pay increase or through a manual salary increase. Such increases are administered via one of two ways:

- Home→Workforce Administration→Job Information→Job Data
- Pay Rate Change

It is important that these increases be accurately entered into the system to avoid overpayment or excessive salary increases that are not within management intentions or financial budgets.

Master Data Maintenance: Key Controls

Key controls over the maintenance of payroll master data include:

1.1.1 Access should also be restricted to authorized personnel to support segregation of duties for the following:

- Defining HRMS business rules via Home→Set Up HRMS
- Administration of employee payroll data via Home→Workforce Administration
- Compensation via Home→Compensation
- Global Payroll via Home→Global Payroll
- North American Payroll via Home→North American Payroll

Add/correction/update access to Set Up HRMS should be restricted to the payroll administrator only. Row-level security should be set up to prevent payroll and HR users from having access to update their own payroll data. An error message should be displayed informing users that they do not have access to make such changes. The main tables to be restricted are:

- PS_JOB
- PS_EMPLOYMENT

- PS_EARNINGS_TBL
- PS_GENL_DED_TBL
- PS_FED_TAX_DATA
- PS_STATE_TAX_DATA
- PS_GARN_SPEC
- PS_ADDL_PAY_DATA
- PS_PAYGROUP_TBL
- PS_DEPT_TBL
- PS_COMPANY_TBL
- PS_LOCATION_TBL
- PS_INSTALLATION
- PS_JOBCODE_TBL

1.2.1 To ensure that all data needed to complete a Payroll table are entered, the PeopleSoft system will not allow the table to be saved unless all necessary data have been entered.

1.3.1 It is necessary to determine whether edit and validation checks should be implemented. Changes to job codes should be validated against the job code table to ensure that the code exists and the system issues a warning to the user if an invalid code is chosen. In addition, bank branch ID numbers entered are validated against a list of valid numbers to ensure that EFT payments are made to legitimate banks. It should be noted that many of the data entry fields in PeopleSoft are populated via drop-down boxes or have look-up tables or prompt lists that detail all possible values. PeopleSoft also stores the date of the last pay increase for a particular employee under the employment data component held within the Job Data menu item (Home→Workforce Administration→Job Information→Job Data→Employment Data). It should be noted that this stores changes only as a result of the following action/action reasons:

- PRO and any action reason (promotion)
- PAY and MER (merit)
- PAY and PRO (promotion)
- PAY and SPG (special increase)
- PAY and no action reason

1.3.2 Audit logs should be kept of changes to employee master data and reviewed by management on a periodic basis.

1.4.1 The Earnings table allows earning types to be created for employees. The Maximum Yearly Earnings (EARN_YTD_MAX) field restricts employees from being paid more than the amount specified. This field should be used for all allowances created.

1.5.1 The Salary Increase Matrices should be set up defining guidelines for salary increases via Home→Compensation→Salary Planning→Salary Planning Administration→Define Salary Increase Matrix. This should define the minimum and maximum salary for a particular salary plan or grade. When a compensation rate is changed, the system should perform a comparison against the Salary Increase Matrices. If the change falls outside the parameters defined, a warning message should display.

Master Data Maintenance: Testing Techniques

Testing techniques for payroll master data controls include:

1.1.1 Review access security matrices and access assignment documentation to gain an understanding of the security design. Corroborate this understanding by generating lists of users with access to the WorkForce Administration, Compensation, Set Up HRMS and Global Payroll Rules menus and reviewing their level of access by writing the following query in PeopleSoft Query Manager:

```
SELECT A.OPRID, A.OPRDEFNDESC, A.ACCTLOCK,
B.ROLENAME, C.CLASSID, D.MENUNAME, D.BARNAME,
D.BARITEMNAME, D.PNLITEMNAME, D.DISPLAYONLY,
D.AUTHORIZEDACTIONS

FROM PSOPRDEFN A, PSROLEUSER B, PSROLECLASS C,
PSAUTHITEM D

WHERE A.OPRID = B.ROLEUSER AND B.ROLENAME =
C.ROLENAME AND C.CLASSID = D.CLASSID AND
D.MENUNAME = 'SETUP_HRMS'
```

Order by A.OPRID, B.ROLENAME, C.CLASSID, D.MENUNAME to ensure that the user IDs (OPRID), roles (ROLENAME), permission lists (CLASSID) and components (MENUNAME) are listed in alphabetical order.

Also, generate a list of users with access to the setup pages within PeopleSoft menus (and the roles that provide such access), and review their level of access by writing the following query in PeopleSoft Query Manager:

```
SELECT A.OPRID, A.OPRDEFNDESC, A.ACCTLOCK,
B.ROLENAME, C.CLASSID, D.MENUNAME, D.BARNAME,
D.BARITEMNAME, D.PNLITEMNAME, D.DISPLAYONLY,
D.AUTHORIZEDACTIONS

FROM PSOPRDEFN A, PSROLEUSER B, PSROLECLASS C,
PSAUTHITEM D

WHERE A.OPRID = B.ROLEUSER AND B.ROLENAME =
C.ROLENAME AND C.CLASSID = D.CLASSID AND D.BARNAME
LIKE '%SETUP%'
```

The column D.AUTHORIZEDACTIONS will contain values that represent the action types the user is authorized to perform. For a list of descriptions for each numeric AUTHORIZEDACTION code, refer to the appendix.

History Note: The D.DISPLAYONLY COLUMN will have value of 0 or 1. A value of 1 means all fields in the page are "display only" to the user, and a value of 0 means this setting is turned off and the action type codes indicate the level of access granted.

Generate a list of users and the row-level security defined by writing the following query in PeopleSoft Query Manager:

```
SELECT A.OPRID, A.OPRDEFNDESC, A.ACCTLOCK, B.SETID,
B.DEPTID, C.DESCR, B.ACCESS_CD,
TO_CHAR(B.TREE_EFFDT,'YYYY-MM-DD'),
B.TREE_NODE_NUM, B.TREE_NODE_NUM_END, C.SETID,
C.DEPTID, TO_CHAR(C.EFFDT,' YYYY-MM-DD')
FROM PSOPRDEFN A, PS_SCRTY_TBL_DEPT B, PS_DEPT_TBL C
WHERE A.ROWSECCLASS = B.ROWSECCLASS
AND B.SETID = C.SETID
AND B.DEPTID = C.DEPTID
AND C.EFFDT =
(SELECT MAX(C_ED.EFFDT) FROM PS_DEPT_TBL C_ED
WHERE C.SETID = C_ED.SETID
AND C.DEPTID = C_ED.DEPTID
AND C_ED.EFFDT <= SYSDATE)
```

Order by A.OPRID, C.DESCR to ensure that the user IDs (OPRID) and department descriptions (DESCR) are listed in alphabetical order.

Select a sample of payroll users and assess whether they have access to update their own payroll data (i.e., salary, job) by observing them attempting to make such changes.

Review the PSOPRDEFN records to determine if each ID has been assigned an emplID.

1.2.1 Complete the following:

- Review security design documentation detailing the configured controls implemented in the system and approved by management. In particular, check the configuration controls designed for the mandatory fields in payroll table data entry.
- Observe a system administrator delete one of the mandatory fields and attempt to save the change. See if a warning/error message is displayed.

Note: Ensure that the original data stored within the mandatory field are reset.

1.3.1 Review security design documentation detailing the configured and customized controls implemented in the system and approved by management, particularly the online edit and validation checks and range checks.

For either a sample of the edit and validation checks or for the entire population, enter changes to employee data and observe the success or failure of these attempts. For example, attempt to change the bank ID and branch ID of an employee's bank information via Home→Workforce Administration→Personal Information→Biographical→Bank Accounts.

Change the bank ID and/or branch ID to an erroneous value and observe whether a warning message is displayed.

Attempt to change the employee's pay group via Home→Workforce Administration→Job Information→Job Data→Payroll. Change the pay group field to an erroneous value and observe whether a warning message is issued.

Review the Date Last Increase field via Home→Workforce Administration→Job Information→Job Data→Employment Data (at the bottom of the page) and determine whether this corresponds to the last authorized pay increase. It should be noted that not all potential pay increase scenarios impact this date change.

For a sample of employees, generate a compensation history by writing the following query in Query Manager:

```
SELECT A.EMPLID, TO_CHAR(A.EFFDT,'YYYY-MM-DD'),
A.ACTION, A.ACTION_REASON, A.ANNUAL_RT,
A.CHANGE_AMT
FROM PS_JOB A, PS_EMPLMT_SRCH_QRY A1
WHERE A.EMPLID = A1.EMPLID
AND A.EMPL_RCD = A1.EMPL_RCD
AND A1.ROWSECCLASS = 'HCDPALL'
AND A.CHANGE_AMT <> 0
```

Note: The PS_EMPLMT_SRCH_QRY table will vary depending on row-level security configuration.

Review the compensation history and investigate the validity of the changes.

Organizations may be reluctant to allow auditors to have the ability to make test changes in the production environment. Consequently, perform the following audit tests in the Test or QA environment. Corroborate that the configuration of controls in the Test/QA environment are the same as those in the production environment.

1.3.2 Review security design documentation detailing the configured controls implemented in the system and approved by management, particularly the way in which the audit trails are set up. Determine with relevant management the procedures in place for generating, reviewing and investigating audit reports showing changes to employee master data. Inspect a sample of audit trail reports for evidence of review and rectification of exception items identified.

1.4.1 Review security design documentation detailing the configured controls implemented in the system and approved by management. In particular, review the online edit and validation checks and range checks.

For a sample of employee data or for the entire population, enter changes to employee data, test for edit and validation checks, and observe the success or failure of these attempts.

1.5.1 Review security design documentation detailing the configured controls implemented in the system and approved by management, particularly the online edit and validation checks and range checks. Corroborate this understanding by inspecting the Salary Increase Matrix tables via Home→Compensation→Salary Planning→Salary Planning Administration →Define Salary Increase Matrix, and compare the limits configured to those defined in the security design documentation.

For either a sample of the salary plans or for the entire population, enter changes to compensations rates for employees enrolled in those plans, and observe the success or failure of these attempts.

Recording Attendance and Leave Processing

Recording Attendance and Leave Processing: Risks

Significant risks associated with recording attendance and leave processing include:

2.1 **Access to Record Attendance**—The time that employees spend at work is dependent on their job responsibilities. Consequently, the mechanisms by which their time is captured in the system may be different. For example, some employees may simply work a standard number of hours a week and, unless leave is applied for, the organization will assume that the standard hours have been worked. These are classified as exceptions time reporters. Other types of employees, such as those paid on an hourly basis, may have to submit time sheets detailing the hours they work in a particular week. These would then have to be entered into the system. These are referred to as positive time reporters.

It is important that employees be paid only for the time they spent working. This is not an access risk, but an integrity risk. Users must not have access to enter their time directly in the system without some form of authorization by a supervisor or manager prior to the time and associated cost being recorded in the system and the time reporter being paid. Equally, it is important that time reporters not have access to approve their own time entries. If access to approve one's own time reported is allowed, time reporters could be inaccurately paid for the time they work or, more important, the risk of overpayment may be increased.

2.2 **Access to Process Leave**—Employees take leaves of absence, either planned (e.g., a vacation) or unplanned (e.g., sick leave), for a number of reasons. During the course of their employment, employees also accrue leave entitlements. If access to leave adjustments and/or leave accruals is not restricted, employees may inaccurately accrue leave, leading to an overstatement of an organization's leave liability. Also, if access to leave entitlements is not restricted, employees may be granted inappropriate and excessive leave.

Depending on the procedures in place and the extent of the PeopleSoft implementation within an organization, employees may apply for a leave of absence via manually approved forms or the self-service functionality within the system. If the latter option is in place, the leave request should be approved online by an appropriate official. It is important to restrict access to the approval of leave requests to avoid an employee requesting and approving his/her own leave.

2.3 Time submitted by positive time reporters should be approved via the time administration process to ensure attendance submitted is valid and approved before the system converts it into payable time. This is to ensure that the time submitted and paid for is valid, and that only active time reporters are paid, and paid only for the time actually worked.

2.4 In addition to the validity and accuracy of the time submitted, it is important to ensure that the time is processed so that time reporters are paid and the associated cost of the work performed is reflected in the payroll costs and GL on a timely basis. If not, any management reporting may be inaccurate for decision-making purposes and unpaid employees may be disgruntled.

2.5 There are two main categories of leave: general and vacation. Vacation leave is normally planned and, therefore, requires preapproval; certain types of general leave, such as sick leave, are not planned and, therefore, may not be subject to prior approval. However, it may be necessary to approve the details of either category of leave prior to input to the system to ensure that leave entitlements and accruals are updated, appropriate follow-up is actioned (e.g., doctor's certificate obtained), and any regulations or guidelines are followed. For instance, certain types of leave may have a maximum number of days allowable, after which point either annual (vacation) leave entitlements must be used or leave without pay must be taken. The payroll must be adequately maintained to ensure that any leave that should be unpaid is not inadvertently paid.

Recording Attendance and Leave Processing: Key Controls

Key controls over the processing of attendance and leave include:

2.1.1 Access to enter approved time worked for employees should be restricted to authorized personnel only and adequately segregated from incompatible duties. For example, an employee who is allowed to submit his/her own time to the system should not be allowed to approve that time in the system. Equally, an approver of time worked should not have access to submit or modify that time in the system. These controls may be implemented in a number of ways, depending on the processes in place within an organization. Access to enter time worked may be limited to a number of users based on approved manual time sheets. The time worked of the users entering the time sheet details may be independently and retrospectively reconciled to their time sheets.

2.2.1 If leave approvals are based on manual forms, access to enter approved leave for employees should be restricted to authorized personnel only. If leave requests are submitted online via PeopleSoft self-service, access to approve leave should be restricted to authorized personnel only and segregated from incompatible duties. For example, an employee should not be allowed to submit his/her own leave request to the system and approve that request in the system. As with the controls surrounding submission of time detailed previously, these controls may be implemented in a number of ways depending on the processes in place within an organization.

The updates to leave accruals in the GL should form part of the GL run control process. Access to perform this process via Home→Global Payroll→Time & Labor/GL Costs→Send Costs to GL→General Ledger Run Control should be restricted to authorized personnel only.

2.3.1 The controls implemented should be dependent on the processes in place to record attendance. If time recording is performed on the basis of manual time sheets, these should be manually approved prior to input. Access to perform rapid (time) entry is addressed under control and testing technique 2.1.1. The system automatically performs validations to ensure that time reporters are active. If the system is used to approve time online, this must be set up at the work group level. A manager must approve time online prior to the payment for time submitted, and this should be done via Home→Manager Self Service→Time Management→Approvals→Approve Payable Time.

2.4.1 Procedures should be in place to ensure the timely submission, approval and input of time sheets, whether manual or online. These procedures should include the time administration batch process, converting reported time into payable time (via Home→Time and Labor→Process Time→Request Time Administration) to ensure that it is run according to a strictly defined and communicated processing time table.

2.4.2 A manager should review and investigate the exceptions generated via the Manage Time Exceptions (Home→Manager Self Service→Time Management→Approvals→Manage Individual Exceptions) and Manage

Group Exceptions (Home→Manager Self Service→Time Management→Approvals→Manage Group Exceptions) pages and resolve exceptions via the Weekly Elapsed, Weekly Punch or Rapid Entry pages. The time submission must then be reprocessed.

2.5.1 A manager should review and approve leave of absence requests via Home→Workforce Administration→Absence and Vacation→Create Vacation Schedule→Request/Approve Vacation and check the employee's leave balance to ensure that excessive leave is not taken. The vacation accrual process should be run before the approval to ensure that an employee's leave balance is up to date.

2.5.2 The system automatically checks that the leave code entered is a valid leave code. The entry of an invalid leave code results in an error message displayed on-screen to the user.

2.5.3 The system automatically checks the vacation request against the employee's leave balance and issues a warning message if the leave request exceeds the leave balance entitlement.

2.5.4 For instances where leave without pay is taken due to, for example, an insufficient paid leave balance, HR officers should manually change an employee's salary to a nominal figure until the date the employee is due to return.

Recording Attendance and Leave Processing: Testing Techniques

Testing techniques for recording attendance and leave processing include:

2.1.1 Review access security matrices and access assignment documentation to gain an understanding of the security design. Corroborate this understanding by generating lists of users with access to the menus:

- Enter Time:
  - Home→Time and Labor→Report Time→Report Rapid Time
  - Home→Employee Self Service→Time Recording→Report Time→Report Weekly Punch Time
- Approve Time:
  - Home→Manager Self Service→Time Management→Approvals→Approve Payable Time
  - Home→Time and Labor→Approvals→Approve Time by Time Reporter

Review users' level of access by writing the SQL query detailed in 1.1.1 (under Master Data Maintenance Testing Techniques) in PeopleSoft Query Manager.

2.2.1 Review access security matrices and access assignment documentation to gain an understanding of the security design. Corroborate this understanding by generating lists of users with access to the following pages:

- Enter and Approve Leave (or Vacation) Requests via Home→Workforce Administration→Absence and Vacation→Create Vacation Schedule→Request/Approve Vacation

- Self Service Absence Request via Home→Employee Self Service→Time Recording→Report Time→Review/Request Absence
- Self Service Absence Approval via Home→Manager Self Service→Time Management →Approvals→Approve Absence Request

Review the users' level of access by utilizing the query in PeopleSoft detailed in test 1.1.1 (Master Data Maintenance).

2.3.1 Review business process documentation to determine the procedures in place for submitting and approving time and attendance. Corroborate this understanding by observing the submission and approval process of time reporter attendance.

Review the work group settings via Home→Set Up HRMS→Product Related →Time and Labor→Rules and Workgroups→Workgroup, and determine whether the work group time sheets are set to Needs Approval.

Alternatively, to analyze this setting for all work groups, use the following query in Query Manager:

```
Select WORKGROUP, DESCR, NEEDS_APPR_FLAG
From TL_WRKGRP_TBL
```

2.4.1 Review business process documentation to determine the procedures in place for submitting and approving time and attendance and the time table in place to run the time administration batch process.

2.4.2 Review business process documentation to determine the procedures in place for identifying and rectifying time and attendance exceptions.

Corroborate this understanding by reviewing the manage time pages for a sample of time exceptions reports via Home→Time and Labor→ Approvals →Manage (Individual/Group) Exceptions to ensure that no exceptions were left unresolved.

2.5.1 Review business process documentation to determine the procedures in place for the submission and approval of leave of absence. Corroborate this understanding by observing the submission and approval of vacation and general leave requests.

2.5.2 Create a dummy leave request via Home→Workforce Administration →Absences and Vacation→Create Vacation Schedule→Request/ ApproveVacation, and attempt to enter a fictitious leave code. Observe the success or failure of the result.

2.5.3 Create a dummy leave request via Home→Workforce Administration →Absences and Vacation→Create Vacation Schedule→ Request/ApproveVacation, and attempt to enter a leave period greater than the available leave balance. Observe the success or failure of the result.

Note: Ensure that the vacation accrual run has been processed beforehand to update the leave accrual. Vacation accrual is run via Home→Workforce Administration→Absences and Vacation→Create Vacation Schedule→Accrue Vacation.

2.5.4 Determine the processes and procedures in place over employees taking leave without pay. If a notional salary is entered into the system during the period of leave, corroborate this by inspecting the employee's salary records.

Alternatively, review audit logs of changes to employee records.

Calculating and Disbursing Payroll

Calculating and Disbursing Payroll: Risks

Significant risks associated with calculating and disbursing payroll include:

3.1 **Access to Payroll Processing**—Although much of the payroll processing is derived from information held within the Payroll Master Data discussed previously, access to the Payroll processing functions within PeopleSoft is restricted to authorized personnel and segregated from incompatible duties. The identification of payees and the Payroll calculation (i.e., the application of deductions and taxes) should be performed by suitably trained personnel and appropriately reviewed and approved. If not, unauthorized payees could be included in the pay run, and subsequent pay calculations may be made, leading to incorrect or inappropriate payments occurring. In addition, these functions should be separated from access to maintain employee records in the system. This applies for both the on-cycle and off-cycle pay run functionality.

All phases of the Global Payroll process are accessed via the menu path Home→Global Payroll→Absence and Payroll Processing→Calculate Absence and Payroll.

This includes:

- Payee Identification
- Payroll Calculation
- Payroll Confirmation

The phases of the North American Payroll are accessed via the menus:

- Paysheet Creation (payee identification): Home→North American Payroll→Payroll Processing→Create Initial Paysheets
- Payroll Calculation: Home→North American Payroll→Payroll Processing→Calculate Pay
- Payroll Confirmation (Finalization): Home→North American Payroll→Payment Processing→Confirm Pay

3.2 **Access to online checks**—Online checks may be written instantly to the system and are typically used for emergency or urgent payments when the normal pay run timing may not be appropriate. Access to this function is obtained via Home→North American Payroll→Periodic Payroll Events→Single Check→Create Single Check. Access to this function is restricted to avoid the production of inappropriate and unauthorized checks.

3.3 **Access to the banking process**—The bank run control process finalizes the payment to employees, recipients, etc. There are two major stages to this process:
- Bank run control process
- EFT process

The processing of the bank run process is based on the assumption that the Payroll process has been confirmed and finalized, exceptions have been investigated and rectified, and the payments have been approved. Consequently, it is important to restrict access to this function; otherwise, payments may be made that are not authorized. Furthermore, access to the EFT process should be restricted. If access to the EFT process and the EFT payment file itself is not restricted, unauthorized amendments may be made to payments, thereby circumventing the controls that have been established at the front end of the process.

For the Global Payroll, bank and EFT processing is accessed via Home→Global Payroll→Payment Processing→Create EFT Payment File (Country).

For North American Payroll, bank and EFT processing are accessed via Home→North American Payroll→Payroll Processing→Create Direct Deposit→Direct Deposit File.

3.4 **Discrepancies and exceptions are corrected**—The initial stage of the payroll process involves the identification of payees. As discussed in chapter 5, the pay calculation phase is iterative; results are viewed and verified after each calculation run. This provides the opportunity for adjustments to be made to take into account any last-minute changes for bonuses, commissions, etc. These are also reviewed and approved prior to the payroll finalization stage to avoid any unauthorized amendments being processed.

Results from each phase of the payroll processing are examined using the Process Statistics, Iterative Lists and Results by Calendar pages for Global Payroll.

For the North American Payroll, the Error Message for Employees report (Pay011) should be viewed after each run.

3.5 **Payroll Calculation**—The Payroll Calculation stage applies deductions and relevant taxes for each of the payees. This provides an indication of the payments to be made and the staff costs/payroll expenses that will update the GL, including taxes and deduction payments to third parties (e.g., government agencies, health insurance providers). These are reviewed for reasonableness, and any errors are identified and resultant adjustments approved prior to finalization of the payroll process.

3.6 **Payroll Finalization (Confirmation)**—Payroll Finalization is the final stage of the PeopleSoft Payroll process and results in deduction arrears, leave accruals and balances being updated. This stage of the Payroll process assumes that all errors and exceptions have been investigated and rectified during the payee Identification/Paysheet Creation and Payroll Calculation stages. The payroll administrator and management ensure that all errors and exceptions are addressed prior to the finalization of the payroll to avoid inaccurate or incomplete payroll payments.

3.7 **EFT**—The transfer of the payment file from the PeopleSoft system to the source bank is performed in a number of different ways. Some organizations utilize specialized applications. The transfer of the payment file from PeopleSoft to the bank's application may also be performed in a number of ways. The integrity of the file transfer process (PeopleSoft to bank application to bank) is maintained to ensure that the payroll payments paid reflect the payroll processing performed by PeopleSoft. If not, the payments made by the source bank may be inaccurate or incomplete, resulting in possible discrepancies in the GL reporting and subsequent reconciliations performed.

Calculating and Disbursing Payroll: Key Controls

Key controls over the calculation and disbursement of payroll include:

3.1.1 Security access design documentation approved by management should be in place, defining the access requirements for individual jobs in the payroll function. This should include details regarding the activities and associated pages, menus, permission lists, and roles created and assigned.

Access to payroll processing should be restricted to authorized personnel only and adequately segregated from incompatible duties. This should encompass the following main stages:

- Payee Identification
- Payroll Calculation
- Payroll Confirmation (Finalization)

Users should not have access to identify Payees/Create Paysheets (and make associated adjustments), run the Payroll Calculation, or confirm the payroll. In addition, users should not have access to their own HR and payroll records. If the segregation of this access is not practical, any changes should be independently reviewed and approved.

3.2.1 Access to create and process online checks should be restricted to authorized personnel only and adequately segregated from incompatible duties. Since online checks should be processed only on an exceptions basis, this access should be restricted to only a few members of the payroll function.

3.3.1 Access to the Bank Control Run process should be restricted to authorized personnel only and adequately segregated from incompatible duties. Since this process is run on the basis of the confirmed payroll, access should not be required by more than a few users.

Depending on the mechanisms in place to transfer the payment/bank file from PeopleSoft to the bank, a number of controls may be implemented.

Access to the EFT file should also be restricted. If the file is downloaded from PeopleSoft to the network for transfer to a bank payment application, the file should be stored in a secure directory on the network with access restricted to authorized personnel only. If the transfer from PeopleSoft to the bank application is via the physical transfer of a disk, the transfer should be performed immediately; if not, the disk should be stored in a secure location, such as a lockable cupboard or fireproof safe.

3.3.2 If the organization utilizes a special bank application to transfer the payment file to the bank, access to this application should be restricted to a small number of authorized personnel. The user should be subject to logical access controls when logging onto the bank transfer/interface application, which should include at minimum the use of unique user IDs and password combinations. Audit trail reports should be maintained to log all user activity on the bank transfer/interface application.

3.4.1 Payroll processing procedures and security design documentation should be in place that have been reviewed and approved by management. This documentation should include procedures for:

- Identification of payees
- Calculation of payroll
- Confirmation (finalization) of payroll
- Transmission of payment files to the bank
- Distribution of pay slips
- Processing of online, manual checks
- Identifying and reviewing summary and exception reports

3.5.1 For Global Payroll, the processing statistics should be reviewed after each calculation, and subsequently the Payee Messages and Results by Calendar reports should be reviewed. Any errors identified should be investigated and rectified.

For North American Payroll, the Payroll Error Message for Employees report (PAY011) should be generated and reviewed to identify errors, which should be investigated and rectified.

3.6.1 For PeopleSoft Global Payroll, the processing statistics should be reviewed to ensure that errors are rectified prior to the payroll finalization.

For North American Payroll, the Payroll Error Message for Employees report (PAY011) should be generated. All exceptions identified should have been investigated and rectified during the Payroll Calculation stage, and the PAY011 report should detail any outstanding exceptions. Any outstanding exceptions should have the associated OK to Pay flag set to No to remove these paylines from the final Payroll Confirmation stage.

3.6.2 The payroll administrator or payroll manager should review the following prior to the final processing and authorization of the payment file:

- General deductions by recipient
- Individual deductions by recipient
- Employee net pay

For Global Payroll reports, the menu path Home→Global Payroll→Absence and Payroll Processing→Payroll Reports→Results Register/Results Summary may be used.

3.7.1 Download and transfer of the payment file should be subject to interface controls dependent on the method of transfer to the bank. Header and trailer records should be detailed in the payment file to ensure full inclusion of payment records. The bank's system should provide a positive acknowledgment of receipt of the payment file to the organization. A reconciliation between the payment file transmitted by the organization and the payment file received by the bank's system should be performed. This should be on the basis of the number of records and currency amounts.

The payment file itself should be encrypted during the transfer/interface process.

3.7.2 If there is a time delay between processing of the payment file in PeopleSoft and transmission to the bank, the payment file should be stored in a secure location, such as a restricted access directory on the network accessible by only appropriate members of payroll staff. If the payment file is stored on a physical storage medium, e.g., a floppy disk, it should be stored in a lockable, fireproof location, such as a safe, accessible only to authorized payroll staff.

Calculating and Disbursing Payroll: Testing Techniques

Testing techniques for calculating and disbursing payroll include:

3.1.1 Review access security matrices and access assignment documentation to gain an understanding of the security design. Corroborate this understanding by generating lists of users with access to the following pages:

- For North American Payroll:
  - Create Paysheets: Home→North American Payroll→Payroll Processing→Create Paysheet→Create Initial Paysheets

  - Calculate Payroll: Home→North American Payroll→Payroll Processing→Run Payroll→Calculate Pay
  - Finalize Payroll: Home→North American Payroll→Payment Processing→Run Payroll→Confirm Pay
  - Payroll UnConfirm: Home→North American Payroll→Payroll Processing→Run Payroll→Reverse Pay Confirmation
- For Global Payroll:
  - Home→Global Payroll→Absence and Payroll Processing→Calculate Absence and Payroll

Review the users' level of access by writing the query detailed in 1.1.1 (under Master Data Maintenance Testing Techniques) in PeopleSoft Query Manager.

3.2.1 Review access security matrices and access assignment documentation to gain an understanding of the security design. Corroborate this understanding by generating lists of users with access to the Create Single Check page:
Home→North American Payroll→Periodic Payroll Events→Single Check →Create Single Check.

Review the users' level of access by utilizing the query in PeopleSoft detailed in 1.1.1 (under Master Data Maintenance Testing Techniques).

3.3.1 Review the following:
- Access security matrices and access assignment documentation, to gain an understanding of the security design of any bank transfer/interface application software utilized. Corroborate this understanding via inquiries with the payroll manager and/or payroll administrator.
- Any additional security controls over the bank transfer/interface application (for example, in addition to user ID and passwords, the use of one-time personal identification numbers [PINs]). Corroborate this understanding via observation of the payment file transfer process.
- System-generated access control listing, to determine the appropriateness of access compared with the roles and responsibilities of the individual users
- A sample of security audit trail reports for evidence of independent review and investigation

3.4.1 Review approved payroll processing procedures and security design documentation to gain an understanding of the procedures surrounding the payroll processes. Interview payroll administration staff to determine the audit evidence available for inspection in:
- Global Payroll:
  - Select a sample of pay runs and review the associated processing statistics to identify if errors are resolved prior to payroll finalization.
  - Review the payee messages for evidence of investigation and rectification.

- North American Payroll:
  - Select a sample of pay runs and review the associated Payroll Error Message for Employees report (PAY011) for evidence of investigation and rectification.
  - Determine whether the Payroll Precalculation Audit SQR (PAY035) has been run and reviewed for each pay run prior to the payroll calculation stage.

3.5.1 Review approved payroll processing procedures and security design documentation to gain an understanding of the procedures surrounding the payroll processes. Interview payroll administration staff to determine the audit evidence available for inspection in:

- Global Payroll—Select a sample of pay runs and review the associated processing statistics to verify that there are no remaining errors.
- North American Payroll—Select a sample of pay runs and review the associated Payroll Error Message for Employees report (PAY011) for evidence of investigation and rectification.

3.6.1 Review approved payroll processing procedures and security design documentation to gain an understanding of the procedures surrounding the payroll processes.

Interview payroll administration staff to determine the audit evidence available for inspection. Where possible, select a sample of pay runs and determine whether the payroll administrator or payroll manager reviewed and approved the following, prior to the final processing of the payment file:

- General deductions by recipient
- Individual deductions by recipient
- Employee net pay

3.7.1 Review approved payroll processing procedures documentation to gain an understanding of the procedures surrounding the payroll processes. Specifically, review the mechanisms in place surrounding the transfer of PeopleSoft payment files to the bank, including the encryption of the payment file. Corroborate this understanding through inquiries with the payroll administrator and manager.

For a sample of pay runs, review the payment files for the existence of header and trailer records. Review any associated positive acknowledgment reports/messages from the bank, and compare the number of records and monetary amounts to the payment file. Review any reconciliations performed between the payment files generated by the organization and the files received and processed by the bank for evidence of independent review and investigation of any reconciling items. Inspect the contents of the payment file to determine whether the data are encrypted prior to transmission or remain in a cleartext format.

3.7.2 Review approved payroll processing procedures documentation to gain an understanding of the procedures surrounding the payroll processes. Specifically, review the mechanisms in place surrounding the transfer of PeopleSoft payment files to the bank and the storage of the payment files if there is a time delay between the payroll finalization in PeopleSoft and the transfer/interface with the bank systems. Corroborate this understanding through inquiries with the payroll administrator and manager.

Review the location for storage of the payment files. If it is a network directory, review whether access to the directory is restricted, check the appropriateness of the access granted, and review if access is based on the roles and responsibilities of the users.

If the transfer of the payment files from PeopleSoft to the bank transfer/interface application is a physical transfer of a floppy disk or other medium, determine the storage location and assess whether the physical security of that location is adequate. For example, determine whether the payment file is stored in a fireproof safe/lockable cupboard, and assess who has access to the file and the appropriateness of such access.

Reporting and Reconciliation

Reporting and Reconciliation: Risks

Significant risks associated with reporting and reconciliation include:

4.1 **Access to GL run control processes**—Although PeopleSoft is an integrated system, processes must be run to update the other modules within the system. The Payroll module processes pay calculations, including deduction arrears and leave accruals, but these calculations will not be reflected in the GL until the GL run control process is completed. This must be run for the GL account balances to be updated. Access to this function is restricted to authorized staff. The update of the GL is performed only once the payroll has been finalized, approved and processed. This includes the finalization, approval and processing of any manual online checks or adjustments. If access is not restricted, the GL may be updated with inaccurate or incomplete information regarding the payroll run.

The GL run control process is initiated via one of two menu paths:

- Home→Global Payroll→Time & Labor/GL Costs→Send Costs to GL→General Ledger Run Control
- Home→North American Payroll→Payroll Distribution→Prepare GL Information→ Non-Commit Accounting Info

4.2 **Access to PeopleSoft reporting**—Subprocess 3—Calculation and Disbursement of Payroll—discusses the risks and controls in relation to specific reporting available from the PeopleSoft Payroll modules at each stage of the Payroll process. Payroll management should generate and review such reports at the appropriate stage of the process (i.e., payee identification/paysheet creation, payroll calculation, payroll confirmation) to identify possible errors or exceptions prior to the next stage or final processing of the payments. If this is not done on a timely basis, the payroll may be processed incompletely or inaccurately or may not be processed at all, due to a lack of data integrity in the system. Access to such reports should be configured adequately, to ensure that relevant management is provided with sufficient payroll/HR information to manage its responsibilities, and restricted so that inappropriate parties do not obtain access to sensitive information.

4.3 **GL reconciliation**—As mentioned in 4.1, Access to GL run control processes, the Payroll module processes pay calculations, but they will not be reflected in the GL until the GL run control process is completed. If this is not performed on a timely basis, the data held in the GL may be incomplete or inaccurate, and management decisions based upon this information may not be appropriate at that point. In addition, statutory or federal reporting, including financial statements and tax liabilities produced from the GL, may be inaccurate.

4.4 **Bank reconciliation**—All payroll expenses, including payments to employees, government agencies and third-party providers, are eventually paid out of an organization's source bank(s). This is done on a weekly, biweekly, monthly, quarterly or even annual basis. Controls are in place to mitigate the risk of inaccurate calculations and payments being processed or incomplete transfer of payment information to the source bank(s). However, these payments are accurately reflected in the bank's own records and compared to the organization's GL balances. If this is not done, any discrepancies as a result of incomplete data transfers, inaccurate payroll calculations or even misappropriation of funds may not be identified and investigated on a timely basis.

Reporting and Reconciliation: Key Controls

Key controls over reporting and reconciliation processes include:

4.1.1 Approval of security access design documentation should be made by management defining the access requirements for individual jobs in the payroll function. This should include details regarding the activities and associated pages, menus, permission lists and roles created and assigned.

Access to update the GL with payroll data via the GL run control process should be restricted to authorized personnel only and adequately segregated from incompatible duties.

4.2.1 Refer to test 4.1.1. The security access design should include access to all reporting tools available, including standard online reporting via the report activity components of the PeopleSoft menu, PeopleSoft Query, PS nVision, etc.

Access to PeopleSoft reports should be restricted to authorized personnel only and adequately segregated from incompatible duties.

4.3.1 A payroll processing and period-end time table should be defined and approved. The specified dates when the GL run control processes are to be executed/processed should also be defined and approved.

A reconciliation should be performed between the Payroll module and the GL that is independently reviewed and approved. This reconciliation should cover employee pay, deductions, leave accruals, taxation liabilities, etc., and all reconciling items should be investigated.

4.4.1 Month-end procedures should be defined and approved and include the performance of reconciliations between the GL and the relevant bank statements for all source bank accounts. All reconciling items should be investigated, and the reconciliation should be independently reviewed and approved.

Reporting and Reconciliation: Testing Techniques

Testing techniques for the reporting and reconciliation processes include:

4.1.1 Review access security matrices and access assignment documentation to gain an understanding of the security design. Corroborate this understanding by generating lists of users with access to the following pages:

- Home→Global Payroll→Time & Labor/GL Costs→Send Costs to GL→General Ledger Run Control
- Home→North American Payroll→Payroll Distribution→Prepare GL Information→ Non-Commit Accounting Info

Review the users' level of access by writing the query detailed in 1.1.1 (under Master Data Maintenance Testing Techniques) in PeopleSoft Query Manager.

4.2.1 Review payroll procedural documentation, access security matrices and access assignment documentation to gain an understanding of the key payroll reports available and generated as well as the security design around such reports.

Corroborate this understanding by generating lists of users with access to:

- Home→Global Payroll→Absence and Payroll Processing→Payroll Reports→Payroll Register/Payroll Summary
- Home→North American Payroll→Payroll Processing→Reports→Payroll Register/Payroll Summary

Review the users' level of access by utilizing the query in PeopleSoft detailed in 1.1.1 (under Master Data Maintenance Testing Techniques).

4.3.1 Review period-end and payroll procedural documentation to gain an understanding of the processes surrounding the reconciliation of the Payroll module and the GL.

For a sample of periods, review the reconciliations for evidence of timely performance, independent review and approval, and the investigation and clearance of reconciling items. Inquire with management the reasons for large and/or recurring reconciling items.

4.4.1 Review period-end procedural documentation to gain an understanding of the processes surrounding the reconciliation of the GL to the various bank statements received from the organization's source banks.

For a sample of periods, review the reconciliations for evidence of timely performance, independent review and approval, and the investigation and clearance of reconciling items. Inquire with management the reasons for large and/or recurring reconciling items.

Summary

This chapter outlined the risks, key controls and testing techniques surrounding the PeopleSoft Payroll business cycle. Among the key risks are unrestricted access to payroll setup tables and payroll processing, leading to inappropriate and/or unauthorized modifications made to payroll master data and pay calculations, and failure to reconcile the payroll expenses in the GL to bank records.

9. PeopleSoft Application and Technical Infrastructure

This chapter provides an overview of the PeopleSoft Technical Infrastructure business cycle, introducing important PeopleSoft utilities and functionality.

PeopleSoft Architecture

PeopleSoft is based on a three-tier architecture, using the principles of a client-server configuration. Client-server is a style of computing that distributes the workload of a computer application across several cooperating computer programs within a network of personal computers/workstations. It is a design model that describes how the various components of a computer application will be deployed in a given processing environment. Client and server are roles in which processes communicate. The client requests services, and the server provides them. All PeopleSoft releases after and including PeopleSoft 8 must be run with a configuration using an application server, database server and web server in addition to a web browser installed on all workstations from which the PeopleSoft application must be accessed. The client is a "thin" client, and the architecture is not client-server architecture in the traditional sense. The PeopleSoft tiered architecture is depicted in **figure 9.1**

Figure 9.1—PeopleSoft Internet Architecture

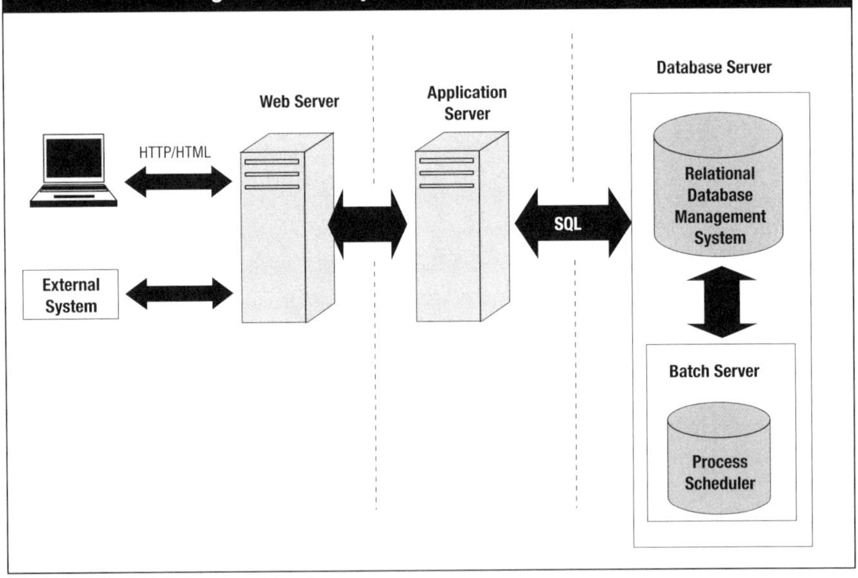

Users interact with the PeopleSoft software via a web browser. For the purposes of this guide, only PeopleSoft version 8.8 architecture components are considered. The PeopleSoft version 8 Internet-based architecture requires a java-enabled web server to support the web browser and transfers the data entered by users to the application server. No object definitions are stored on the workstation; the web browsers receive only HTML, Javascript and cookies from the application server. The application layer consists of one or more application servers. An application server (normally a BEA Tuxedo application server) manages the web browser transaction requests from users, maintains the SQL connection to the database, and runs the PeopleSoft application programs that manipulate data obtained from the user and the database. Each application server consists of multiple services (a particular task to be performed) and server processes (executable code that processes requests). A set of server processes facilitating transactions with the database is called an application server domain. Each application server domain can connect to only one database, although a database may connect to multiple domains. This may be the case for organizations with high volumes of transactions, high demand or high performance expectations. Each application server domain has a separate configuration file, configured using the PSADMIN utility.

The database layer consists of the relational database management system (RDBMS, e.g., DB2/MVS®, Oracle®, Informix®, Microsoft SQL Server®) used by the application server. The database server is the central source of information for an organization's business data as well as the container of user information, software components, object definitions, business rules, business transactional data and administrative statistical data to be used when managing or monitoring the system. The application server and database server can be physically separated and reside on different server machines, or logically separated on the same server machine, as shown in **figure 9.2**.

Each PeopleSoft installation normally has more than one database "instance," i.e., a copy of the underlying database. Most organizations should have as a minimum:

- Demonstration (DEMO) instance—The PeopleSoft-delivered environment
- Development (DEV) instance—An environment in which all system modifications are made and performed
- Test (TST) instance—An environment for testing the modifications
- Quality assurance (QUAL) instance—A copy of production used for user acceptance testing and quality assurance purposes
- Production (live) instance—The environment used by the business to process and hold day-to-day transactions

A complex implementation may have multiple instances of each of the environments; for example, there may be multiple test, development and production environments. There may also be environments for conversion and/or user training (it is important to have a specific environment with dummy data for

Figure 9.2—Physical vs. Logical Architecture

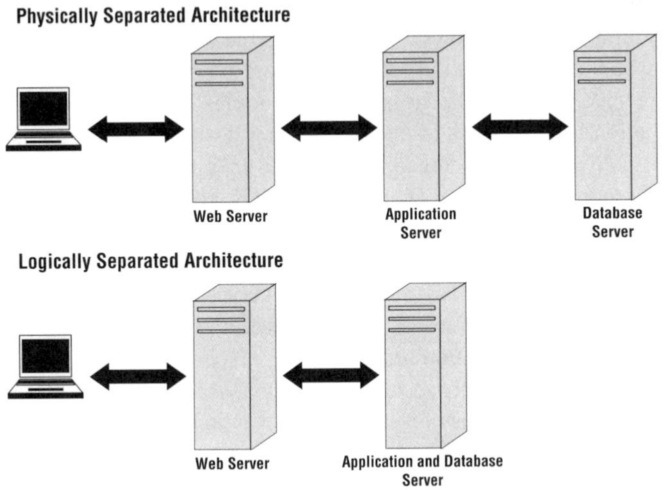

training purposes to keep sensitive HR data confidential). Whether these environments reside on the same database server or on separate physical servers is dependent on the performance, data storage and usage requirements. Auditors should be aware of all environments and include these in their testing where appropriate.

There are a number of advantages of the PeopleSoft Internet Architecture (essentially a thin client-server) approach. Some of the major advantages are:
- Flexible configuration—There are many possibilities for configuring an installation, from a centralized configuration to a distributed system, using communication interfaces.
- Workload distribution—Application servers can be configured to operate in parallel and communicate with the database server. They can be located in business areas to improve response times for users.
- Workload high-scalability—This permits users to adapt the capacity of their hardware according to the performance needs of their businesses, such as by adding application servers for additional users or when adding other modules.
- Ease of deployment—End users do not need client software installed on their PCs to access PeopleSoft. They can gain access to the PeopleSoft system by typing in an appropriate URL via a web browser and signing on using a valid user ID and password.

PeopleSoft is also based on an open system's "platform-neutral" philosophy allowing the application to run on multiple operating systems (e.g., various forms of UNIX or Windows NT®), databases (e.g., Oracle, Microsoft SQL Server) and user interfaces (e.g., personal computer, Macintosh®).

PeopleSoft Application Infrastructure

PeopleTools is PeopleSoft's proprietary toolset. It encompasses development tools, administration and upgrade tools, reporting and analysis tools, and integration tools. PeopleTools provides the means for administering the PeopleSoft application infrastructure. The key components of significance from an audit perspective include:

- Development and integration tools
- Data management tools
- Operations tools
- Security administration tools
- Reporting tools

Each of these areas is considered in more detail in the following paragraphs.

Development and Integration Tools

The PeopleSoft system may have a number of different database instances (e.g., DEMO, DEV, TST, QUAL, PROD). The production instance is the live environment where all business transaction processing is performed. All development and maintenance of PeopleSoft objects and functions should be performed in the development (DEV) instance and migrated through test (TST), quality (QUAL) and eventually the production (PROD) instance. The most common tools used for developing the system are:

- Application Designer—This is an interactive suite of PeopleTools and utilities used in tailoring the PeopleSoft application to suit the business needs. This may include defining menus, pages, records, fields, objects and/or business processes. The Application Designer is discussed in more detail later in this section.
- Application Engine—This is a tool used to develop programs that process data and transactions in the background. These programs reside in the database along with the business rules and definitions developed using the Application Designer.
- Business Process Designer—As discussed in chapter 2 in the Navigating the PeopleSoft System section, a business process represents an entire end-to-end process in an organization and is depicted graphically in the system by a business process map (or workflow map). PeopleSoft provides this as an alternative (to menu components) method of navigating the system. When the Business Process icon is selected, the activities that make up the business process are displayed. The Business Process Designer is a tool that allows developers to define the activities, events, decision points and steps that compose a particular business process.
- Workflow Administrator—Workflow enables the integrations of the automated processes within PeopleSoft with the business processes of an organization. The tasks of individual users are normally part of a larger business process involving multiple users across potentially multiple departments. Workflow enables the

results of these tasks (workflow items) to be routed to the subsequent user in the process (e.g., a purchase requisition once approved by one user is then automatically routed to the purchase order clerk for submission to the supplier). The Workflow Administrator provides the tools and utilities to set up and define workflow users, events and approval processes and to monitor workflow.
- Query Writer—Query Writer allows queries to be written for general business tasks or specific individuals needs.
- Report Manager—Report Manager helps manage any reports produced in the system and enables them to be sent to specific users using a given criteria in the system.

Note that the workflow and business process maps are developed via the Application Designer.

To a large extent, these tools have an impact on:
- How business processes are carried out
- How reporting and consolidation are accomplished
- What business objects are used (e.g., sales orders, purchase orders)
- How PeopleSoft functionality will meet the business requirements
- How data are defined in the system (e.g., the complexity of data input, the size of master data files)
- How cross-company processing will take place

As mentioned, the Application Designer is used to tailor the PeopleSoft application to meet the needs of the organization. PeopleCode is the primary programming language used to develop the application environment; this is used extensively with the SQL editor to extend the functionality of the system. An important aspect of the development of PeopleSoft is the change control methodology. The implementation of common change control procedures in the PeopleSoft environment aids in:
- Communicating changes to all affected stakeholders
- Coordinating the implementation of the changes across environments
- System availability
- Providing a detailed audit trail of modifications to all PeopleSoft environments

Application Designer includes change tracking and change control features, which can maintain version control over the changes made and manage development in a structured manner. It is possible to choose enabling of change tracking, change control or both.

Change tracking provides an audit trail of changes made to the PeopleTools objects and facilitates the identification and monitoring of the objects that have been modified.

Change control helps maintain version control and restricts who can make changes and how much information is captured about each change. An aspect of the change control function is the ability to lock objects, which give a developer exclusive control over a particular object being changed. Only the user ID that locks the object is able to modify that object. Furthermore, other than the change control administrator, only the user ID that locked the object may unlock it. It should be noted that while change control helps maintain version control, in that only one person can modify an object, it does not facilitate regression back to the original version in the event of an error during development.

It is also possible to lock the entire database using the change control administrator. This locks all database objects and is normally used during upgrades to prevent development from being performed during an upgrade process. Change Control History allows comments to be inserted regarding the development performed on the objects. This identifies the user who performed the change, the date the change was made and the type of change performed. It is important for the security administrator (see later section) to ensure that only appropriate users have access to the change control functionality. There are three levels of change control access that should be considered:

- Restricted access restricts users from locking or unlocking objects. When Change Control locking is enabled, users with restricted access can open Application Designer development objects only in read-only mode.
- Developer access allows a user to lock any unlocked definitions and unlock any definitions they have locked. They can then manipulate object definitions, as allowed in Maintain Security. Users can also view and enter object history comments.
- Supervisor access allows a user to unlock any locked definitions, regardless of who has locked them. Supervisors also have access to the Change Control Administrator dialog, which allows the user to lock/unlock all objects at one time and enable/disable Change Control locking and History. Note, however, that if Change Control locking is disabled, these access levels have no security value. If History is disabled, developer- and supervisor-access users can still view the History dialog; however, restricted-access users will not be able to view it.

Data Management: Tools

The PeopleSoft database tables contain objects definitions, business rules and business transaction data. The main data management tools are:

- Data Mover—Used to transfer data between databases and platforms, e.g., between development and test environments
- Mass Change—Used to generate multiple SQL statements that update data in the database. Although Mass Change is similar to other utilities and functions in PeopleSoft in that it updates the database and applies SQL statements to data, it is predominantly used for high-volume transactions and copying data from one table to another.

- Cube Manager—A suite of tools that is used to define analytical data stores, sometimes referred to as Online Analytical Processing (OLAP) cubes. These are simply databases that have a number of dimensions, such as product, time and region. Cube Manager facilitates the creation and analysis of the data cubes.
- Application Designer—Discussed in the previous section
- Integration Broker—Manages changes in data from one module to another within PeopleSoft

PeopleSoft also provides tools, such as SQR Alter and DDDAudit. SQR and SYSAudit.SQR are reports that can be used to verify the integrity of data stored in the database tables. While the majority of changes to the system should be made through the application front end, it is possible to make changes directly at the database level. Both SQL Alter tool and the Data Designer/Database Audit (DDD Audit) report help maintain the consistency between the PeopleTools record and index definitions and the underlying database objects. The System Audit (SYSAUDIT) report identifies "orphaned" objects (e.g., record definition fields that do not exist in the Record Definition table) or other anomalies (e.g., queries with the name "Untitled"). Both the SYSAUDIT and DDDAudit are often run at an appropriate time before go-live as part of a preimplementation review.

Operation Tools

The operational performance of the PeopleSoft system is controlled and administered by two main components:
- Process Schedule Manager
- PeopleSoft Administration

The PeopleSoft Administration profile facilitates the administration of the application servers and application server domains and is a superuser, which by default has access to the entire PeopleSoft system. In a production environment, it is important for this ID to be stripped down of its full administration access rights and tightly controlled with a complex password that is changed frequently and not shared.

The Process Scheduler Manager is used to manage batch processing and recurring tasks within the PeopleSoft system. The increased efficiency is derived from the reduction of user involvement in these processes and enables the user to:
- Schedule recurring tasks or processes
- Create groups of tasks or processes, i.e., jobs
- Schedule jobs

Processes and jobs are identified by a run control ID that is used with a user ID as a key to determine the parameters of a process, such as output type.

As mentioned, the PeopleSoft profile facilitates the administration of the application servers and application server domains.

The Process Scheduler Manager's primary functions include (for specific databases):

- Start a Process Scheduler server
- Stop a Process Scheduler server
- Configure a Process Scheduler server
- Create a Process Scheduler server configuration
- Delete a Process Scheduler server configuration
- Edit a Process Scheduler configuration file
- Show status of a Process Scheduler server

Security Administration Tools

Within an ERP environment such as PeopleSoft, there are multiple access points to the data held within the system. PeopleSoft Application Security is one of several security components that need to be considered in an audit of a PeopleSoft environment, as depicted in **figure 9.3**. Other components that need to be secured and subject to independent review include:

- Operating Environment Security
- Technology Infrastructure Security

Figure 9.3—Key ERP Security Components

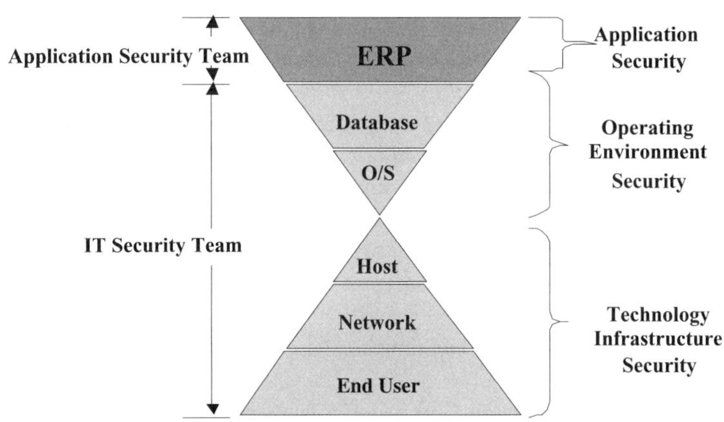

PeopleSoft security administration is performed using the PeopleTools Security component accessed via Home→PeopleTools→Security, as shown in **figure 9.4**.

It is appropriate at this stage to discuss the user identification and authentication, i.e., the sign-in process. A user accesses the PeopleSoft system by entering his/her unique user ID and password at the sign-in page. The application server then connects to the Relational Database Management System (RDBMS) using the Connect ID. The Connect ID performs the initial connection between the application server and the RDBMS and has only limited access to certain

Figure 9.4—PeopleTools Security Component

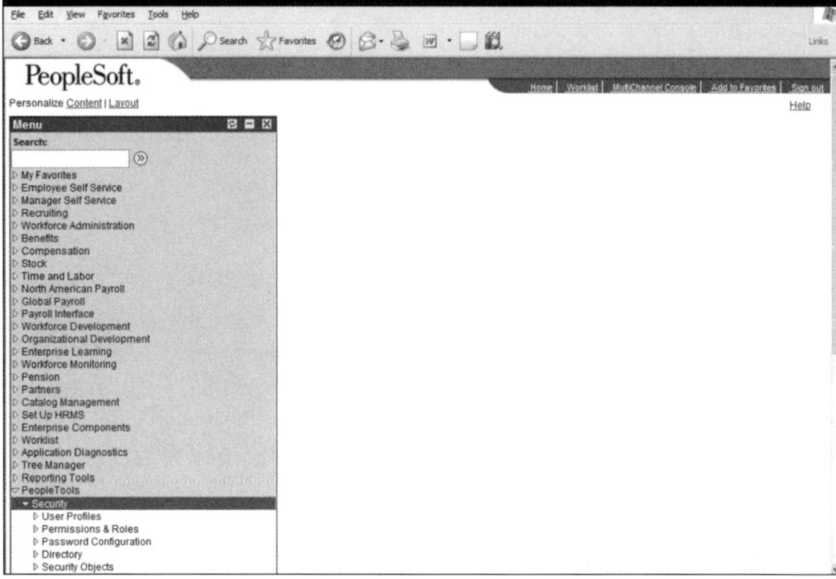

database tables for the authentication process. The application server passes the user ID and password onto the database for validation against various database tables, such as PSOPRDFN and, if verified, retrieves the associated Access ID and password information from the PSACCESSPRFL table. The application server then logs off as the Connect ID and reconnects using the Access ID. The application server maintains a continuous connection using the database server with the Access ID, which has administrator access to the RDBMS. User access is restricted via PeopleSoft Application Security.

This process differs (within PeopleSoft, not to the end user) if an LDAP authentication or single sign-on configuration is enabled. These features are discussed in chapter 11, New Directions for PeopleSoft and ERP Audit.

Chapter 4 introduced the PeopleSoft Security Authorization concept and defined the main application security object types:
- User profile
- Roles
- Permission lists

Users are identified within PeopleSoft by a user ID, which is associated with a user profile. The user profile defines access to the system, which is restricted by limiting the pages (or screens) that a user is able to access. In many cases, the security requirements of groups of users may be common, and roles and permission lists are created to aid the administration of individual's access security rights. A role generally equates to a job (e.g., accounts payable clerk, payroll manager, global payroll administrator or benefits administrator), and roles are subsequently linked to permission lists. Permission lists control which pages (or menu items), processes and tools that a role (and, therefore, a user) has access to, in addition to other parameters such as the time of the day that the user may log into the system or the maximum period of inactivity before the user is automatically timed out of the system. Authorizations are defined at the page level and identify the type of access that a role has been granted for that page.

Figure 9.5—Roles Assigned to Users

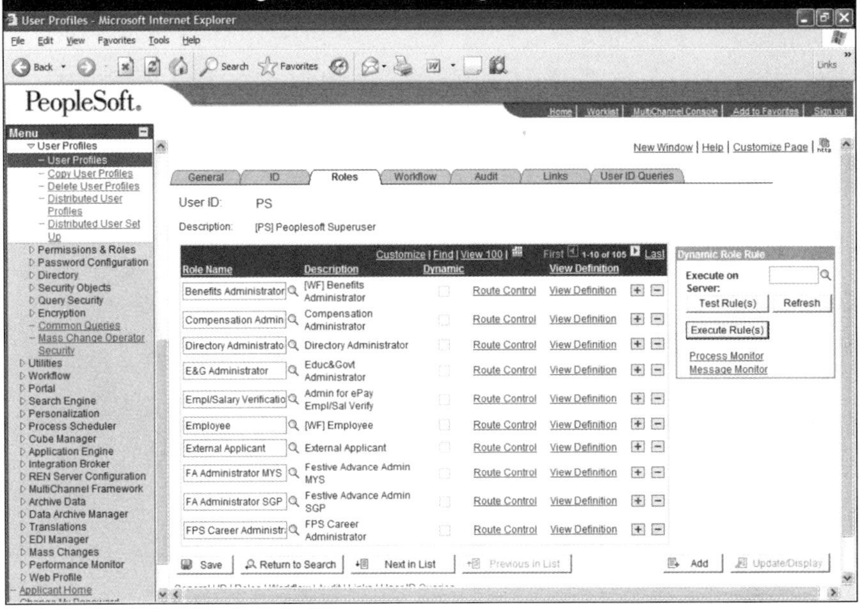

Figure 4.4 in chapter 4 shows the relationships among user profiles, roles and permission lists. **Figure 9.5** depicts where roles are assigned to a user. **Figures 9.6**, **9.7** and **9.8** show how users are assigned roles and lists of permissions that determine the specific access that a user has. **Figure 9.9** shows the assignment of authorizations (Update/Display, Correction, etc.) for a page. The design, administration and approval of user access should be in tune with the business requirements so that operational access requirements can be incorporated and segregation of duties can be maintained. Segregation of security administration duties is also important to prevent any one individual from having excessive access within the system. Depending on the size of the organization, it is usually desirable to segregate the following three functions:

- Creation and maintenance of roles and permission lists
- Migration of roles and permission lists into the production (PROD) instance
- Creation and maintenance of user profiles

Figure 9.6—Permission Lists

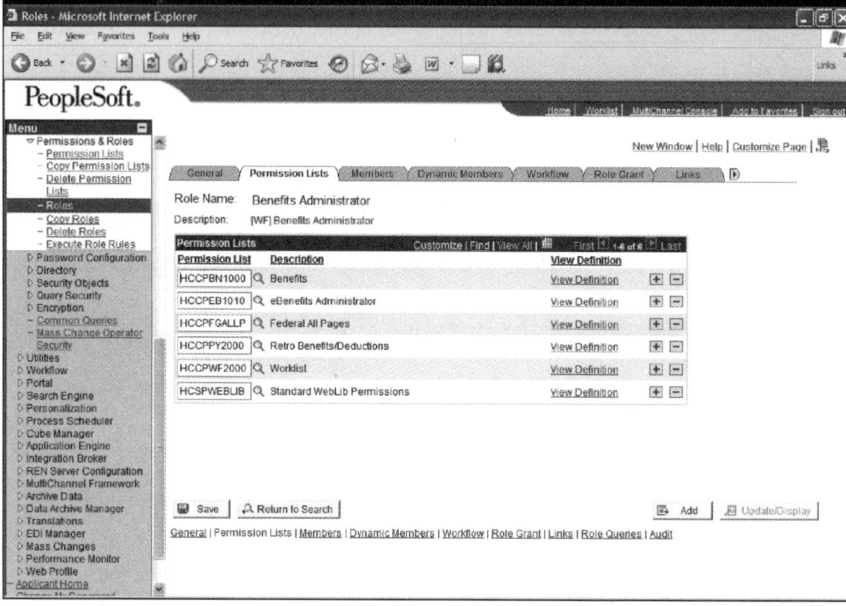

Figure 9.7—PeopleTools

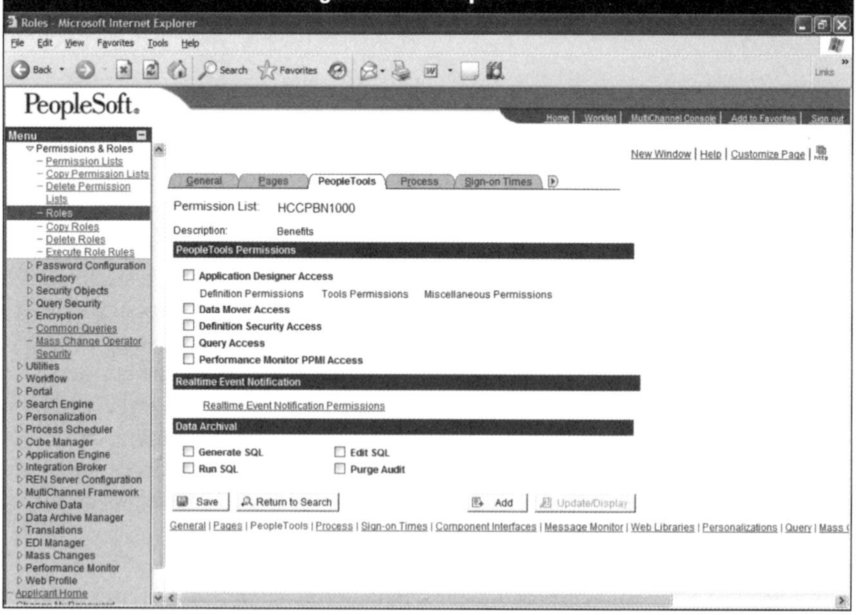

Figure 9.8—Pages

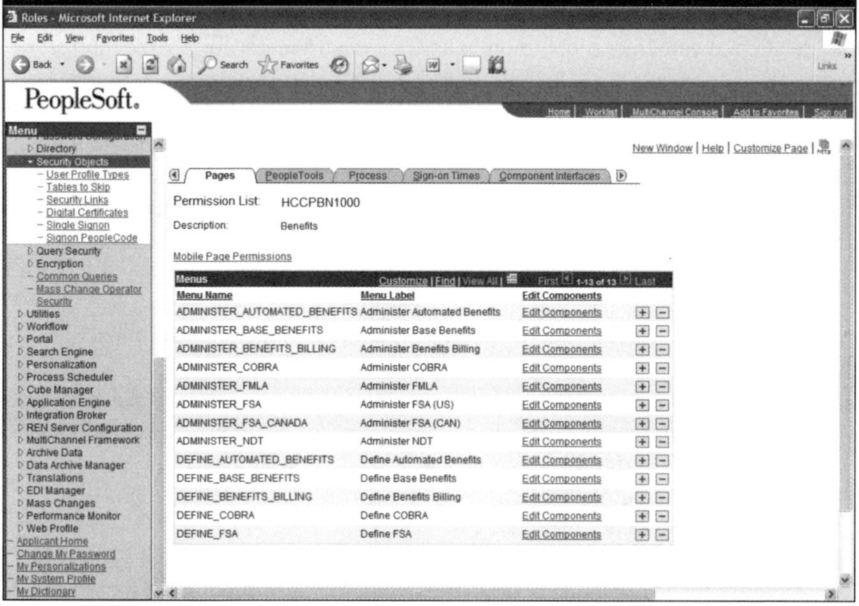

Figure 9.9—Page Permissions

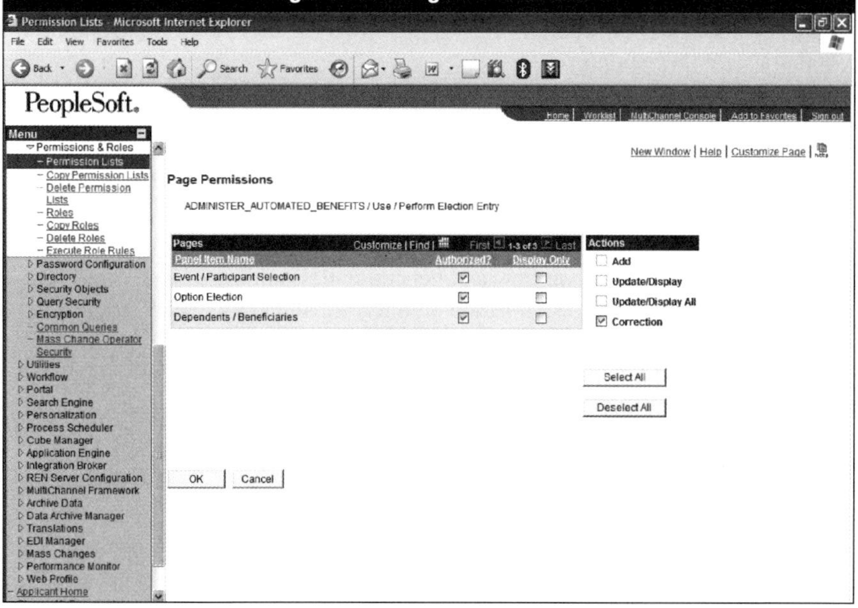

Appropriate segregation of these functions mitigates the risk that a security administrator can maintain user profiles, migrate roles and permission lists, and maintain roles and permission lists. End users must not have access to maintain roles, profiles and permission lists.

Audit Implications

As mentioned earlier, it is common in an ERP environment for a large number of the controls to be automated using access security or configuration settings. An understanding of the PeopleSoft security concepts and the PeopleSoft Application Infrastructure tools (e.g., development and integration tools, operations tools, security administration tools) is essential in identifying the risks and understanding the controls and techniques for testing them. An understanding of the PeopleSoft architecture and an organization's particular systems landscape is also essential in determining an effective audit approach.

Some of the audit aspects that the previously described factors may impact include:

- Testing of security parameters—How many PeopleSoft servers are there, and have security parameters been synchronized across all servers? If not, security parameters may need to be tested on each server or a sample of servers.
- Infrastructure testing requirements—How many systems are there, and which systems are running production?
- Testing under rotation plan—Is an audit rotation plan operating and, if so, what systems are relevant? Is the rotation plan operating at the technical security infrastructure level, the business cycle level or both? What technical security areas are due for testing under rotation? What business cycles are due for testing under rotation, and on what systems or platforms are they running? What countries are they supporting?
- Specific, identified risks—Have systems been upgraded? Have there been any country-specific changes?

Summary

This chapter provided an overview and general understanding of the PeopleSoft technical infrastructure and application architecture and key PeopleSoft components, including:

- Development and integration tools
- Data management tools
- Operations tools
- Security administration tools

10. Auditing PeopleSoft Application Security

This chapter provides a sample tool set for use in auditing PeopleSoft Application Security, including:
• Specific risks in the PeopleSoft Application Infrastructure
• Automated control activities to manage these risks
• Sample assurance techniques

Chapter 9 outlined the main PeopleSoft Application Infrastructure components. PeopleTools is a tool set packaged with all PeopleSoft applications, encompassing development tools, administration and upgrade tools, reporting and analysis tools, and integration tools. These are categorized into the following:
• Development and integration tools
• Data management tools
• Operations tools
• Security administration tools

It should be noted that these are broad categories and the tools may be utilized in a number of these areas.

Development and Integration Tools

Development and Integration Tools: Risks

The development and integration activities within PeopleSoft and the associated security risks and controls may be categorized into the following:
• Development and integration tools
• Definition (object) security

Significant risks associated with development and integration include:

1.1 **Tools**—As discussed in chapter 9, the PeopleSoft system may have a number of different database instances (e.g., DEMO, DEV, TST, PROD). The production instance is the live environment where all business transaction processing is performed. All development and maintenance of PeopleSoft definitions and functions are performed in the development (DEV) instance; testing of such changes is performed in a test (TST) instance and migrated through to the production (PROD) instances. The most common tools utilized for this are:
• Application Designer
• Application Engine
• Workflow Administrator
• Query Manager
• Business Process Designer

Note that the workflow and business process maps are developed via the Application Designer.

If access to development functions is available in the production instance or preproduction instances (e.g., QA instance), unauthorized or inappropriate changes may be made, bypassing established procedures and controls. Bypassing established procedures may relate to the approval and testing stage. Consequently, this may have a detrimental impact on the integrity of the system and data.

1.2 **Risks related to definition (object) security**—Definition security dictates access to the PeopleTools object definitions (e.g., tree structures, records, fields). These are created using tools such as Application Designer and stored in underlying PeopleTools tables.

There are two steps involved in establishing definition security:
• Creation of definition groups
• Assignment of definition groups to permission lists

A definition group is a collection of one or more definitions that form a logical group for security purposes. Definitions not associated with a specific definition group are included in the *All Definitions* "catch-all" group and are accessible by anyone who has access to this group and the tools that can modify them. Once an object is associated with a definition group, it can only be accessed by users who have been assigned access to the corresponding definition group. Users receive access to definition groups via the primary permission list that has been assigned directly to their user profile.

Definition security is configured to prevent unauthorized or inappropriate modifications to definitions. The following definition types may be secured:
• Activities
• Application engine programs
• Application packages
• Approval rule sets
• Business interlinks
• Business processes
• Components
• Component interfaces
• Fields
• File layouts
• HTML
• Images
• Menus
• Message channels

- Messages
- Mobile pages
- Pages
- Problem types
- Projects
- Queries
- Records
- SQL
- Style sheets
- Tree structures
- Trees
- Translate tables

Object definitions may be accessed using the following tools:
- Application Designer
- Tree Manager
- Query Manager

There are two default definition groups delivered with PeopleSoft:
- PEOPLETOOLS
- *ALLDEFINITIONS*\

Development and Integration Tools: Key Controls

Key controls over development and integration include:

1.1.1 Access to the following development and integration tools in the production environment should be restricted to authorized users and segregated from incompatible duties:
- Application Designer
- Application Engine
- Workflow Administrator
- Query Manager
- Business Process Designer

1.2.1 Security documentation should be compiled to define the PeopleTools definition-level security design and procedures for creation and modification of object definitions, in line with management intentions. Definition security should be implemented to restrict access to object definitions via the tools listed in 1.1.1 and to ensure that every high-risk object definition has been assigned to a definition group.

Development and Integration Tools: Testing Techniques

Testing techniques for development and integration controls include:

1.1.1 Review access security matrices and access assignment documentation to gain an understanding of the security design. Corroborate this understanding by generating lists of users with access to the Application

Designer and Application Engine menus, and review their level of access by writing and executing the following query in PeopleSoft Query Manager:

```
SELECT A.OPRID, A.OPRDEFNDESC, A.ACCTLOCK,
B.ROLENAME, C.CLASSID, D.MENUNAME, D.BARNAME,
D.BARITEMNAME, D.PNLITEMNAME, D.DISPLAYONLY,
D.AUTHORIZEDACTIONS
FROM PSOPRDEFN A, PSROLEUSER B, PSROLECLASS C,
PSAUTHITEM D

WHERE A.OPRID = B.ROLEUSER AND B.ROLENAME =
C.ROLENAME AND C.CLASSID = D.CLASSID
```

Order by A.OPRID, B.ROLENAME, C.CLASSID, D.MENUNAME to ensure that the user IDs (OPRID), roles (ROLENAME), permission lists (CLASSID) and components (MENUNAME) are listed in alphabetical order.

The authorized actions column will contain values that represent the action types that the user is authorized to perform. A listing and description of these actions is detailed at the end of this chapter. The auditor should determine which of the values are considered high risk within the organization.

The display only column will have a value of either:

- 1—All fields in the page are display-only to the user.
- 0—This setting is turned off, and the action type codes indicate the level of access granted.

A.ACCTLOCK will have a value of either:

- 1—The user ID is locked from system entry.
- 0—The user ID is available for use.

Use caution if filtering users who are locked out. Users can be temporarily locked out for an excessive number of incorrect password attempts. As such, users with access to sensitive pages should not be discounted from the above query until it is confirmed that they no longer require access to PeopleSoft. In addition to locking the account, it is good practice to remove all roles and permission lists from a user profile when that access is no longer required.

1.2.1 Review security documentation to gain an understanding of the definition security design. Corroborate by generating a list of users with access to definition groups.

This can be generated by writing the following SQL into Query Manager:

```
SELECT A.OPRID, A.OPRDEFNDESC, A.ACCTLOCK, B.CLASSID,
B.OBJGROUPID, B.DISPLAYONLY FROM PSOPRDEFN A,
```

```
PSOPROBJ B WHERE A.OPRCLASS = B.CLASSID
```

Note: In the event that a user belongs to multiple definition groups and more than one group provides access to a definition, the level of access provided to the user will be determined by the definition group with the highest level of access (i.e., the least restrictive fashion).

Generate a list of definition groups and the definitions defined in them by writing the following query in Query Manager:

```
SELECT A.OBJGROUPID, A.ENTTYPE, A.ENTNAME
FROM PSOBJGROUP A
```

Alternatively, the following query could be used for increased detail:

```
SELECT PSOPRDEFN.OPRID, PSOPRDEFN.OPRDEFNDESC,
PSOPROBJ.CLASSID, PSOPROBJ.OBJGROUPID,
PSOPROBJ.DISPLAYONLY, PSOPROBJ.VERSION,
PSOBJGROUP.ENTTYPE, PSOBJGROUP.ENTNAME,
PSOBJGROUP.VERSION, PSOPRDEFN.ACCTLOCK,
PSOPROBJ.CLASSID

FROM PSOBJGROUP INNER JOIN (PSOPROBJ INNER JOIN
PSOPRDEFN ON PSOPROBJ.CLASSID = PSOPRDEFN.OPRCLASS)
ON PSOBJGROUP.OBJGROUPID = PSOPROBJ.OBJGROUPID;
```

At minimum, the PSOPRDEFN and PSOPROBJ classes must be joined to obtain a report on user IDs with the definition groups that they have been assigned.

Review the output from both queries to determine appropriateness and compliance with security documentation.

Generate a list of users with access to PeopleTools menus via the query detailed in 1.1.1 (under Development and Integration Tools: Testing Techniques).

Data Management Tools

Data Management Tools: Risks

Significant risks associated with data management include:

2.1 **Data integrity**—The PeopleSoft database tables contain object definitions, business rules and business transaction data. Consequently, if access to the database and the PeopleTools available to manipulate the data are not restricted, the integrity of the database structure and definitions may be inappropriately modified. Access to modify object definitions has already been discussed in the previous test. The main data management tools within PeopleSoft are:

- Data Mover
- Mass Change
- Cube Manager
- Application Designer (relevant for restricting access to object definitions)

PeopleSoft provides tools that can be utilized to verify the integrity of data stored in the database tables. It should also be noted that it is possible to obtain direct access to the database and, consequently, gain complete assurance over the integrity of data. All data access paths should be identified, and security reviews should be performed at the database and operating system levels.

Data Management Tools: Key Controls

Key controls over data management include:

2.1.1 Access to the following pages in production should be restricted to authorized users and segregated from incompatible duties:

- Data Mover
- Mass Change
- Cube Manager
- Application Designer (relevant for restricting access to object definitions)

The DDDAudit.SQR and SYSAudit.SQR reports should be generated on a regular basis and independently reviewed by management. Any exceptions should be investigated, and corrective action should be taken on a timely basis.

Note: It is also necessary to consider access controls over the network folders that may contain Data Mover scripts or data to be imported/moved.

Data Management Tools: Testing Techniques

Testing techniques for data management include:

2.1.1 Review access security matrices and access assignment documentation to gain an understanding of the security design. Corroborate this understanding by generating lists of users with access by running the SQL query detailed in 1.1.1 (under Development and Integration Tools: Testing Techniques) and reviewing users with access to the above menus and pages.

Review security procedures created by management that identify whether the SQR Alter tool and DDDAudit.SQR and SYSAudit.SQR reports are run and independently reviewed and investigated by management. Corroborate by selecting a sample of reports and reviewing them for evidence of independent review and follow-up of exceptional items.

Operations Tools

Operations Tools: Risks

The operational performance of the PeopleSoft system is controlled and administered by two main components:

- Process Schedule Manager
- PeopleSoft Administration

The PeopleSoft Administration profile facilitates the administration of the application servers and is a superuser with access to the entire PeopleSoft system. The risks, controls and testing techniques associated with superuser access are addressed in the security administration section later in this chapter.

Significant risks associated with operations include:

3.1 **Process Schedule Manager**—The process scheduler is used to manage batch processing and recurring tasks within the PeopleSoft system. The increased efficiency is derived from the reduction of user involvement in these processes. If access to process scheduler functions and process requests is not restricted, the processes may not run as intended or in the correct order, or the output may not be sent to the correct destination.

Operation Tools: Key Controls

Key controls over operations include:

3.1.1 Access to the Process Schedule Manager functions should be restricted to authorized users.

Process group permissions and process profiles should be established and assigned to permission lists in line with the security design and management intentions.

Operation Tools: Testing Techniques

Testing techniques for operation tools include:

3.1.1 Review the system design documentation relating to access security (design of roles and permission lists); any established policies, procedures, standards and guidance related to the maintenance of roles/permission lists; and, in particular, the design and assignment of Process Scheduler access, process groups and process profiles.

Corroborate this understanding by generating and reviewing a list of user IDs with access to functionality under the Process Scheduler menu. The list can be generated by writing the following query in PeopleSoft Query Manager:

```
SELECT A.OPRID, A.OPRDEFNDESC, A.ACCTLOCK,
B.ROLENAME, C.CLASSID, D.MENUNAME, D.BARNAME,
D.BARITEMNAME, D.PNLITEMNAME, D.DISPLAYONLY,
D.AUTHORIZEDACTIONS
```

```
FROM PSOPRDEFN A, PSROLEUSER B, PSROLECLASS C,
PSAUTHITEM D

WHERE A.OPRID = B.ROLEUSER AND B.ROLENAME =
C.ROLENAME AND C.CLASSID = D.CLASSID
```

Order by A.OPRID, B.ROLENAME, C.CLASSID, D.MENUNAME to ensure that the user IDs (OPRID), roles (ROLENAME), permission lists (CLASSID) and components (MENUNAME) are listed in alphabetical order

The authorized actions column will contain values that represent the action types. These values are detailed at the end of this chapter.

Generate and review a list of process group permissions assigned to user IDs by writing the following query:

```
SELECT A.OPRID, A.OPRDEFNDESC, A.ACCTLOCK, B.PRCSGRP
FROM PSOPRDEFN A, PSAUTHPRCS B WHERE A.OPRCLASS =
B.CLASSID
```

Order by A.OPRID to ensure that the user IDs (OPRID) are listed in alphabetical order.

Generate and review a list of process group permission contents by writing the following query:

```
SELECT A.PRCSTYPE, A.PRCSNAME, A.PRCSGRP
FROM PS_PRCSDEFNGRP A
```

Generate and review a list of users and their process profile configurations by writing the following query:

```
SELECT A.OPRID, A.OPRDEFNDESC, A.ACCTLOCK, B.CLASSID,
B.SRVRDESTFILE, B.SRVRDESTPRNT, B.CLIENTDESTFILE,
B.CLIENTDESTPRNT, B.OVRDOUTDEST, B.OVRDSRVRPARMS,
B.RQSTSTATUSUPD, B.RQSTSTATUSVIEW, B.SRVRSTATUSUPD,
B.SRVRSTATUSVIEW, B.MVSJOBNAME, B.MVSJOBACCT,
B.RECURUPD FROM PSOPRDEFN A, PSPRCSPRFL B
WHERE A.PRCSPRFLCLS = B.CLASSID
```

Order by A.OPRID to ensure that the user IDs (OPRID) are listed in alphabetical order.

Note: The ProcessSchedulerAdmin role grants users access to override controls established via Process Profile permission lists. Therefore, the following query should be executed to identify users who have been assigned this access:

```
SELECT A.OPRID, A.OPRDEFNDESC, A.ACCTLOCK,
```

```
C.ROLENAME, C.DESCR
FROM PSOPRDEFN A, PSROLEUSER B, PSROLEDEFN C
WHERE A.OPRID = B.ROLEUSER
AND B.ROLENAME = C.ROLENAME
AND C.ROLENAME = 'ProcessSchedulerAdmin'
```

Security Administration Tools

PeopleSoft Application Security can be separated into application online security (functionality) and application data security (data). The release of PIA supports the implementation of single sign-on across different applications (e.g., HRMS and Financials), allowing the user to access different application without having to sign on multiple times. Auditing security in a PeopleSoft environment requires expert knowledge, as well as knowledge of the organization's approach to security.

Security Administration Tools: Risks

Significant risks associated with security administration include:

4.1 **Security administration profiles**—Security administration functions control the access to the applications and data stored within PeopleSoft and support the confidentiality and integrity of that data. Access to security functions may not be appropriately assigned to be compatible with an individual's roles and responsibilities.

4.2 **Authorization documentation**—During the implementation of PeopleSoft, organizations should have developed adequate documentation that describes the design and assignment of permission lists and roles, and a procedure should have been developed for the maintenance of this documentation. Without detailed documentation of how the permission lists and roles were developed and implemented, it may be difficult to adequately monitor and control security, as irregularities may not be able to be traced back to their root causes. In addition, without documentation it is difficult to determine if security has been implemented to maintain segregation of duties and in accordance with management's intentions.

4.3 **Superuser access**—PeopleSoft comes with a number of powerful security authorizations:

- SYSADM access profile
- PeopleSoft Administration user ID
- PeopleSoft Administrator role

Default user IDs are discussed at the end of this chapter.

SYSADM provides superuser-level access to the underlying database. The PeopleSoft Administration user ID and the PeopleSoft Administrator role provide users with access to all menus and pages in the system. If improperly controlled, these could be used to access the system and perform unauthorized processing of transactions that may circumvent established controls in the system.

The bullet list represents some of the PeopleSoft-delivered security authorizations. Many organizations disable the functionality of these security authorizations and reassign the privileges to specific individuals responsible for performing that role within the organization. The auditor should be wary of security administration staff whose access has been modelled on the above-delivered functionality, as this could provide more access than intended or required.

Access to functionality under the following menus is generally considered powerful:

- APPLICATION_DESIGNER
- APPLICATION_ENGINE
- DATA_MOVER
- DEFINITION_SECURITY
- QUERY or QUERY_MANAGER
- MAINTAIN_SECURITY
- MASS_CHANGE
- PROCESS_SCHEDULER
- NVISION
- QUERY or QUERY_MANAGER
- TREEMANAGER
- UTILITIES

PeopleSoft is delivered with a number of user IDs providing superuser access to specific applications in the system. Some of the common delivered user IDs for the HRMS application are detailed at the end of this chapter. Inappropriate assignment and use of superuser access may result in the input and processing of unauthorized or invalid transactions or loss of data.

Note: The items listed above represent some of the critical menus where controls should be in place to ensure data integrity. However, there may be additional sensitive functional menus/panels that need to be controlled within a specific organization's implementation.

4.4 **Default users**—The PeopleSoft software is delivered with a set of standard user IDs and passwords that should be secured appropriately, removed or locked, and the passwords changed as part of the implementation process. The risk is increased since the default passwords are often the same as the user IDs. If these passwords are left unchanged, they provide a way for unauthorized users to gain access to the system. In addition, the use of default user IDs reduces the ability to establish accountability within the application.

4.5 **Powerful roles and permission lists**—In addition to the PeopleSoft Administrator role and PSADMIN permission list, PeopleSoft delivers additional permission lists that provide powerful levels of access to select modules in the system. A listing of delivered permission lists is provided at the end of this chapter. If these permission lists are inappropriately assigned, users may obtain excessive access within the system, leading to unauthorized transactions or processing, or a breakdown in segregation of duties.

4.6 **User identification, authentication and security parameters**—User identification and authentication is a critical control process in restricting access to systems and data. All users of the system are identified by a user ID. If user IDs are not unique, individual accountability of activity on the system may be lost. User authentication on PeopleSoft is via a user ID/password combination. Inadequate password controls may lead to unauthorized access to the system, data and functions.

4.7 **Correct history (Correction Mode)**—Correction Mode access allows a user to view, modify, insert and delete rows of data, regardless of the effective date. This is one of the most powerful levels of access that can be assigned in the PeopleSoft application and can be used to alter historic, current or future effective-dated data, without the creation of an audit trail. Consequently, data integrity, audit trails and management reporting from the system may be adversely affected. Since Correction Mode can be used to make changes without an audit trail, the ability to detect, identify and investigate inappropriate changes is severely diminished.

4.8 **Query security**—PeopleSoft provides the ability to run and create *ad hoc* queries to report data (in the form of SQL queries) via the Query tool facility. If access to the Query tool and the data records/tables upon which queries are run is not restricted, users may have inappropriate access to information on the system. Query security restricts access at the row level in the PeopleSoft tables. Although queries do not allow the user to modify data, inadequate security over the access to queries and data may lead to a breakdown over the confidentiality of the information held on the system. In addition, access to change workflow queries could potentially impact approval routings if workflow is misconfigured.

System performance may be adversely impacted if inexperienced users are allowed to create and run poorly designed queries. Granting user IDs access to use PeopleSoft's Query functionality is accomplished by:

- Granting access to the Query tools via roles and permission lists
- Setting up Query profiles, which define the query functions available to the users assigned the Query tools
- Setting up and assigning Query access groups, which restricts the tables accessible for users of Query tools. Access groups are represented by nodes on a Query tree.

4.9 **Table logging and audit trails**—The PeopleSoft system does not have standard security logging features. It is possible to log changes to database tables, but this has to be set up manually. If auditing is not set or if the audit logs are not reviewed, unauthorized modifications to data and tables may not be identified and rectified on a timely basis. Consequently, data integrity and management reporting may be adversely affected.

Once auditing is enabled, appropriate security should be enabled to prevent unauthorized alterations of the audit logs.

Security Administration Tools: Key Controls

Key controls over security administration include:

4.1.1 Security administration profiles should be appropriately segregated and assigned to system management staff.

Where segregation of duties is not practicable due to resource restrictions, audit reports can be set up to allow management to independently review system administration changes.

System audits can be set up on security tables at the field level or the record level. The Audit page under user profiles and permission lists identifies the last user to make a change and the time of the change.

4.2.1 Original documentation of the PeopleSoft Access Security design should be developed and signed off by management during the implementation. Documentation should be maintained that identifies all changes made to roles and permission lists. In addition, copies of all such documentation should be kept offsite for use in the event of a disaster.

4.3.1 The following measures should be implemented:

- Remove the delivered PeopleSoft Administration ID.
- Properly segregate PeopleSoft Administration capabilities across newly created profiles with less functionality.
- Restrict assignment of the PeopleSoft Administrator role.

If a decision is made to keep the delivered PeopleSoft Administration user ID unlocked, a new password must be created and should be stored confidentially until an emergency arises to warrant its use.

4.4.1 The remaining delivered PeopleSoft user IDs should be removed or locked, where possible.

4.5.1 The assignment of powerful roles and permission lists should be restricted in line with the approved security design documentation and management intentions.

4.6.1 Password controls should be established to enforce stronger passwords and help reduce risks of unauthorized access. Standards should be developed and communicated to end users to ensure that passwords remain confidential. In addition to governing the parameter settings in PeopleSoft, these standards and policies should include guidance on choosing passwords (i.e., should not be easily guessable) and prohibiting the sharing of passwords, and they should include the use of other controls (e.g., password protected screen savers). **Figure 10.1** illustrates the password parameters available.

Figure 10.1—Password Parameters

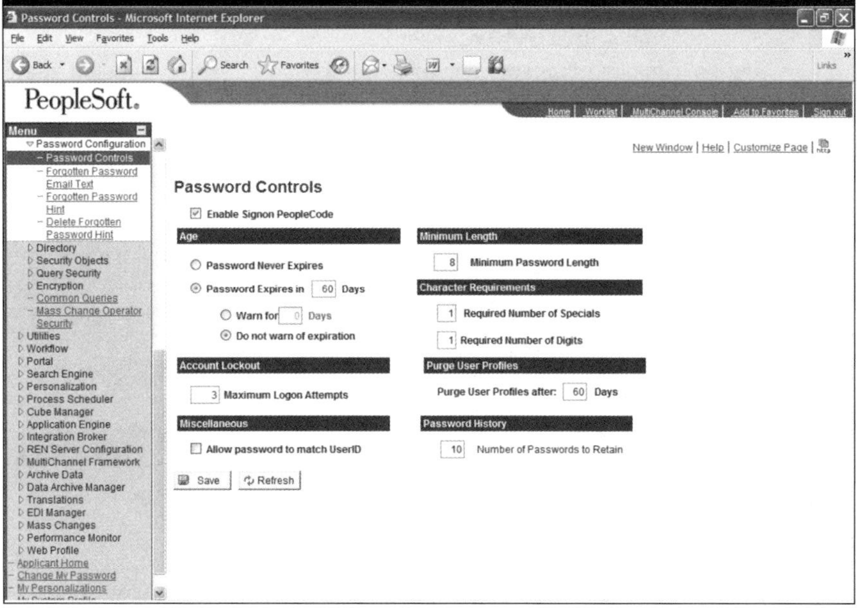

On the Password Controls page, the following password controls should be enabled by checking (ticking) the box to be operational:

- Password Expiration—PeopleSoft provides password expiration capability, and users are able to define the password validity period (1 to 365 days). This should be dependent on organizational requirements and policies, but should be set between 30 days and 90 days.

It is also possible for the system to display a warning message to inform users when their password is due to expire. This can have a value from 1 to 365 days. Again, this should be set in line with the security policy.

- Account Lock-out—This defines the maximum number of login attempts before a user is locked out of the system. This is usually set as three to five attempts.
- Allow Password to Match User ID—It is important that a user's password be distinct from his/her user ID. This parameter ensures that the password defined does not match the user ID.
- Minimum Length—This defines the minimum character length that a password should be. If a password specified by the user does not meet this requirement, a message is displayed. The character length should be set at six or eight characters as a minimum.

- Character Requirements—It is possible to further strengthen password controls by dictating how many special characters (e.g., $ or @) and/or numbers must be included in the password.
- Password History—This defines the number of passwords PeopleSoft will remember. This parameter ensures that a user's password is not reused until after a specified number of password changes. This should be set according to an organization's security policy, although it is usually set to remember the last 10 passwords.
- Sign-on Time and Time-out Parameters—It is possible to define the time period during which a user ID is allowed to sign on to the PeopleSoft system. This interval is adjustable, and user IDs are not granted access to the system outside these periods. This should be dependent on the specific user's responsibilities. Users could have their access restricted to 08:30 to 18:30, Monday to Friday, if they are not expected to work beyond these hours. Other users may require unrestricted access (see **figure 10.2**).

Figure 10.2—Sign-on Times

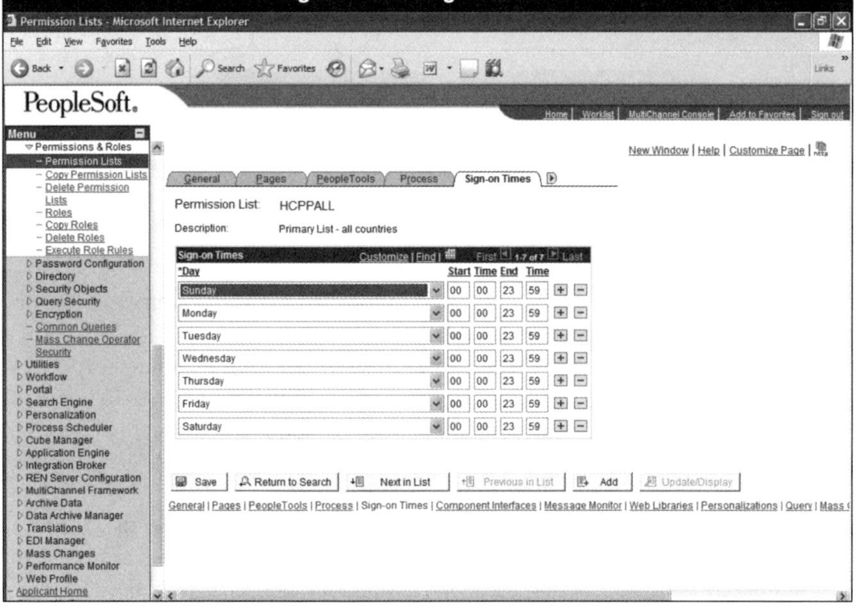

In addition, it is possible to define a maximum period (in minutes) of idle time (Specific Time-out) before a user ID is automatically disconnected by the system, as shown in **figure 10.3**.

Note: Both these parameters are set at the permission list level. Time-outs can also be set at the application server and web server levels. If multiple permission lists assigned have differing time-out periods and sign-on times, the greatest values are adhered to by the system. For example, if permission list A100 provides unrestricted access and permission list

Figure 10.3—Time-out Minutes

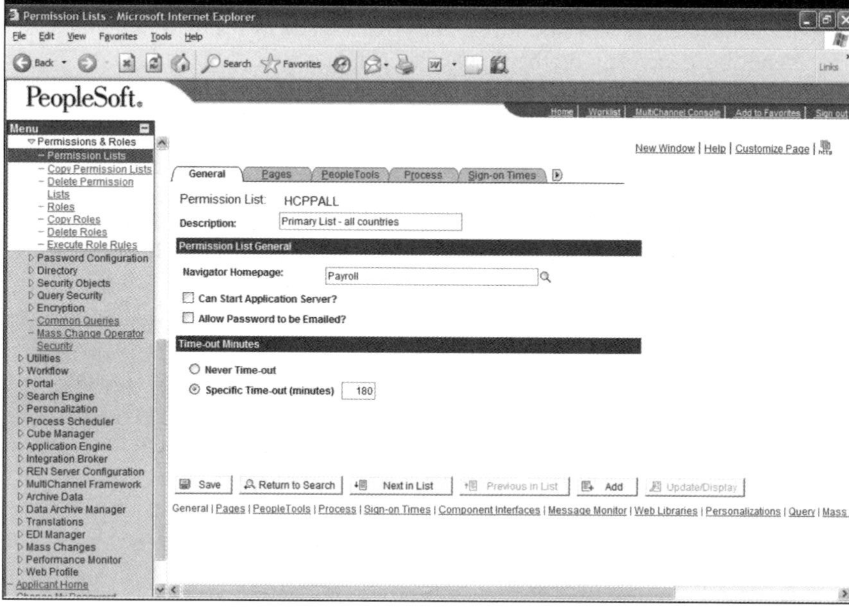

B100 provides access from 09:00 to 17:30, Monday to Friday, the user has unrestricted access.

4.7.1 Security policies and procedures should include specific guidance on the use of Correction Mode, i.e., restrictions on assignment to user profiles, procedures for assigning Correction Mode, situations where it is appropriate to assign it, and comparison of intended use with actual use. The assignment of Correction Mode should be minimized and additional approval sought, if this action type is requested.

The PeopleSoft Auditing functionality should be turned on for objects that are accessible via the Correct History action.

4.8.1 Security documentation should define query-level security design, policies and procedures in line with management intentions.

Query security should be established to restrict access to appropriate and authorized users commensurate with their roles and responsibilities. This should be set up in three stages:

1. Access to the query manager tool is restricted.
2. Query profiles are defined to restrict access to Query functions.
3. Access to specific tables is restricted via assignment of access groups, and access to data rows is restricted via Query Record Security Definitions.

4.9.1 Policies and standards should be documented to define the critical records and record fields that are to be logged for changes; this should take into account the performance requirements and operational and database constraints at the organization.

PeopleSoft provides auditing capability to track changes to security tables. These should be set at the record or field level; however, they should also be enabled at the database level. The effectiveness of the audit logging as a control is dependent on the timely, independent review of the logs produced. All changes to the critical PeopleSoft records and fields are logged by the system, and the periodic review of these logs forms part of the security procedures for the organization.

It should be noted that these audit options apply only to data that are manipulated on a normal PeopleSoft Application page through page processing. These options do not apply to data that are added using SQLExec in PeopleCode or by some other means. The user ID, date and time fields are modified, and the old values and new values are logged in the PSAUDIT table. Tables should be set up to store record-level audits.

Access to the PSAUDIT table should be appropriately restricted to ensure that unauthorized changes to the audit logs are not made.

Security Administration Tools: Testing Techniques

Testing techniques for security administration include:

4.1.1 The following menu names are associated with security administration:

- MAINTAIN_SECURITY
- DEFINITION_SECURITY
- TREEMANAGER
- UTILITIES

The migration of objects among database instances (DEV to TST to PROD) requires access to the Application Designer. The relevant menu names (components) for migration are:

- APPLICATION_ DESIGNER
- DATA_MOVER

Determine whether the security administration functions have been assigned appropriately and administrator tasks have been segregated. Review access security matrices and access assignment documentation to gain an understanding of the security design. Corroborate this understanding by generating lists of users with access to the above menu names and reviewing their level of access by performing the test described in 1.1.1 (under Development and Integration Tools: Testing Techniques).

If full segregation is not possible due to resource issues, consider one of the following scenarios:

- The ability to create/maintain roles or permission lists and assign them to user profiles is included in the user profile of Security Administrator 1. The ability to migrate roles, permission lists and user profiles to the production instance is contained in the user profile of Security Administrator 2

- The ability to migrate roles and permission lists into production and assign Authorization Profiles to user master records are included in the user master record of Security Administrator 1, and the ability to create/maintain Activity Groups or Authorization Profiles is contained in the user master record of Security Administrator 2. This scenario is acceptable but may cause some control concerns, as this may be more difficult to implement appropriately.

If segregation of duties options are practicable, assess the hard copies of reports generated detailing changes to security tables (e.g., PSROLEUSER, PSROLECLASS, PSAUTHITEM, PSOPRCLS, PSOPRDFN) and user profiles (via the audit tab) for evidence of review and action by management.

Note: The review of changes to security tables assumes that logging of activity on specific tables has been set up.

4.2.1 Review the system design documentation relating to access security (design of roles and permission lists) and any established policies, procedures, standards and guidance related to the maintenance of roles/permission lists and the list of roles/permission lists and their assignment to user IDs defined in the system. Ascertain from management whether this documentation has been maintained accurately since implementation.

Perform two tests to corroborate the understanding gained through review of the documentation to ensure the accuracy of the documentation and the effectiveness of compliance with the established policies:

- Generate a list of user IDs and the roles, permission lists and subsequent menu items assigned to them by writing the following query in PeopleSoft Query Manager:

```
SELECT A.OPRID, A.OPRDEFNDESC, A.ACCTLOCK,
B.ROLENAME, C.CLASSID, D.MENUNAME, D.BARNAME,
D.BARITEMNAME, D.PNLITEMNAME, D.DISPLAYONLY,
D.AUTHORIZEDACTIONS

FROM PSOPRDEFN A, PSROLEUSER B, PSROLECLASS C,
PSAUTHITEM D
WHERE A.OPRID = B.ROLEUSER AND B.ROLENAME =
C.ROLENAME AND C.CLASSID = D.CLASSID
```

Order by A.OPRID, B.ROLENAME, C.CLASSID, D.MENUNAME to ensure that the user IDs (OPRID), roles (ROLENAME), permission lists (CLASSID) and components (MENUNAME) are listed in alphabetical order.

Perform further investigation on an individual user profile basis manually or externally in Excel, Access or ACL.

Alternatively, to identify users and roles only, use the following query:

```
SELECT A.ROLEUSER, A.ROLENAME, A.DYNAMIC_SW
FROM PSROLEUSER A
```

Take a representative sample of user profiles from the system and confirm them against the original documentation. Any discrepancies should be resolved with management.

- Test changes to roles, permission lists and user profiles since the implementation of the system. Changes to tables in PeopleSoft are reflected by the addition of a new row if they are specifically set to be audited. This applies only to effective-dated data; this does not apply to security changes unless the security tables are specifically audited.

Note: A query has to be written to download the security table to be reviewed (e.g., PSAUTHITEM). This involves taking a sample of changes from the system and tracing them back to current documentation. Management should also be able to provide source documentation for the authorization of these changes. The effectiveness of this test is dependent on management implementing the system audits on the relevant tables. See also Security Administration Tools: Risks, 4.9 Table Logging and Audit Trails.

4.3.1 Review the PeopleSoft Administration password to ensure that it has been changed from the default. Alternatively, attempt to sign on to the system using the PeopleSoft Administration password, and observe the success or failure of this attempt.

Generate lists of users with access to the above menu names by writing the query detailed in 1.1.1 (under Development and Integration Tools: Testing Techniques) in PeopleSoft Query Manager. Review the output for appropriateness of the access provided, focusing on user IDs with combinations of the menu names detailed.

4.4.1 Determine the policies and procedures in place regarding the use of default user IDs and changing the default passwords. Attempt to gain access to the PeopleSoft system using the default user IDs and passwords.

4.5.1 Generate lists of users and their access by writing the query detailed in 1.1.1 (under Development and Integration Tools: Testing Techniques) in PeopleSoft Query Manager. Review the output for appropriateness of the access provided, focusing on user IDs containing the powerful roles and permission lists. Check the user list identified by this test to ascertain whether individuals who have access to the aforementioned functionality require this access based on their job responsibilities and established policies, procedures, standards and guidance.

4.6.1 Gain an understanding of the authentication techniques and controls by reviewing documented security policies governing password controls and required parameter settings. Corroborate this understanding by reviewing the password parameter settings configured on the system (Home→PeopleTools→Security→Password Configuration→Password Controls):

- Check the ENABLE SIGNON PEOPLECODE box to see if it is checked.
- Review the parameter settings for compliance with security policies and standards and against accepted best practice.

The following SQL can be used to report on password controls that have been configured:

```
SELECT A.PSWD_CNTRL_ON, A.PSWDEXPIRESDAYS,
A.PSWDWARNDAYS, A.MINPSWDLENGTH, A.PSWDREQSPECIAL,
A.PSWDREQDIGITS, A.ALLOWOPRID, A.LOGINATTEMPTS,
A.LOCKOUTDURATION, A.PURGE_DAYS,
A.PASSWORD_HISTORY FROM PSSECOPTIONS A
```

It is also worth noting that many organizations integrate PeopleSoft with LDAP directories to store user IDs and passwords; therefore, these directories need to be audited to determine the level and adequacy of password controls.

Select a sample of permission lists (Home→PeopleTools→Security→Permissions & Roles→Permission Lists), and review the time-out values under the General Attributes page for compliance with security policies. Alternatively, write the following query in Query Manager to obtain a list of sign-on times by user ID:

```
SELECT B.OPRID, A.DAYOFWEEK, A.STARTTIME, A.ENDTIME
FROM PSAUTHSIGNON A, PSOPRDEFN B
WHERE B.OPRCLASS = A.CLASSID
```

Order by A.OPRID to obtain an output with the user IDs (OPRID) in alphabetical order. Note that the DAYOFWEEK code range is 0-6 corresponding to Sunday to Saturday and the start time of 0 = 00:00 hours and end time of 1439 = 23:59 hours.

4.7.1 Review security documentation to gain an understanding of the policy regarding the use of Correction Mode. Generate lists of users with access to the menu names in 4.1.1 by writing the query detailed in 4.1, Security Profiles, in PeopleSoft Query Manager. Review the output for appropriateness of the access provided, focusing on user IDs with authorized actions values of: 8, 9, 10, 11, 12, 13, 14, 15, 136, 137, 138, 139, 140, 141, 142 and 143. A detailed list of authorized actions and their values is provided at the end of this chapter.

Alternatively, the following query could be used:

```
SELECT A.OPRID, A.OPRDEFNDESC, A.ACCTLOCK,
B.ROLENAME, C.CLASSID, D.MENUNAME, D.BARNAME,
D.BARITEMNAME, D.PNLITEMNAME, D.DISPLAYONLY,
D.AUTHORIZEDACTIONS FROM PSOPRDEFN A, PSROLEUSER B,
PSROLECLASS C, PSAUTHITEM D
WHERE A.OPRID = B.ROLEUSER AND B.ROLENAME =
C.ROLENAME AND C.CLASSID = D.CLASSID
AND D.AUTHORIZEDACTIONS BETWEEN 7 AND 16
OR D.AUTHORIZEDACTIONS > 135
```

Determine whether these users should have correction mode access as part of their roles and responsibilities.

4.8.1 To understand the intended query security design, review security documentation using the following steps:

- Generate a list of users with access to the Query Manager menu, utilizing the query detailed in 1.1.1 (under Development and Integration Tools: Testing Techniques).
- Generate a list of query profiles using the following query:

```
SELECT A.OPRID, A.OPRDEFNDESC, A.ACCTLOCK,
B.ROLENAME, C.CLASSID, E.CLASSID, E.VERSION,
E.QRY_RUN_ONLY, E.QRY_CREATE_PUBLIC,
E.QRY_CREATE_WFLOW, E.QRY_MAX_FETCH,
E.QRY_MAX_RUN, E.QRY_ADV_DISTINCT,
E.QRY_ADV_ANY_JOIN, E.QRY_ADV_SUBQUERY,
E.QRY_ADV_UNION, E.QRY_ADV_EXPR, E.QRY_MAX_JOINS,
E.QRY_MAX_IN_TREE, E.QRY_OUT_LISTBOX,
E.QRY_OUT_NVISION, E.QRY_OUT_CRYSTAL,
E.QRY_ADM_AUTOPUBLIC, E.QRY_ADM_AUTOPRIV,
E.QRY_ADM_LIMUNAPPRV, E.QRY_ADM_UNAPP_ROWS FROM
PSOPRDEFN A, PSROLEUSER B, PSROLECLASS C,
PS_SCRTY_QUERY E WHERE A.OPRID = B.ROLEUSER
AND B.ROLENAME = C.ROLENAME AND C.CLASSID =
E.CLASSID
```

- Generate a list of user access to query trees and the access groups assigned to them by writing the following query in Query Manager. This determines the tables that a user may access when maintaining his/her queries.

```
SELECT A.OPRID, A.OPRDEFNDESC, A.ACCTLOCK,
B.ROLENAME, C.CLASSID, D.CLASSID, D.TREE_NAME,
D.ACCESS_GROUP, D.ACCESSIBLE FROM PSOPRDEFN A,
PSROLEUSER B, PSROLECLASS C, PS_SCRTY_ACC_GRP D
WHERE A.OPRID = B.ROLEUSER AND B.ROLENAME =
C.ROLENAME AND C.CLASSID = D.CLASSID
```

4.9.1 Review security procedures created by management that identify what critical records and fields are being logged and how often these logs are reviewed by management. For the critical records and record fields identified, check that the following audit settings have been configured appropriately in Application Designer.

- Record-level auditing—Choose the Objects workspace and open the record. Check the Use Properties field of the record and review the audit options selected:
  - Audit Record Add—Inserts an audit table row whenever a new row is added to the table
  - Audit Record Change—Inserts one or two audit table rows whenever a row is changed on the table
  - Audit Record Selective—Inserts one or two audit table rows whenever a field that is also included on the record definition for the audit table is changed
  - Audit Record Delete—Inserts an audit table row whenever a row is deleted from the table
- Record field-level auditing—For the record fields chosen, check the Use Properties field of the different field type (character, number, date/time) options and review the audit options selected:
  - Field Add—Audits this field whenever a new row of data is added
  - Field Change—Audits this field whenever the contents are changed
  - Field Delete—Audits this field whenever a row of data is deleted

Default User IDs

PeopleSoft comes delivered with default user IDs, providing superuser-type access to specific applications within the system. **Figure 10.4** lists some of the more powerful user IDs.

Figure 10.4—HRMS Default User IDs

BELHR	GER	PSESP	UKHR
CAN	GRHR	PSFRA	UKNI
CFR	JCADMIN1	PSGER	USA
CNHR	NLDHR	PSINE	USHR
ESP	PS	PSJPN	WEBGUEST
FRA	PSCFR	PSPOR	WEBMODEL
FRHR	PSDUT	TIME	

PeopleSoft is delivered with a number of default permission lists providing superuser-type access to various applications in the system. These permission lists are shown in **figure 10.5**.

Figure 10.5—HRMS Default Permission Lists					
HHR_TRN	HHR_VC04	HPI_KCI001	HTL	PSAPPS	PSQRY
HHR_VC01	HHR_VC05	HPY	KRONOS	PSBASS	
HHR_VC02	HPA	HPYCFR	MOBILE	PSDEV	
HHR_VC03	HPI	HST	PS	PSEM	

Authorized Actions

Figure 10.6 is a listing of standard action types that can be assigned and corresponding descriptions for each. This listing can be obtained by querying the PSPGEACCESSDESC table.

Figure 10.6—Action Types

Auth Action	Description
1	Add
2	Update/Display
3	Add Update/Display
4	Update/Display All
5	Add Update/Display All
6	Update/Display Update/Display All
7	Add Update/Display Update/Display All
8	Correction
9	Add Correction
10	Update/Display Correction
11	Add Update/Display Correction
12	Update/Display All Correction
13	Add Update/Display All Correction
14	Update/Display Update/Display All Correction
15	Add Update/Display Update/Display All Correction
128	Data Entry
129	Add Data Entry
130	Update/Display Data Entry
131	Add Update/Display Data Entry
132	Update/Display All Data Entry
133	Add Update/Display All Data Entry
134	Update/Display Update/Display All Data Entry
135	Add Update/Display Update/Display All Data Entry
136	Correction Data Entry
137	Add Correction Data Entry
138	Update/Display Correction Data Entry
139	Add Update/Display Correction Data Entry

Figure 10.6—Action Types *cont.*	
Auth Action	**Description**
140	Update/Display All Correction Data Entry
141	Add Update/Display All Correction Data Entry
142	Update/Display Update/Display All Correction Data Entry
143	Add Update/Display Update/Display All Correction Data Entry

Figure 10.7 is a listing of action types and corresponding descriptions that are associated with the Application Designer definition, tools and miscellaneous permissions that can be assigned. Note: The same numerical value may translate into different access when associated with different Application Designer permissions.

Figure 10.7—Application Designer Action Types	
Auth Action	**Description**
0	No Access
1	Read-Only (Note that read-only access for Application Designer is determined by the Authorized Action field, whereas read-only access to pages is determined by the Display Only field.)
2	Update Translate Values Only (applies to the Field Definition permission)
2	Data Admin Only (applies to the Record Definition permission)
2	Restricted Access Only (applies to the Change Control Tools permission)
2	Build Scripts Only (applies to the Build/Data Admin Tools permission)
3	Developer Access Only (applies to the Change Control Tools permission)
3	Build Online (applies to the Build/Data Admin Tools permission)
4	Supervisor Access Only (applies to the Change Control Tools permission)
4	Full Data Admin (applies to the Build/Data Admin Tools permission)

Summary

This chapter provided an approach to identify the risks, key controls and various testing techniques that are part of the PeopleSoft Application Security Infrastructure. The chapter provided a sample tool set that can be used in auditing the PeopleSoft Application Security Infrastructure. It includes:

- Specific risks that are part of the PeopleSoft Application Security Infrastructure
- Automated control activities
- Sample assurance techniques

11. New Directions for PeopleSoft and ERP Audit

This chapter looks ahead at two major new directions that are emerging, namely the need for:

- Continuous assurance techniques in the traditional ERP environment
- An extension to the traditional ERP control framework to encompass the emerging e-enabled ERP environment

Available tools for continuous assurance in a PeopleSoft environment are overviewed in this chapter, and a sample control framework for the e-ERP environment is provided.

Tools for Continuous Assurance in a PeopleSoft Environment

Effective audit in the ERP environment requires new automated diagnostic tools for:

- Application security assurance
- Data integrity assurance

Application Security Assurance

ERPs have powerful and complex security arrangements. Testing security is not just a matter of reviewing the security matrix of users to functions. Activity groups or composite security profiles may be used, and unravelling these to find out who has access to what often requires automated diagnostic tools to complete the task effectively. Security exposures also can arise from the combination of different security profiles assigned to a user. For example, a page or permission list in one profile combined with the permission list from another may inadvertently provide a user with excessive access, contrary to management's intentions. To effectively identify and assess this type of exposure, automated security diagnostic tools are required.

Automated security diagnostic tools are needed to:

- Provide a historic view, e.g., identifying when security parameters were changed
- Unravel complex security profiles
- Provide dynamic documentation of user access
- Produce plain language output
- Promote independence (i.e., permissions are developed independently to access the required data)

- Be noninvasive (i.e., there is minimal disruption to the operation of the production system, usually through extracting and downloading the required information offline for subsequent evaluation)

The Application Security Assurance Toolkit is evolving. Third-party products are available that run on an independent server and extract security information from PeopleSoft for offline analysis.

Data Integrity Assurance

Despite the deployment of business process and application security controls, transactions inconsistent with management's intentions may continue to be processed.

Duplicate payments can and do occur in an ERP environment. Therefore, data assurance techniques are needed to control and test specific, identified risks associated with the data in an ERP environment. Knowledge of PeopleSoft tables, data structures, reports, programming techniques and data extraction techniques is needed so that data may be extracted in the most cost-effective manner for analysis. Tools in this area are evolving. Audit Command Language (ACL®), for instance, has established a mechanism for extracting information from ERP systems for offline analysis. Some of the audit and consulting firms have tools and techniques for extracting information from the logistics modules required, for example, to obtain information on purchases and duplicate payments. Data quality plays a key role in the new PIA. An overall data management strategy is needed to manage data as a corporate asset, and key data quality standards such as those below should be considered from the beginning:

- Establish a formal group to own and define data and quality standards.
- Allow the group to define data standards and requirements for front-office and back-office data quality.
- Develop and deploy enterprisewide data quality standards and approaches.
- Define data quality measurement.
- Develop enterprise data models/definitions.
- Ensure that structures are published and disseminated.
- Define transaction processing/data needs.
- Define data stores/repositories.
- Define retention, statutory and recovery requirements.

There is an increased need to implement capabilities for measuring and monitoring data quality on an ongoing basis to promote sustainability of data quality in the new PeopleSoft application environment. Key considerations should revolve around continuous data monitoring and data ownership and may include:

- Leveraging existing activities and deliverables developed to enhance data quality
- Establishing a center of expertise with enterprisewide approaches and best-of-breed tools
- Establishing a data integrity group to be responsible for data quality on an ongoing basis

- Ensuring that this group has authority to effect change
- Reassessing data quality through application of monitoring activities
- Applying corrective actions as required

E-enabled ERP Audit

Just as audit professionals begin to reach and pursue continuous assurance in an ERP environment, the ERP environment is changing with the development of the networked economy and e-enabled ERPs. In the past, the focus from a business perspective has been on achieving efficiencies within the organization through implementation of enterprise applications. Now the focus has shifted to outside the organization and to e-enabled ERP applications. The e-economy can be grouped into five key elements:

- Sell-side—E-customer solutions and services focus on the sales, marketing and service processes and leverage customer relationship management (CRM), web-based and call center technologies to achieve an effective total customer experience. These technologies improve multichannel transactions and relationships with customers, expand marketing and sales reach, and empower customers to serve themselves.
- Buy-side—E-supply chain solutions and services focus on supply chain processes, including procurement, and leverage supply chain optimization, e-procurement and other Internet technologies to enhance transactions and relationships with suppliers. They automate and optimize processes across the enterprise and drive efficiencies across the entire value chain.
- Inside—E-transformation solutions and services focus within the firewalls of an enterprise on the management, financial and HR processes. They leverage core ERP, Internet and other technologies to enhance and build intellectual capital, process transactions, develop employees, and improve decision making and productivity.
- Exchanges—These marketplace solutions and services focus on digital trading exchanges. They leverage Internet-based technologies to create virtual business communities that facilitate commerce and collaboration, reduce costs, and link fragmented networks of buyers and sellers.
- Outside—These solutions and services extend to sell-side, inside and buy-side solutions by enabling businesses to focus on core strengths and transfer technology and/or business processes to an external service provider. This offering extends across areas such as outsourcing and business acceleration services.

Figure 11.1 shows an example of what the e-enabled ERP enterprise may look like. **Figure 11.2** shows an example network overview for an ERP and the Internet. PeopleSoft version 8 has a number of enhancements that facilitate Internet connectivity. The introduction of the web browser-based user interface means that no data are stored on the workstation, unlike previous versions where object definitions were cached. This enables low-cost rollout to multiple locations, since all that is required is a web browser on each workstation/client.

Figure 11.1—E-enabled ERP Systems

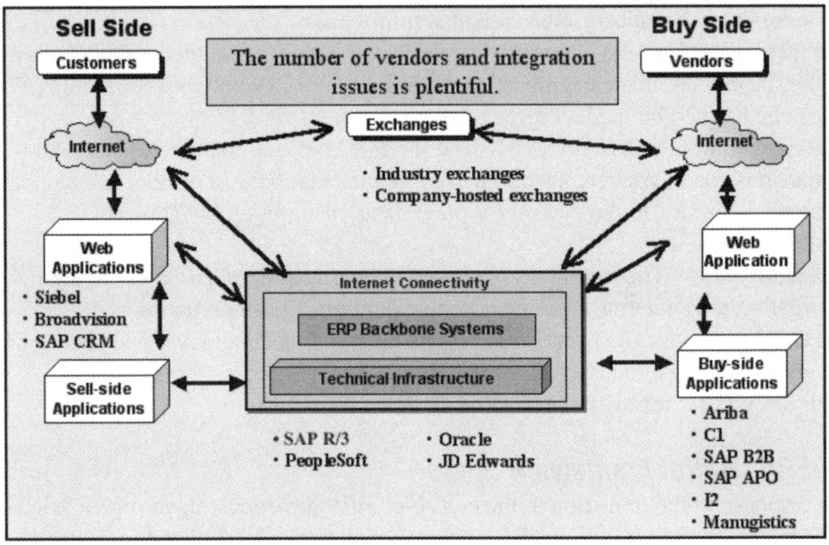

Figure 11.2—Example Network Overview of ERP and the Internet

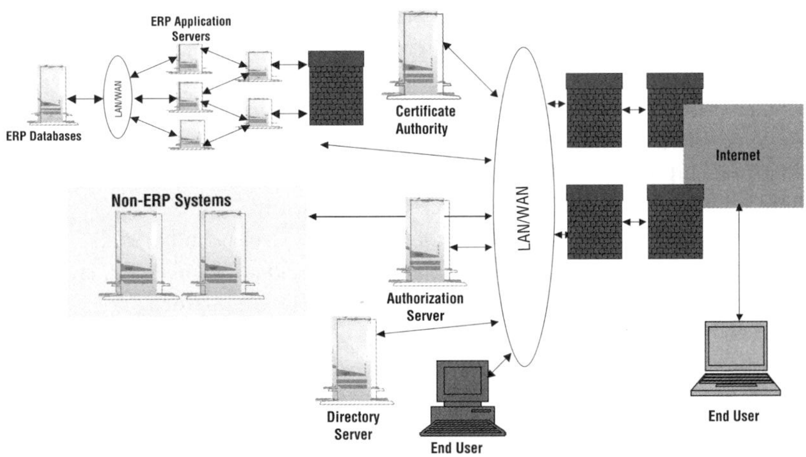

The audit professional has been moved back down the growth continuum to the earlier stages of growth, as organizations face increased risk associated with e-business and must develop control solutions to keep those risks in check. New risks or new flavors of risk associated with e-business include:

- Legal risk—Part of the Internet service may break local or foreign laws. This includes the supply of incorrect information to the customer or unauthorized use of credit card details or other personal information.
- Image risk—Hackers can vandalize web sites, making unauthorized changes to the site content that can embarrass the organization. The organization's image can be harmed by media coverage of a hacking attempt.
- Repudiation of transaction risk—The Internet does not guarantee successful transmission of packets; therefore, transactions that are lost or rejected may not be retransmitted to the system for processing, resulting in incomplete transactions.
- Security risk—The Internet can be used to gain unauthorized access to the organization's internal systems or to the systems of business partners.
- Denial of service (disruption risk)—Disruptions to technology could shut down online business processes. This includes system shutdowns due to natural disasters, fire, terrorism, etc.

E-ERP Control Framework

In response to the transition to the e-enabled ERP environment, an organization needs to extend its traditional ERP control framework. As depicted in **figure 11.3**, the traditional control framework should be extended to include the following areas to address the risks arising from e-commerce:

- Identity management—Are we dealing with whom we think we are? Appropriate management of participant identities enables building a trusted exchange community. Single sign-on facilities can facilitate identity management and greatly reduce security administration costs. However, it may also increase the risk, as a user may inadvertently be assigned access to several systems.
- Content quality—Is the information that is being used internally and provided to customers and vendors accurate, timely, pertinent and current? When making enterprise information available to external parties, the importance of providing timely and correct information increases dramatically.
- Privacy/confidentiality—Is information restricted to only authorized organizations and individuals? Are customers' personal details (e.g., credit card numbers, spending habits, addresses) appropriately safeguarded?
- Collaborative commerce—Do the extended electronic business processes, incorporating customers and suppliers, have the appropriate integrity and security controls built in (e.g., how a credit limit will be checked when purchasing goods via the web)?
- Integration integrity—Are all elements of transactions fully and completely processed throughout the extended value chain (e.g., appropriate control totals, data editing criteria and security between program interfaces)?

Figure 11.3—Risk and Controls Environment

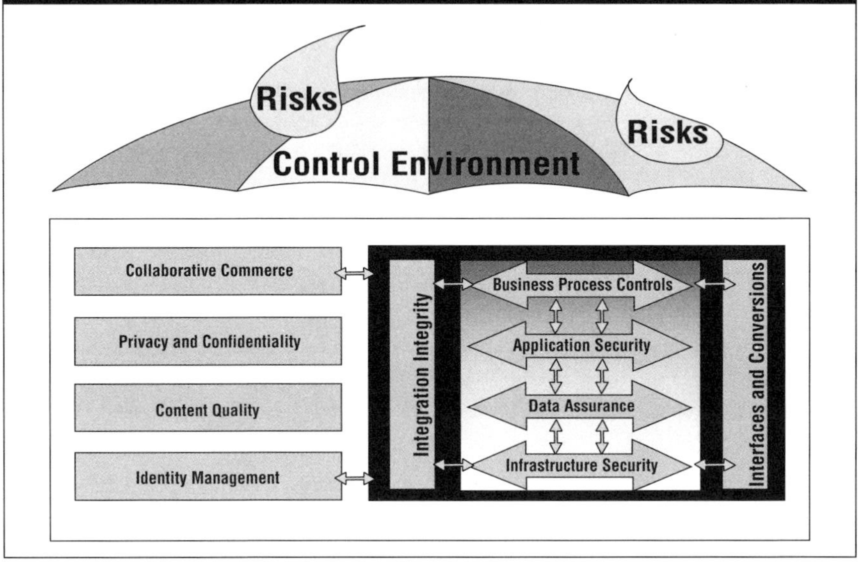

The Changing Compliance Landscape

Increased pressures from government regulations, financial markets and shareholders, combined with corporate collapses and acts of management fraud in recent years have resulted in a new focus on corporate governance and risk management. The result has been a landslide of corporate regulations around the world with significant implications for financial reporting:

- US Sarbanes-Oxley Act of 2002—One of the most far-reaching pieces of legislation to impact financial reporting, Sarbanes-Oxley compliance efforts have focused on sections 404 and 302 of the Act. Section 404 requires the management of all companies registered with the SEC to provide an annual report on their assessment of internal controls over financial reporting, and attestation of the existence of these controls by an independent auditor. Section 302 requires quarterly reporting on any control deficiencies that have the potential to impact the financial statements. Section 409 of the Act requires "real-time issuer disclosures" on a "rapid and current basis" that may include trend and qualitative information along with graphic presentations. In real terms, this is an additional continuous reporting requirement.
- SEC Financial Statement Logging Date Requirement—At the same time the Sarbanes-Oxley Act was introduced, the US Securities and Exchange Commission (SEC) introduced a requirement that will progressively shorten the "grace" period between the end of the financial year and the due date for the logging of financial statements with the SEC. This accelerated reporting

schedule will require changes to, and automation of, significant aspects of the financial reporting process. ERPs, particularly PeopleSoft, have an important role in this regard.
- Basel Capital Accord (Basel II)—Basel II requires banks to maintain minimum levels of capital with the objective of better aligning regulatory capital measures with the inherent risk profile of a bank considering credit, market, operational and other risks. If the bank can demonstrate a risk management and control regime that reduces its risk profile, the Accord allows for a reduction in the level of capital held.
- International Financial Reporting Standards (IFRS)—Although not a recent regulation, the focus has recently shifted toward the global implementation of IFRS. IFRS promote the adoption of a single set of global accounting standards that require high-quality, transparent and comparable information in the company's financial statements. This means that companies may be required to make changes to the way account balances are presented in the financial statements (e.g., elimination of internally generated goodwill) and provide additional disclosures in the notes to their annual report, where appropriate.
- European Union Directives on Financial Reporting—The Directives are designed to promote transparent, high-quality financial reporting across the EU nations. This is similar to the initiatives of the IFRS regulation.

To support corporate governance reforms, such as Sarbanes-Oxley, many organizations around the world have adopted an internal controls framework, such as COSO, COCO or Turnbull. The COSO framework (discussed in chapter 3) is commonly used by organizations to define an internal control framework and methodology and can be adapted to manage the financial reporting risks associated with an ERP environment. The framework covers five interrelated components:
1. Control environment—Tone at the top
2. Risk—Assessment, identification and analysis
3. Control activities—Process-level controls in support of significant accounts in the financial statements, e.g., review of control system, segregation of duties
4. Information and communication—Identification, capture and reporting of financial and operating information that is useful to control the organization's activities
5. Monitoring—Assessment of the robustness and relevance of the internal control activities

An internal control system is judged to be effective if the five components are present and functioning effectively for operations, financial reporting and compliance.

As organizations have scrambled their way toward compliance with a plethora of regulations, the role of IT in meeting the requirements of these regulations has been highlighted. **Figure 11.4** illustrates how IT controls are embedded within each element of an organization's business. The role of the ERP is particularly

Figure 11.4—Common Elements of Organizations

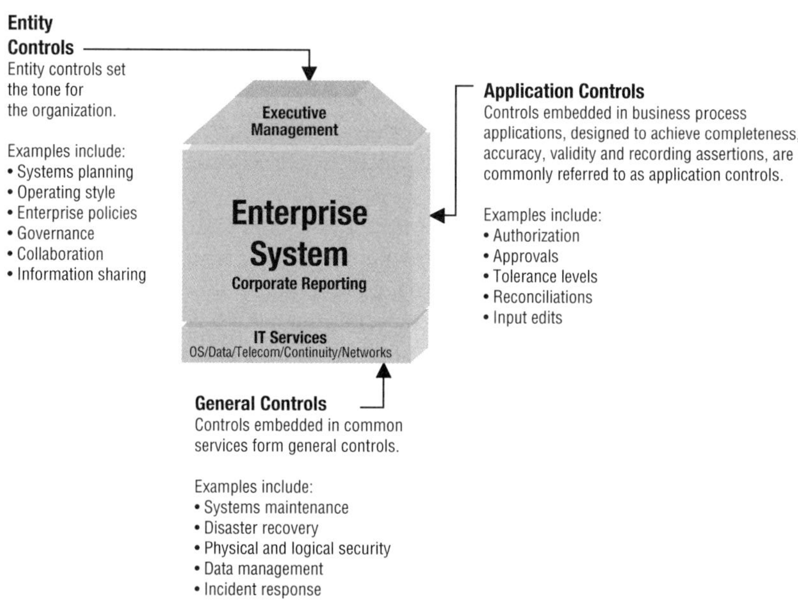

Source: IT Governance Institute, *IT Control Objectives for Sarbanes-Oxley*, 2004

important at the IT application control level, as data from numerous business processes are integrated, becoming a direct input into the financial statements. As such, the ERP is at the heart of the control requirements of the corporate governance and risk management regulations that affect the financial reporting process.

When designing internal controls using the COSO framework, companies should consider enabling certain functionalities in their ERP system or implementing new technology to achieve the following objectives:
• Effectiveness and efficiency of operations[9]
• Reliability of financial reporting
• Compliance with the applicable laws and regulations

The key areas that should be considered by organizations to ensure compliance with financial reporting regulations include:
• Data capture capability—The ability of the ERP system to capture sufficient information to meet the requirements of corporate governance regulations, such as IFRS. A risk management system designed to identify, assess, monitor and manage risk and inform investors of material changes to the company's risk profile[10] should be implemented.

[9] COSO, *Internal Control–Integrated Framework*, 2004
[10] Group of 100, "Guide to Compliance with ASX Principle 7: 'Recognise and Manage Risk'," 2003

- Data integrity—Ensures authenticity of data across an ERP
- Reporting functionality—The ability of the ERP system to extract meaningful information for internal and external reporting purposes
- Accountability—The ability of the ERP system to provide adequate and sufficient evidence of automated controls, such as digital sign-off, automated reconciliations and logs of changes to key data. This also assists with providing greater visibility over the segregation of duties in the underlying business processes that support the significant accounts in the financial statements.

The potential for control automation is the largest benefit of using ERP systems to support corporate governance and financial reporting control. When organizations design any form of internal control, they must first consider the potential for automating the required control through the ERP. Control automation can reduce the impact on worker productivity by eliminating additional effort associated with manual controls. The effectiveness of the control can be enhanced by automatically enforcing security restrictions and ensuring that a complete record of the controls history is maintained for auditing requirements.

In addition to the benefits associated with automated controls, ERP vendors, such as PeopleSoft, have begun to introduce specific functionality and tools to address the increasingly complex corporate governance requirements.

Using PeopleSoft Tools to Support Compliance

In response to the changing global compliance landscape, organizations are looking to their application systems to drive internal controls and manage compliance to legislation such as the Sarbanes Oxley Act, the IFRS and Basel II. Organizations can leverage PeopleSoft to support compliance in the following ways:

- Identity management—Effectively authenticating users to a PeopleSoft application ensures that accountability within the application is maintained. PeopleSoft provides a number of authentication options that can be tailored to an organization's overall identify management solution, including:
  - LDAP directory services—Enabling PeopleSoft's LDAP directory services integration allows an organization to authenticate PeopleSoft users against their corporate LDAP-compliant directory server (e.g., Microsoft's Active Directory, Novell NDS). This approach streamlines an organization's security policy implementation by centralizing management of password settings and administration.
  - PeopleCode—The PeopleSoft proprietary programming language can be used to customize any component of a PeopleSoft application. Where the above (supplied) identity solutions do not meet an organization's requirements, PeopleCode can be used to design a customized solution, such as biometrics integration.

- PeopleSoft Financial Management Blueprint and Sarbanes-Oxley compliance—In 2003 PeopleSoft released an application architecture designed to help customers comply with their governance requirements by providing stronger internal controls, auditable processes, reporting capabilities, and increased transparency and visibility of data. PeopleSoft led the way to governance in developing the PeopleSoft Financial Management Blueprint, shown in **figure 11.5**. The architecture responded to disparate systems and complex business processes with a consolidated transaction and reporting application.

Figure 11.5—PeopleSoft Financial Management Blueprint

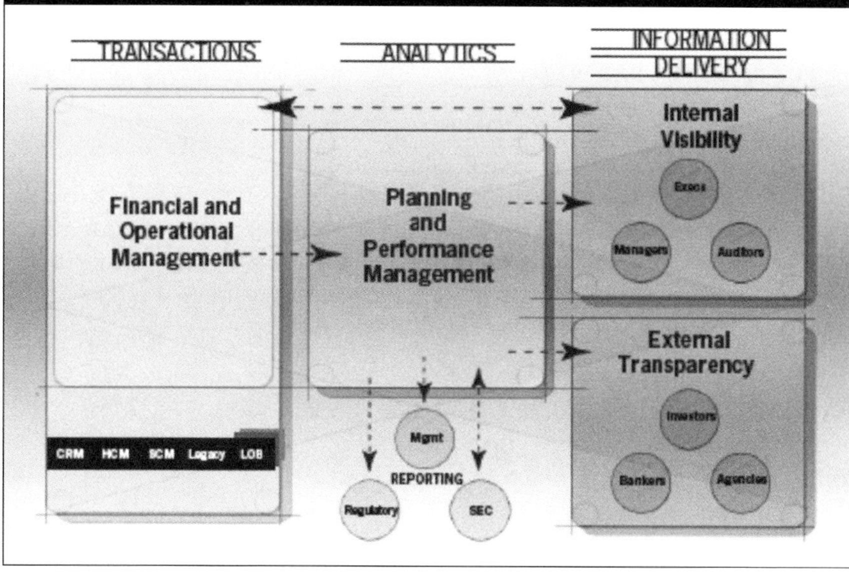

- PeopleSoft Internal Controls Enforcer—PeopleSoft's Internal Controls Enforcer (ICE) was designed to assist organizations in complying with section 404 of the Sarbanes-Oxley Act. Released as an optional additional component to PeopleSoft Financial Management System, ICE provides the following key features:
  - Diagnostic and survey tools—Provide continuous monitoring of the PeopleSoft environment and automated alerts of system changes
  - Compliance framework for project management—Provides management with the tools to track compliance projects and manage accountability of compliance projects
  - Real-time compliance monitoring—Provided through live dashboards that provide real-time visibility of internal controls
  - A COSO-based data model—Allows organizations to map their "financial statement elements to entities, processes and sub-processes";[11] document business process; define risks, testing plans and narratives
  - Risk library import

[11] PeopleSoft, Internal Controls Enforcer Datasheet, 2005

- Third-party tools—Can be integrated with a PeopleSoft environment and used for continuous monitoring of the adequacy of security access. Tools from Virsa (*www.virsa.com*) and Approva (*www.approva.net*) provide real-time preventive controls so that as access is granted to new or existing users, automated checks against their segregation of duty tables are executed, which may prevent inappropriate access from being granted (depending on configuration of tools). This may be tailored in both vendor cases to allow segregation of duties conflicts upon adoption of certain predefined and approved mitigating controls. Both come with workflow approval solutions, a full suite of reporting capabilities and business process control automation techniques that are extensive, can be easily tailored to a business's specific needs, and offer closed-loop remediation techniques to:
  - Identify potential control issues
  - Route the details to the appropriate individuals
  - Capture their corrective action plans
  - Monitor progress over time in addressing the issue

Organizations need to be aware that software tools and architecture alone are not sufficient to achieve compliance. Tools and architecture can be used to support and enable compliance; however, achieving compliance requires a balanced combination of software, architecture and business discipline.

Product and Technology Changes

Industry Consolidation

Over the past two years, Oracle has undertaken an aggressive corporate acquisition strategy, acquiring leading enterprise software application vendors PeopleSoft and Siebel. JD Edwards was acquired through its earlier acquisition by PeopleSoft. Oracle's application consolidation strategy has been further supplemented by an extended purchasing period for a variety of best-of-breed middleware and infrastructure software vendors.

Project Fusion

Having acquired a variety of enterprise software application vendors and their application suites, Oracle embarked on the ambitious software engineering exercise of rearchitecting each of the disparate application suites into a consolidated application suite. The name given by Oracle to this next generation enterprise application suite is Fusion Applications. Fusion Applications succeeds the Oracle E-Business Suite, Siebel's Customer Relationships Management Suite, PeopleSoft Enterprise Applications, and JD Edwards' World and EnterpriseOne Application Suites. They will variously employ Oracle's own Fusion Middleware technologies; in a departure from Oracle's usual approach, they also claim to be able to support technology platforms from traditional competitors such as Microsoft and IBM.[12] The tasks related to rearchitecting its portfolio of enterprise application suites supported by the targeted adoption of Fusion Middleware technologies are collectively referred to by Oracle as Project Fusion.

Pre-Fusion Application Releases

Over the next three to five years, Oracle intends to transition each of its disparate application suites, including the current Oracle 11i E-Business Suite, to Fusion Applications, as shown in **figure 11.6**. In doing so, it has also committed to meeting the published application road maps of each of the subsumed application vendors. It is not known whether awareness of the upcoming Fusion Applications release will cause organizations to balk at upgrading to the pre-Fusion application releases that Oracle has committed to releasing in 2006. Specific versions stated for calendar year 2006 availability are:

- Oracle E-Business Suite 12
- JD Edwards EnterpriseOne 8.12
- PeopleSoft Enterprise 9.0 (PeopleSoft 8.9 was released in the latter half of 2005)

Figure 11.6—Oracle Upgrade Paths

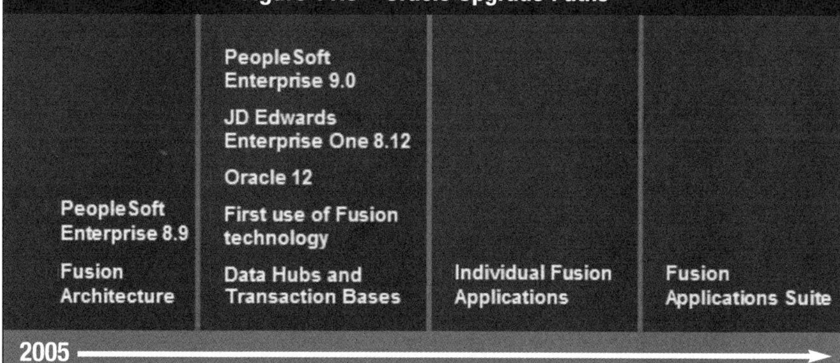

Source: Oracle Applications Strategy Publication, 2006

Supported Upgrade Paths to Fusion Applications

To encourage existing clients to upgrade existing installed base applications to current versions, Oracle has also committed to direct migrations paths to Fusion Applications from the following relatively current or pending application suite versions:

- PeopleSoft Enterprise 8.8, 8.9 and 9.0
- Oracle E-Business Suite 11i release 10, 12
- JD Edwards 8.11, 8.12
- JD Edwards World A7.3 and A8.1 and 2006 World Release

[12] Oracle, "Oracle Applications: Committed to Your Success," 2006

Oracle has also announced a plan to continue to enhance and support existing PeopleSoft and JD Edwards product lines until 2013.[13] Consequently, customers are able to assess the appropriateness of migrating or upgrading their existing application suites to Fusion Applications.

Monitoring the Adoption of Fusion Middleware in Preparation of Fusion Applications

This publication addresses security, audit and control features for the Oracle E-Business Suite series of ERP systems. As the migration to Fusion Applications accelerates, the implications for auditors will become clearer. It is likely that ERP audit frameworks and audit techniques will have to be reconsidered. Particular emphasis will need to be given to the platformwide use of business process management technology and consolidated identity management infrastructure being implemented within the Fusion Application's architecture.

One of the most important aspects of the Fusion Application ERP products is the enablement of business process integration and enterprise identity management. As Oracle's portfolio of application suites has evolved, enhancements have enabled increasing business process integration beyond enterprise boundaries. In contrast, the inherent design of Fusion applications combined with new Fusion functionalities, enables extended and collaborative business process integration with suppliers, business partners, customers and internal organizations. This integration is made possible through Oracle's Fusion middleware platform architecture and its associated functions. Oracle is recommending that several Fusion middleware architectural components be reviewed for pre-Fusion applications implementation.[14] Several implications for security and audit processes are presented by the adoption of the following tools:

- Business process orchestration (BPO)—Tools to define, automate and execute enterprise business processes to interact with multiple technology systems, workflows, manual operations and human interactions in a standards-based manner. BPO encapsulates business processes and increases automation of systems and process integration. Accordingly, auditors must be aware of risks of inappropriately designed or implemented processes. Auditors are also presented with a mechanism to assess and monitor process compliance and exceptions.
- Business activity monitoring (BAM)—Tools to collect data from multiple operational and analytical sources of information from across the enterprise and present them to decision makers in graphical format to assist real-time decision making. BAM provides auditors with a mechanism for capturing operational status of operational processes and risk profiles across the enterprise.
- Identity management (IM)—Tools to centrally define and administer identities, their authorization and access policies, and provisioning and deprovisioning across enterprise processes and systems. The implementation of identity management suites, such as the one provided by Oracle Fusion Middleware,

[13] Oracle, "Oracle Applications: Committed to Your Success," 2006

[14] Oracle, "Oracle Fusion Architecture and Oracle Fusion Applications: Technology," 2006

enables auditors to more readily attest to the compliance of security policies across a larger breadth of enterprise interactions and activities, particularly those that relate to system interactions and information access.

Conclusion

This guide discussed earlier how the advent of ERPs necessitated a change in the audit approach (i.e., toward a business process focus and a greater emphasis on application security, configurable controls and continuous assurance). In the same manner, the advent of collaborative commerce and e-enabled ERPs will necessitate a change in the organization's concept of its audit universe. The existing focus and paradigms may need further development to audit in the new e-enabled ERP environment. New tools and techniques may need to be adopted for e-business. Auditors have an excellent opportunity to get involved early in the second wave of ERP development and assist their organizations to maximize the very real and tangible business benefits that can be achieved with enterprise applications and collaborative commerce.

Appendix A—Frequently Asked Questions

1. Should the PeopleSoft administrator have access to functional modules in the PeopleSoft software?

   No. The PeopleSoft administrator's role should be restricted to administration of the system and maintaining user access as requested by the data owners.

2. Should the authorization to develop queries be given freely to all the users?

   No. Incorrectly structured queries can adversely affect system performance. Further, in the PeopleSoft environment, the query requirements of users may be predetermined. Therefore, queries should be created on the development client and fully tested on the integration client. Users should have access only to run, not develop, queries on the production system.

3. Should a separate user account be created for batch process? Does this account require administrator access?

   It is considered better practice to create a separate user account for running batch processes; however, this account should not have administrator access. Accounts for processing batches should have only the minimum level of access required to complete the batch process.

4. Is evaluating the PeopleSoft software performance the responsibility of IS auditors?

   In an ERP environment, the IS auditor should look beyond security and controls and indeed suggest options for system performance improvement. PeopleSoft does have quite a few system performance monitoring tools, and an auditor should point out the need for appropriate procedures for review of these measures by the system administrator.

   A few tips to ensure performance efficiency are:
   - Scheduling high-volume processes (e.g., generation of trial balance report, stock valuation and purchase orders clearing) during off-peak periods
   - Restricting the number of sessions a user can initiate[15]

[15] *www.theiia.org/itaudit/index.cfm?fuseaction=forum&fid=65*

5. What are some important controls that should be looked at when auditing PeopleSoft HR and Payroll?

   Three basic, but important, controls that should be looked at are:
   - Separation of duties—To audit persons who perform specific functions within PeopleSoft, either query PSOPERDEFN and PSAUTHITEM tables or review individual user profiles and permission lists through Security Administrator.
   - Access controls—Access authority is assigned as follows:
     - Add—Allows addition of new data
     - Update/Display—Allows the ability to review and/or change data already in the system
     - Update/Display All—Allows the ability to review and/or change historical (effective-dated) data
     - Correction—Allows all access authority

     Furthermore, the auditor should also review row-level security to ensure that the permission list access rights to business units are as identified in the security tree.
   - Management controls, including:
     - PeopleCode Edits—The auditor should review for appropriateness all fields that have PeopleCode edits attached.
     - Record Auditing—The auditor should discuss audited records with the PeopleSoft administrator.
     - Field Auditing—The auditor should ensure that the audit log is being reviewed and archived as necessary.
     - Workflows—With the assistance of the PeopleSoft administrator, the auditor should review the workflows for appropriateness and/or efficiency. In addition, the auditor should ensure that only authorized persons have access to create/modify workflows and those workflows are tested within a nonproduction environment.

   To perform a complete PeopleSoft audit/review, the audit should also include:
   - Change control management
   - Query security
   - Process group security
   - Object security

Appendix B—Recommended Reading

Anderson, Lynn; *Understanding PeopleSoft*, Sybex Inc., Cap Gemini and Ernst & Young US LLC, 2001

Bilbrey, Darrell; *PeopleSoft Administrator's Guide: The Essential Resource for Implementation and Administration*, Sybex Inc., 1999

Bryan, M.; "ERP Mayday," *MIS Australia*, November 1998

Davenport, T.; "Putting the Enterprise into the Enterprise System," *Harvard Business Review*, July-August 1998, p. 121-131

Deloitte Consulting, "ERP's Second Wave: Maximizing the Value of ERP-Enabled Processes—Including Deloitte Consulting's Perspective on Making ERP Spell ROI," USA, 1998

Deloitte Consulting, "Under Control: Sustaining Compliance with Sarbanes-Oxley in Year Two and Beyond," USA, 2005

Gartner Group, *www3.gartner.com/init*, June 2001

Gillespie, Richard; JoAnn Gillespie; *PeopleSoft Developer's Handbook*, McGraw Hill, USA, 1999

Greenberg, Paul; Michael Fauscette; Scott Fletcher, *et al; Special Edition Using PeopleSoft*, Que Corporation, 2000

ISACA, *Security, Audit and Control Features Oracle® Applications: A Technical Risk Management Reference Guide, 2nd Edition*, USA, 2006

ISACA, *Security, Audit and Control Features SAP® R/3®: A Technical Risk Management Reference Guide, 2nd Edition*, USA, 2005

Wagle, D.; *The Case for ERP Systems*, McKinsey & Company, 1998

Wheatley, M.; "ERP Training Stinks," *CIO Magazine*, July 200

Appendix C—HR Cycle Audit Program

<table>
<tr><th>Control Objective/Test</th><th>Documentation/
Matters Arising</th><th>COBIT
References</th></tr>
<tr><td colspan="3">Preliminary Audit Steps</td></tr>
<tr><td colspan="3">Gain an understanding of the PeopleSoft environment.</td></tr>
<tr><td>a. The same background information obtained for the PeopleSoft Application Security audit plan is required for, and relevant to, the business cycles. In particular, the following information is important:
• Determine the version and release of the PeopleSoft software implemented (by holding Ctrl-J on any PeopleSoft page).
• Determine the total number of named users (for comparison with logical access security testing results).
• Determine the number of PeopleSoft instances.
• Determine the operating systems and database management systems running within the environment.
• Identify the modules that are being used.
• Determine if there have been any locally developed reports or tables created by the organization.
• Obtain details of the risk assessment approach taken by the organization to identify and prioritize risks.
• Obtain copies of the organization's key security policies and standards.
• Obtain a copy of any service level agreements.
• Obtain a copy of the contingency/ backup plan.
• Review outstanding audit findings, if any, from previous years.</td><td></td><td>PO2
PO3
PO4
PO6
PO9
AI2
AI6
DS2
DS5
ME1
ME2</td></tr>
</table>

Control Objective/Test	Documentation/ Matters Arising	COBIT References
Preliminary Audit Steps *cont.*		
b. In addition: • Obtain details of the organizational model as it relates to HR activity, i.e., HR organization unit structure in the PeopleSoft software and HR organization chart (required when evaluating the results of access security control testing). • Interview the systems implementation team, if possible, and obtain process design documentation for HR. • Review the training program to ensure that it is adequate and addresses all functional areas.		AI1 DS5 DS6
Identify the significant risks and determine the key controls.		
c. Develop a high-level process flow diagram and overall understanding of the HR processing cycle, including the following subprocesses: • Master Data Maintenance • Commencements • Personal Development • Terminations		PO9 AI1 DS13
d. Assess the key risks, determine key controls or control weaknesses, and test controls (refer to the following sample testing program and chapter 4 for techniques for testing configurable controls and logical access security) in regard to the following factors: • The controls culture of the organization • The need to exercise judgment to determine the key controls in the process and whether the controls structure is adequate (Any weaknesses in the control structure should be reported to executive management and resolved.)		PO9 DS5 DS9 ME2

	Control Objective/Test	Documentation/ Matters Arising	COBIT References
1.	**Master Data Maintenance**		
1.1	***Access to HR setup tables and master file transaction is appropriately restricted.***		
	Review access security matrices and access assignment documentation to gain an understanding of the security design. Corroborate this understanding by generating lists of users with access to the Workforce Administration, Compensation, Set Up HRMS and Global Human Resources Rules menus, and reviewing their level of access by writing the following query in PeopleSoft Query Manager: SELECT B.OPRID, B.OPRCLASS, A.MENUNAME, A.BARNAME, A.BARITEMNAME, A.PNLITEMNAME, A.AUTHORIZEDACTIONS, A.DISPLAYONLY FROM PSAUTHITEM A, PSOPRCLS B WHERE A.CLASSID = B.OPRCLASS Order by B.OPRID, B.OPRCLASS, A.MENUNAME to ensure that the user IDs (OPRID), permission lists (OPRCLASS) and components (MENUNAME) are listed in alphabetical order. Also, generate a list of users with access to the setup pages within PeopleSoft menus, and review their level of access by writing the following query in PeopleSoft Query Manager: SELECT B.OPRID, B.OPRCLASS, A.MENUNAME, A.BARNAME, A.BARITEMNAME, A.PNLITEMNAME, A.DISPLAYONLY, A.AUTHORIZEDACTIONS		AI2 AI6 DS5 DS6 DS11 DS13

	Control Objective/Test	Documentation/ Matters Arising	COBIT References
1.	**Master Data Maintenance *cont.***		
1.1 *cont.*	FROM PSAUTHITEM A, PSOPRCLS B WHERE A.CLASSID = B.OPRCLASS AND A.BARNAME LIKE 'SETUP%' Order by B.CLASSID to ensure that the user IDs (OPRID) are listed in alphabetical order. The column A.AUTHORIZEDACTIONS will contain values that represent the action types that the user is authorized to perform, where high-risk values are: • 8—Corrections • 9—Add Correction • 10—Update/Display, Corrections • 11—Add Update/Display, Correction • 12—Update/Display, All Correction • 13—Add Update/Display, All Correction • 14—Update/Display, Update/Display, All Correction • 15—Add Update/Display, Update/ Display, All Correction • 136—Correction, Data Entry • 137—Add Correction, Data Entry • 138—Update/Display, Correction, Data Entry • 139—Add Update/Display, Correction, Data Entry • 140—Update/Display All, Correction, Data Entry • 141—Add Update/Display All, Correction, Data Entry • 142—Update/Display, Update/Display All, Correction, Data Entry • 143—Add Update/Display, Update/ Display All, Correction, Data Entry Note: The A.DISPLAYONLY column will have a value of 0 or 1. A value of 1 means that all fields in the page are display-only to the user, and a value		

	Control Objective/Test	Documentation/ Matters Arising	COBIT References
1.	**Master Data Maintenance *cont.***		
1.1 *cont.*	of 0 means this setting is turned off and the action type codes indicate the level of access granted. Generate a list of users and the row-level security defined by writing the following query in PeopleSoft Query Manager: SELECT C.OPRID, A.DEPTID, B.SETID, B.DESCR, A.ACCESS_CD, A.TREE_NODE_NUM, A.TREE_NODE_NUM_END FROM PS_SCRTY_TBL_DEPT A, PS_DEPT_TBL B, PSOPRDEFN C WHERE A.SETID = B.SETID AND A.DEPTID = B.DEPTID AND B.EFFDT = (SELECT MAX(B_ED.EFFDT) FROM PS_DEPT_TBL B_ED WHERE B.SETID = B_ED.SETID AND B.DEPTID = B_ED.DEPTID) AND A.ROWSECCLASS = C.ROWSECCLASS Order by B.OPRID, B.DESCR to ensure that the user IDs (OPRID) and descriptions (DESCR) are listed in alphabetical order. Select a sample of HR users and assess whether they have access to update their own HR data (i.e., job) by observing them attempting to make such changes.		
1.2	***Access to make changes to employee HR master data is appropriately restricted***		
1.2.1	Review security design documentation detailing the configured controls implemented in the system and approved by management. In particular, review the online edit and validation checks and range checks.		PO9 AI2 AI6 DS6 DS9

	Control Objective/Test	Documentation/ Matters Arising	COBIT References
1.	**Master Data Maintenance *cont.***		
1.2.1 *cont.*	For either a sample of the edit and validation checks or for the entire population, enter changes to employee data and observe the outcome to these attempts. Organizations may be reluctant to allow auditors to have access to make test changes in the production environment. Consequently, perform audit tests in the Test or QA environment. Corroborate that the configuration of controls in the Test/QA environment is the same as that in the production environment. For example, attempt to change the bank ID and branch ID of an employee's bank information via Home→Workforce Administration→Personal Information→Biographical→Bank Accounts. Change the bank ID and/or branch ID to an erroneous value, and observe whether a warning message is displayed. Attempt to change the employee's pay group via Home→Workforce Administration→Job Information→Job Data→Payroll. Change the pay group field to an erroneous value, and observe whether a warning message is issued. Review the Date Last Increase field via Home→Workforce Administration→Personal Information→Job Data→Employment Data (at the bottom of the page), and determine whether this corresponds to the last authorized pay increase.		

Control Objective/Test	Documentation/ Matters Arising	COBIT References
1. Master Data Maintenance *cont.*		
1.2.1 *cont.* Note that not all potential pay increase scenarios impact this date change. Therefore, in addition to the above, generate a compensation history by writing the following query in Query Manager: SELECT JO.EFFDT, JO.ACTION, JO.ACTION_REASON, JO.ANNUAL_RT, JO.EMPLID FROM PS_JOB JO WHERE JO.CHANGE_AMT <> 0 AND JO.EMPLID = 'specific EmplID' Order by JO.EFFDT to ensure that the output is in effective-date (EFFDT) order. Review the compensation history and investigate the validity of the changes.		
1.2.2 Review security design documentation detailing the configured controls implemented in the system and approved by management, in particular the audit trails setup. Determine with relevant management the procedures in place for generating, reviewing and investigating audit reports showing changes to employee master data. Inspect a sample of audit trail reports for evidence of review and rectification of exception items identified.		AI4 DS9 ME4
2. Commencements		
2.1 Access to the hiring process is appropriately restricted.		
2.1.1 Review access security matrices and access assignment documentation to gain an understanding of the security design. Determine if the documentation was authorized by management prior to implementation.		PO10

Control Objective/Test	Documentation/ Matters Arising	COBIT References
2. Commencements *cont.*		
2.1.2 Generate lists of users with access to the Workforce Administration, Workforce Development, Recruiting and Applicant Contract Data menus, and review their level of access by writing the SQL query detailed in chapter 6, Master Data Maintenance: Testing Techniques 1.1.1 in PeopleSoft Query Manager. Select a sample of HR users and assess whether they have access to update their own HR data (i.e., job) by observing them attempting to make such changes.		DS5 DS11
2.2 Access to make changes to employee contract data is appropriately restricted.		
2.2.1 Review security design documentation detailing the configured controls implemented in the system and approved by management, particularly the online edit and validation checks, range checks, etc. For either a sample of the edit and validation checks or for the entire population, enter changes to employee contract data (via Home→Workforce Administration→Job Information→Contract Administration→Update Contracts) and observe the success or failure of these attempts and whether a warning message is displayed. Note that the above menu navigation path is different from Home→Recruiting→Hire Applicants→Prepare for Hire→Create Employment Contracts, which is for creating applicant contracts. The first menu path described is for access to employee contracts.		AI1 DS11 DS13

	Control Objective/Test	Documentation/ Matters Arising	COBIT References
2.2	***Access to make changes to employee contract data is appropriately restricted. cont.***		
	Organizations may be reluctant to allow auditors to have the access to make test changes in the production environment. Consequently, perform the following audit tests in the Test or QA environment. Corroborate that the configuration of controls in the Test/QA environment is the same as those in the production environment.		
3.	**Personal Development**		
3.1	***Access to career planning is appropriately restricted.***		
	Review access security matrices and access assignment documentation to gain an understanding of the security design. Determine if the documentation was authorized by management prior to implementation. Generate lists of users with access to the Career Planning page via Home→Workforce Development→Career Planning→Prepare→Create Career Plan. Review their level of access by writing the SQL query detailed in chapter 6, Master Data Maintenance Testing Technique 1.1.1, in PeopleSoft Query Manager. Select a sample of HR users and assess whether they have access to update the strengths and development area pages of their own career plans by observing them attempting to make such changes.		DS5 DS11
3.2	***Access to succession planning is appropriately restricted.***		
3.2.1	Review access security matrices and access assignment documentation to gain an understanding of the security design. Determine if the documentation was authorized by management prior to implementation.		PO4 PO8 AI1 AI2 DS5

	Control Objective/Test	Documentation/ Matters Arising	COBIT References
3.	**Personal Development *cont.***		
3.2.1 *cont.*	Generate lists of users with access to Succession Planning via Home→ Organizational Development→ Succession Planning→Create Succession Plan. Review their level of access by writing the SQL query detailed in chapter 6, Master Data Maintenance Testing Technique 1.1.1, in PeopleSoft Query Manager. Select a sample of HR users and assess whether they have access to update the succession plans by observing them attempting to make such changes.		
3.3	***Access to training administration is appropriately restricted.***		
3.3.1	Review access security matrices and access assignment documentation to gain an understanding of the security design. Determine if the documentation was authorized by management prior to implementation. Generate lists of users with access to the Training Administration functions through one of the following paths: • Home→Enterprise Learning→Define Course/Cost Details→Program Information • Home→Enterprise Learning→Define Course/Cost Details→Courses Also review the users' level of access by writing the SQL query detailed in chapter 6, Master Data Maintenance Testing Technique 1.1.1, in PeopleSoft Query Manager.		AI2 AI4 DS5

	Control Objective/Test	Documentation/ Matters Arising	COBIT References
4.	**Terminations**		
4.1	***Access to process terminations is appropriately restricted.***		
4.1.1	Review access security matrices and access assignment documentation to gain an understanding of the security design. Determine if the documentation was authorized by management prior to implementation.		PO7 DS13
4.1.2	Generate lists of users with access to terminate employees on the system via Home→Workforce Administration → Job Information→Job Data. Review their level of access by writing the SQL query detailed in chapter 6, Master Data Maintenance Testing Techniques 1.1.1, in PeopleSoft Query Manager.		PO7 DS5 DS11

Appendix D—HR Cycle Audit ICQ

Control Objective/Test		Response			Comment	COBIT References
		Yes	No	N/A		
1.	**Master Data Maintenance**					
1.1	***Access to HR setup tables and master file transaction is appropriately restricted.***					
1.1.1	Are there security matrices and documentation in place that define roles, permission lists, menus and pages per job function for HR? Who has access to define business rules and administration of employee HR data? Are these users appropriate? Who has access to add/correct/update access to Define Business Rules? This should be restricted to the HR administrator.					PO7 DS5 DS11
1.2	***Access to make changes to employee HR master data is appropriately restricted.***					
1.2.1	Have edit and validation checks been implemented to ensure valid data changes? What type of edit and validation checks are in place? Who has access to make changes to the employee HR master data? Are these users appropriate?					DS11
1.2.2	Are audit logs of changes to employee master data reviewed by management on a periodic basis?					DS13 ME1

	Control Objective/Test	Response: Yes	Response: No	Response: N/A	Comment	COBIT References
2.	**Commencements**					
2.1	***Access to the hiring process is appropriately restricted.***					
2.1.1	Are there security matrices and documentation in place that define roles, permission lists, menus and pages per job function for HR? Has this documentation been reviewed and approved by management prior to implementation?					PO7 DS4 DS5
2.1.2	Who has access to the function to hire employees and maintain employee contract information? Are these users appropriate, and have duties been appropriately segregated?					PO4 DS4
2.2	***Access to make changes to employee contract data is appropriately restricted.***					
2.2.1	Has the security design documentation detailed the configured controls in the system? Was this documentation approved by management? What types of edit and validation checks are in place?					PO4 AI2 DS9
3.	**Personal Development**					
3.1	***Access to career planning is appropriately restricted.***					
3.1.1	Are there security matrices and documentation in place that define roles, permission lists, menus and pages per job function for HR?					PO7 AI4 ME1

	Control Objective/Test	Response			Comment	COBIT References
		Yes	No	N/A		
3.	**Personal Development *cont.***					
3.1.1 *cont.*	Has this documentation been reviewed and approved by management prior to implementation?					
3.1.2	Who has access to maintain the employee strengths and development areas as part of an employee's career plan? Are these users appropriate HR personnel?					DS5
3.2	***Access to succession planning is appropriately restricted.***					
3.2.1	Who has access to succession planning? Are these users appropriate HR personnel?					PO7
3.3	***Access to training administration is appropriately restricted.***					
3.3.1	Who has access to maintain the Training Course table? Are these users appropriate HR personnel?					PO7 DS5 DS11
4.	**Terminations**					
4.1	***Access to process terminations is appropriately restricted.***					
4.1.1	Are there security matrices and documentation in place that define roles, permission lists, menus and pages per job function for HR? Has this documentation been reviewed and approved by management prior to implementation?					PO7
4.1.2	Who has access to the terminations process? Are these users appropriate HR personnel?					PO7 DS5

Appendix E—Payroll Cycle Audit Program

Control Objective/Test	Documentation/ Matters Arising	COBIT References
Preliminary Audit Steps		
Gain an understanding of the PeopleSoft environment.		
a. The same background information obtained for the PeopleSoft Application Security audit plan is required for, and relevant to, the business cycles. In particular, the following steps are important: • Determine what version and release of the PeopleSoft software has been implemented (by holding Ctrl-J on any PeopleSoft page). • Determine the total number of named users (for comparison with logical access security testing results). • Determine the number of PeopleSoft instances. • Identify the modules that are being used. • Determine whether the organization has created any locally developed reports or tables. • Obtain details of the risk assessment approach taken in the organization to identify and prioritize risks. • Obtain copies of the organization's key security policies and standards. • Review outstanding audit findings, if any, from previous years.		PO2 PO3 PO4 PO6 PO9 AI1 AI2 AI6 ME2
b. Obtain details: • Of the organizational model as it relates to payroll activity, i.e., payroll organization unit structure in the PeopleSoft software and payroll organization chart (required when evaluating the results of access security control testing).		AI1 AI3

	Control Objective/Test	Documentation/ Matters Arising	COBIT References
Preliminary Audit Steps *cont.*			
b. *cont.*	• By interviewing the systems implementation team, if possible, and obtaining process design documentation for payrolls		
Identify the significant risks and determine the key controls.			
c.	Develop a high-level process flow diagram and overall understanding of the payroll processing cycle, including the following subprocesses: • Master Data Maintenance • Recording Attendance and Leave Processing • Calculating and Disbursing Payroll • Reporting and Reconciliation		PO9 AI1 DS13
d.	Assess the key risks, determine key controls or control weaknesses, and test controls (refer to the following sample testing program and chapter 4 for techniques for testing configurable controls and logical access security) regarding the following factors: • The controls culture of the organization • The need to exercise judgment to determine the key controls in the process and whether the controls structure is adequate (Any weaknesses in the control structure should be reported to executive management and resolved.)		PO9 DS5 DS9 ME2

	Control Objective/Test	Documentation/ Matters Arising	COBIT References
1.	**Master Data Maintenance**		
1.1	***Access to payroll setup tables and master file transaction is restricted appropriately.***		
1.1.1	Review access security matrices and access assignment documentation to gain an understanding of the security design. Corroborate this understanding by generating lists of users with access to the WorkForce Administration, Compensation, Set Up HRMS and Global Payroll Rules menus and reviewing their level of access by writing the following query in PeopleSoft Query Manager: SELECT A.OPRID, A.OPRDEFNDESC, A.ACCTLOCK, B.ROLENAME, C.CLASSID, D.MENUNAME, D.BARNAME, D.BARITEMNAME, D.PNLITEMNAME, D.DISPLAYONLY, D.AUTHORIZEDACTIONS FROM PSOPRDEFN A, PSROLEUSER B, PSROLECLASS C, PSAUTHITEM D WHERE A.OPRID = B.ROLEUSER AND B.ROLENAME = C.ROLENAME AND C.CLASSID = D.CLASSID AND D.MENUNAME = 'SETUP_HRMS' Order by A.OPRID, B.ROLENAME, C.CLASSID, D.MENUNAME to ensure that the user IDs (OPRID), roles (ROLENAME), permission lists (CLASSID) and components (MENUNAME) are listed in alphabetical order.		AI2 AI6 DS5 DS6 DS11 DS13

	Control Objective/Test	Documentation/ Matters Arising	COBIT References
1.	**Master Data Maintenance *cont.***		
1.1.1 *cont.*	Generate a list of users with access to the setup pages within PeopleSoft menus (and the roles that provide such access), and review their level of access by writing the following query in PeopleSoft Query Manager: SELECT A.OPRID, A.OPRDEFNDESC, A.ACCTLOCK, B.ROLENAME, C.CLASSID, D.MENUNAME, D.BARNAME, D.BARITEMNAME, D.PNLITEMNAME, D.DISPLAYONLY, D.AUTHORIZEDACTIONS FROM PSOPRDEFN A, PSROLEUSER B, PSROLECLASS C, PSAUTHITEM D WHERE A.OPRID = B.ROLEUSER AND B.ROLENAME = C.ROLENAME AND C.CLASSID = D.CLASSID AND D.BARNAME LIKE '%SETUP%' The column D.AUTHORIZEDACTIONS will contain a numerical value that represents the action type that the user is authorized to perform. Action types are detailed at the end of chapter 10. History note: The D.DISPLAYONLY column will have value of 0 or 1. A value of 1 means all fields in the page are display-only to the user, and a value of 0 means this setting is turned off and the action type codes indicate the level of access granted.		

	Control Objective/Test	Documentation/ Matters Arising	COBIT References
1.	**Master Data Maintenance *cont.***		
1.1.1 *cont.*	Generate a list of users and the row-level security defined by writing the following query in PeopleSoft Query Manager: SELECT A.OPRID, A.OPRDEFNDESC, A.ACCTLOCK, B.SETID, B.DEPTID, C.DESCR, B.ACCESS_CD, TO_CHAR (B.TREE_EFFDT,'YYYY-MM-DD'), B.TREE_NODE_NUM, B.TREE_NODE_NUM_END, C.SETID, C.DEPTID,TO_CHAR (C.EFFDT,'YYYY-MM-DD') FROM PSOPRDEFN A, PS_SCRTY_TBL_DEPT B, PS_DEPT_TBL C WHERE A.ROWSECCLASS = B.ROWSECCLASSAND B.SETID = C.SETIDAND B.DEPTID = C.DEPTID AND C.EFFDT =(SELECT MAX (C_ED.EFFDT) FROM PS_DEPT_TBL C_EDWHERE C.SETID = C_ED.SETID AND C.DEPTID = C_ED.DEPTID AND C_ED.EFFDT <= SYSDATE) Order by A.OPRID, C.DESCR to ensure that the user IDs (OPRID) and department descriptions (DESCR) are listed in alphabetical order. Select a sample of Payroll users, and assess whether they have access to update their own payroll data (i.e., salary, job) by observing them attempting to make such changes. Determine how the system has been configured to use emplIDs which are associated with operator IDs. Review the PSOPRDEFN records to determine if each ID has been assigned an emplID.		

	Control Objective/Test	Documentation/ Matters Arising	COBIT References
1.	**Master Data Maintenance *cont.***		
1.2	***Access to make changes to payroll setup tables is restricted appropriately.***		
1.2.1	Review security design documentation detailing the configured controls implemented in the system and approved by management. In particular, check the configuration controls designed for the mandatory fields in payroll table data entry. Observe a system administrator delete one of the mandatory fields and attempt to save the change. Observe if a warning/error message is displayed. Note: Ensure that the original data stored within the Mandatory field are reset.		AI3 AI6
1.3	***Access to make changes to employee payroll master data is restricted appropriately.***		
1.3.1	Review security design documentation detailing the configured and customized controls implemented in the system and approved by management, particularly the online edit and validation checks and range checks. For either a sample of the edit and validation checks or for the entire population, enter changes to employee data and observe the success or failure of these attempts. For example, attempt to change the bank ID and branch ID of an employee's bank information via Home→ Workforce Administration→ Personal Information →Biographical →Bank Accounts. Change the bank ID and/or branch ID to an erroneous value and observe whether a warning message is displayed.		AI5 AI6 DS5 DS9 DS11

	Control Objective/Test	Documentation/ Matters Arising	COBIT References
1.	**Master Data Maintenance *cont.***		
1.3.1 *cont.*	Attempt to change an employee's pay group via Home→Workforce Administration→Job Information → Job Data→Payroll. Change the pay group field to an erroneous value and observe whether a warning message is issued. Review the Date Last Increase field via Home→Workforce Administration →Job Information→Job Data→ Employment Data (at the bottom of the page), and determine whether this corresponds to the last authorized pay increase. Note that not all potential pay increase scenarios impact this date change. For a sample of employees, generate a compensation history by writing the following query in Query Manager: SELECT A.EMPLID, TO_CHAR (A.EFFDT,'YYYY-MM-DD'), A.ACTION, A.ACTION_REASON, A.ANNUAL_RT, A.CHANGE_AMT FROM PS_JOB A, PS_EMPLMT_SRCH_QRY A1 WHERE A.EMPLID = A1.EMPLID AND A.EMPL_RCD = A1.EMPL_RCD AND A1.ROWSECCLASS = 'HCDPALL' AND A.CHANGE_AMT <> 0 Note that the PS_EMPLMT_SRCH_QRY table will vary depending on row-level security configuration. Review the compensation history and investigate the validity of the changes.		

	Control Objective/Test	Documentation/ Matters Arising	COBIT References
1.	**Master Data Maintenance *cont.***		
1.3.1 *cont.*	Organizations may be reluctant to allow auditors to have the access to make test changes in the production environment. Consequently, perform the following audit tests in the Test or QA environment. Corroborate that the configuration of controls in the Test/QA environment is the same as in the production environment. Alternatively, extract and query the required tables offline using Microsoft Access or ACL.		
1.3.2	Review security design documentation detailing the configured controls implemented in the system and approved by management, particularly the audit trails' setup. Determine with relevant management the procedures in place for generating, reviewing and investigating audit reports showing changes to employee master data. Inspect a sample of audit trail reports for evidence of review and rectification of exception items identified.		AI1 AI4 DS9
1.4	***Online edit and validation checks and ranges checks are configured in the system.***		
1.4.1	Review security design documentation detailing the configured controls implemented in the system and approved by management. In particular, review the online edit and validation checks and range checks. For a sample of employee data or for the entire population, enter changes to employee data and test for edit and validation checks. Observe the success or failure of these attempts.		AI2 DS11

	Control Objective/Test	Documentation/ Matters Arising	COBIT References
1.	**Master Data Maintenance *cont.***		
1.5	***Edit and validation checks are in place for maximum and minimum salary.***		
1.5.1	Review security design documentation detailing the configured controls implemented in the system and approved by management, particularly the online edit and validation checks and range checks. Corroborate this understanding by inspecting the Salary Increase Matrix tables via Home→ Compensation→Salary Planning→ Salary Planning Administration→ Define Salary Increase Matrix, and compare the limits configured to those defined in the security design documentation. For a sample of the salary plans, enter changes to compensation rates for employees enrolled in those plans and observe the success or failure of these attempts.		AI2 DS5 DS11
2.	**Recording Attendance and Leave Processing**		
2.1	***Access to record attendance is restricted appropriately.***		
2.1.1	Review access security matrices and access assignment documentation to gain an understanding of the security design. Corroborate this understanding by generating lists of users with access to the following menus: • Enter Time: – Home→Time and Labor→Report Time→Report Rapid Time – Home→Employee Self Service →Time Recording→Report Time →Report Weekly Punch Time • Approve Time: – Home→Manager Self Service→ Time Management→Approvals→ Approve Payable Time		AI2 DS11

	Control Objective/Test	Documentation/ Matters Arising	COBIT References
1.	**Master Data Maintenance *cont.***		
2.1.1 *cont.*	– Home→Time and Labor→Approvals →Approve Time by Time Reporter Review the users' level of access by writing the SQL query detailed in chapter 6, 1.1.1 Master Data Maintenance Testing Techniques, in PeopleSoft Query Manager.		
2.2	***Access to process leave is restricted appropriately.***		
2.2.1	Review access security matrices and access assignment documentation to gain an understanding of the security design. Corroborate this understanding by generating lists of users with access to the following pages: • Enter and Approve Leave (or vacation) Requests via Home→Workforce Administration→Absence and Vacation →Create Vacation Schedule→Request/ Approve Vacation • Self Service Absence Request via Home→Employee Self Service→Time Recording→Report Time→Review/ Request Absence • Self Service Absence Approval via Home→Manager Self Service→Time Management →Approvals→Approve Absence Request Review the users' level of access by utilizing the SQL query detailed in chapter 6, test 1.1.1 Master Data Maintenance.		DS5 DS10 DS13 ME1
2.3	***Attendance submitted is valid and approved.***		
2.3.1	Review business process documentation to determine the procedures in place for submitting and approving time and attendance. Corroborate this understanding by observing the submission and approval process of time reporter attendance.		DS1 DS3

	Control Objective/Test	Documentation/ Matters Arising	COBIT References
2.	**Recording Attendance and Leave Processing *cont.***		
2.3.1 *cont.*	Review the work group settings (via Home→Set Up HRMS→Product Related→Time and Labor→Rules and Workgroups→Workgroup) and determine whether the work group timesheets are set to Needs Approval.		
2.4	***Valid time worked is processed on a timely basis.***		
2.4.1	Review business process documentation to determine the procedures in place for submitting and approving time and attendance, and the timetable in place to run the time administration batch process.		AI1
2.4.2	Review business process documentation to determine the procedures in place for identifying and rectifying time and attendance exceptions. Corroborate this understanding by reviewing the Manage Time pages for a sample of time exceptions reports (via Home→Time and Labor→ Approvals →Manage [Individual/ Group] Exceptions) to ensure that no exceptions were left unresolved.		AI1 AI4 DS3
2.5	***Leave requests are valid and approved.***		
2.5.1	Review business process documentation to determine the procedures in place for the submission and approval of leaves of absence. Corroborate this understanding by observing the submission and approval of vacation and general leave requests.		AI1 AI4
2.5.2	Create a dummy leave request (via Home→Workforce Administration→ Absences and Vacation→Create Vacation Schedule →Request/Approve Vacation), and attempt to enter a fictitious Leave Code. Observe the success or failure of the result.		DS5 DS11

	Control Objective/Test	Documentation/ Matters Arising	COBIT References
2.	**Recording Attendance and Leave Processing *cont.***		
2.5.3	Create a dummy leave request via Home→Workforce Administration→ Absences and Vacation→Create Vacation Schedule →Request/Approve Vacation, and attempt to enter a leave period greater than the available leave balance and observe the success or failure of the result. Note: Ensure that the Vacation Accrual run has been processed beforehand to update the leave accrual. Vacation Accrual is run via Home→Workforce Administration→Absences and Vacation→Create Vacation Schedule →Accrue Vacation.		DS5 DS11
2.5.4	Determine the processes and procedures in place over employees taking leave without pay. If a notional or temporary salary is entered into the system during the period of leave, corroborate this by inspecting the employee's salary records. Alternatively, review audit logs of changes to employee records.		DS13
3.	**Calculating and Disbursing Payroll**		
3.1	***Access to payroll processing is restricted appropriately.***		
3.1.1	Review access security matrices and access assignment documentation to gain an understanding of the security design. Corroborate this understanding by generating lists of users with access to the following pages: • North American Payroll: – Paysheet Creation via Home→North American Payroll→Payroll Processing→Create Initial Paysheets – Payroll Calculation via Home→ North American Payroll→Payroll Processing→Calculate Pay		PO7 DS4 DS5

	Control Objective/Test	Documentation/ Matters Arising	CobiT References
3.	**Calculating and Disbursing Payroll** ***cont.***		
3.1.1 *cont.*	– Payroll Finalization via Home→North American Payroll→Payment Processing→Confirm Pay • Global Payroll via Home→Global Payroll→Absence and Payroll Processing→Calculate Absence and Payroll Review users' level of access by writing the query detailed in chapter 6, 1.1.1 Master Data Maintenance Testing Techniques, in PeopleSoft Query Manager.		
3.2	***Access to online checks is restricted appropriately.***		
3.2.1	Review access security matrices and access assignment documentation to gain an understanding of the security design. Corroborate this understanding by generating lists of users with access to the Create Single Check page via Home→North American Payroll→Periodic Payroll Events→Single Check→Create Single Check. Review users' level of access by writing the query detailed in chapter 6, 1.1.1 Master Data Maintenance Testing Techniques, in PeopleSoft Query Manager.		DS11 DS13 ME1
3.3	***Access to the banking process is restricted appropriately.***		
3.3.1	Review the following: • Access security matrices and assignment documentation to gain an understanding of the security design of any bank transfer/interface application software utilized. Corroborate this understanding via inquiries with the payroll manager and/or payroll administrator.		PO8 DS5

	Control Objective/Test	Documentation/ Matters Arising	COBIT References
3.	**Calculating and Disbursing Payroll** ***cont.***		
3.3.1 *cont.*	• Any additional security controls over the bank transfer/interface application, e.g., the use of one-time PINs in addition to user ID and passwords. Corroborate this understanding via observation of the payment file transfer process. • System-generated access control listing to determine the appropriateness of access compared with the roles and responsibilities of the individual users • A sample of security audit trail reports for evidence of independent review and investigation		
3.4	***Discrepancies and exceptions are reviewed and corrected.***		
3.4.1	Review approved payroll processing procedures and security design documentation to gain an understanding of the procedures surrounding the payroll processes. Interview payroll administration staff to determine the audit evidence available for inspection. For: • Global Payroll: – Select a sample of pay runs and review the associated processing statistics to identify if errors are resolved prior to payroll finalization. – Review the payee messages for evidence of investigation and rectification. • North American Payroll: – Select a sample of pay runs and review the associated Payroll Error Message for Employees Report (PAY011) for evidence of investigation and rectification.		PO6 AI6 DS5 ME1

	Control Objective/Test	Documentation/ Matters Arising	COBIT References
3.	**Calculating and Disbursing Payroll *cont.***		
3.4.1 *cont.*	Determine whether the Payroll Precalculation Audit SQR (PAY035) has been run and reviewed for each pay run prior to the payroll calculation stage.		
3.5	***Edit and validation rules are in place to identify errors in the payroll.***		
3.5.1	Review approved payroll processing procedures and security design documentation to gain an understanding of the procedures surrounding the payroll processes. Interview payroll administration staff to determine the audit evidence available for inspection. For: • Global Payroll: – Select a sample of pay runs and review the associated processing statistics to identify if errors are resolved prior to payroll finalization. – Review the payee messages for evidence of investigation and rectification. • North American Payroll: – Select a sample of pay runs and review the associated Payroll Error Message for Employees report (PAY011) for evidence of investigation and rectification. Determine whether the Payroll Precalculation Audit SQR (PAY035) has been run and reviewed for each pay run prior to the payroll calculation stage.		AI4 ME1

	Control Objective/Test	Documentation/ Matters Arising	COBIT References
3.	**Calculating and Disbursing Payroll** *cont.*		
3.6	***Payroll runs are reviewed and approved by the payroll administrator/manager.***		
3.6.1	Review approved payroll processing procedures and security design documentation to gain an understanding of the procedures surrounding the payroll processes. Interview payroll administration staff to determine the audit evidence available for inspection. Where possible, select a sample of pay runs and determine whether the payroll administrator or payroll manager reviewed and approved the following, prior to the final processing of the payment file: • General deductions by recipient • Individual deductions by recipient • Employee net pay		DS1 DS3
3.7	***Interface controls are in place for electronic funds transfer (EFT).***		
3.7.1	Review approved payroll processing procedures documentation to gain an understanding of the procedures surrounding the payroll processes. Specifically, review the mechanisms in place surrounding the transfer of PeopleSoft payment files to the bank, including the encryption of the payment file. Corroborate this understanding via inquiries with the payroll administrator and manager.		DS11 DS13 ME1

Control Objective/Test		Documentation/ Matters Arising	COBIT References
3.	**Calculating and Disbursing Payroll *cont.***		
3.7.1 *cont.*	For a sample of pay runs, review the payment files for the existence of header and trailer records. Review any associated positive acknowledgment reports/messages from the bank, and compare the number of records and monetary amounts to the payment file. Review any reconciliations performed between the payment files generated by the organization and the files received and processed by the bank for evidence of independent review and investigation of any reconciling items. Inspect the contents of the payment file to determine whether the data are encrypted prior to transmission or remain in a cleartext format.		
3.7.2	Review approved payroll processing procedures documentation to gain an understanding of the procedures surrounding the payroll processes. Specifically, review the mechanisms in place surrounding the transfer of PeopleSoft payment files to the bank and the storage of the payment files to determine if there is a time delay between the payroll finalization in PeopleSoft and the transfer/interface with the bank systems. Corroborate this understanding via inquiries with the payroll administrator and manager. Review the location for storage of the payment files. If this is a network directory, review whether access to the directory is restricted, check the appropriateness of the access granted, and review if access is based on the roles and responsibilities of the users.		DS1 DS4 DS13 ME1

	Control Objective/Test	Documentation/ Matters Arising	COBIT References
3.	**Calculating and Disbursing Payroll *cont.***		
3.7.2 *cont.*	If the transfer of the payment files from PeopleSoft to the bank transfer/interface application is a physical transfer of a floppy disk or other medium, determine the storage location and assess whether the physical security of that location is adequate. For example, determine whether the payment file is stored in a fireproof safe/lockable cupboard, and assess who has access to the file and the appropriateness of such access.		
4.	**Reporting and Reconciliation**		
4.1	***Access to GL run control processes is restricted appropriately.***		
4.1.1	Review access security matrices and access assignment documentation to gain an understanding of the security design. Corroborate this understanding by generating lists of users with access to the following pages: • For Global Payroll: Home→Global Payroll→Time & Labor/GL Costs→Send Costs to GL →General Ledger Run Control • For North American Payroll: Home→North American Payroll→ Payroll Distribution→Prepare GL Information→Non-Commit Accounting Info Review their level of access by writing the query detailed in 1.1.1 (under Master Data Maintenance Testing Techniques), in PeopleSoft Query Manager.		DS5 ME1
4.2	***Access to PeopleSoft reporting is restricted appropriately.***		
4.2.1	Review payroll procedural documentation, access security matrices and access assignment documentation to gain an understanding of the key payroll reports available and generated as well as the security design around such reports.		DS5 DS13 ME1

	Control Objective/Test	Documentation/ Matters Arising	COBIT References
4.	**Reporting and Reconciliation *cont.***		
4.2 *cont.*	Corroborate this understanding by generating lists of users with access to the pages: • For Global Payroll: Home→Global Payroll→Absence and Payroll Processing→Payroll Reports→Payroll Register/Payroll Summary • For North American Payroll: Home→North American Payroll →Payroll Processing→Reports→ Payroll Register/Payroll Summary Review users' level of access by utilizing the query in PeopleSoft detailed in previous test 3.2.1.		
4.3	***GL reconciliations are performed at period-ends.***		
4.3.1	Review period-end and payroll procedural documentation to gain an understanding of the processes surrounding the reconciliation of the payroll module and the GL. For a sample of periods, review the reconciliations for evidence of timely performance, independent review and approval, and the investigation and clearance of reconciling items. Inquire with management the reasons for large and/or recurring reconciling items.		DS13
4.4	***Bank reconciliations are performed at period-ends.***		
4.4.1	Review period-end procedural documentation to gain an understanding of the processes surrounding the reconciliation of the GL to the various bank statements received from the organization's source banks.		PO6 DS13 ME1

	Control Objective/Test	Documentation/ Matters Arising	COBIT References
4.	**Reporting and Reconciliation *cont.***		
4.4.1 *cont.*	For a sample of periods, review the reconciliations for evidence of timely performance, independent review and approval, and the investigation and clearance of reconciling items. Inquire with management the reasons for large and/or recurring reconciling items.		

Appendix F—Payroll Cycle Audit ICQ

	Control Objective/Test	Response			Comment	COBIT References
		Yes	No	N/A		
1.	**Master Data Maintenance**					
1.1	***Access to Payroll Setup tables and master file transactions is restricted appropriately.***					
1.1.1	Who has access to define business rules, administration of employee payroll data and compensation? Are these users appropriate? Who has add/correction/update access to Set Up HRMS business rules? This should be restricted to the Payroll administrator only. Are error messages displayed when access is denied?					PO10 DS11 ME1
1.2	***Access to make changes to Payroll Setup tables is restricted appropriately.***					
1.2.1	Are validation checks in place to ensure that all mandatory data are input in the Payroll table? Who has access to make changes to the Payroll Setup tables? Are these users appropriate?					DS5

Control Objective/Test		Response: Yes	Response: No	Response: N/A	Comment	COBIT References
1.	**Master Data Maintenance *cont.***					
1.3	***Access to make changes to employee payroll master data is restricted appropriately.***					
1.3.1	Are edit and validation changes in place to ensure that changes made to the employee payroll master data are valid and accurate? If an invalid change is made, is this prevented from being processed, and how is the user alerted? Who has access to make employee payroll master data changes? Are these users appropriate?					DS5 DS11
1.3.2	Are audit logs kept of changes to the employee master data, and are these reviewed by management on a periodic basis?					DS10 DS12
1.4	***Online edit, validation and range checks are configured in the system.***					
1.4.1	How does the organization prevent employees from being paid more than the specified amounts? Is the Maximum Yearly Earnings field utilized?					DS11
1.5	***Edit and validation checks are in place for maximum and minimum salary.***					
1.5.1	How are the Salary Increase matrices set up? Who defines the minimum and maximum salary for a particular salary plan/grade?					DS5 DS13

	Control Objective/Test	Response			Comment	COBIT References
		Yes	No	N/A		
1.	**Master Data Maintenance** ***cont.***					
1.5.1 *cont.*	Does the system perform automatic validation when the compensation rate is changed against the Salary Increase matrices? Is a warning message displayed to notify the user if the change falls outside the parameters? Can this message be ignored/overwritten?					
2.	**Recording Attendance and Leave Processing**					
2.1	***Access to record attendance is restricted appropriately.***					
2.1.1	Are employees classified as exception time reporters or positive time reporters? If the time is recorded manually, who has access to input the manually approved time record? Are these users appropriate? If the time is recorded online, who has access to approve the time online? Are these users appropriate? How does the organization prevent approvers from approving their own time records?					AI4 AI6 DS11 DS13
2.2	***Access to process leave is restricted appropriately.***					
2.2.1	Are there documented procedures in place for processing leave?					AI4 AI6 DS9

Control Objective/Test		Response			Comment	CobiT References
		Yes	No	N/A		
2.	**Recording Attendance and Leave Processing *cont.***					
2.2.1 *cont.*	Is the application for leave of absence performed via manually approved forms or via the Self Service functionality within the system? If the Self Service option is being employed, who has access to approve leave online? Are these users appropriate? Who has access to the GL run control process? Are these users appropriate?					
2.3	***Attendance submitted is valid and approved.***					
2.3.1	For manual attendance, who manually approves the time sheets? In addition, who has access to input the approved time records? Are these users appropriate? Who can approve time online? Are these users appropriate? Does the system automatically perform validations to ensure that time reporters are active?					PO6 DS5
2.4	***Valid time worked is processed on a timely basis.***					
2.4.1	Are there documented procedures in place to ensure the timely submission, approval and input of timesheets, whether manual or online?					AI4

	Control Objective/Test	Response			Comment	COBIT
		Yes	No	N/A		References
2.	**Recording Attendance and Leave Processing *cont.***					
2.4.2	Are exceptions reviewed and investigated? Who performs these reviews, and how often are they performed?					DS3
2.5	***Leave requests are valid and approved.***					
2.5.1	Who reviews and approves leave of absence requests? How does the organization ensure that excessive leave has not been taken?					DS10
2.5.2	Does the system have validation checks in place to ensure that valid leave codes are entered? If an invalid leave code occurs, is the process stopped and the user prevented from proceeding?					AI6 DS11
2.5.3	Does the system automatically check the leave request against the employee's entitled leave balance? If the leave request exceeds the entitlement, can the leave still be approved or does the process cease at this point?					DS11
2.5.4	How does the organization ensure that unpaid leave is not paid out? Is this performed via automatic or manual data parameters on the system?					DS5 DS12

	Control Objective/Test	Response Yes	No	N/A	Comment	COBIT References
3.	**Calculating and Disbursing Payroll**					
3.1	***Access to payroll processing is restricted appropriately.***					
3.1.1	Has security access design documentation defining the access required for individual jobs in the payroll function been approved by management? Who has access to payroll processing? Are these users appropriate? Who has access to create paysheets (and associated adjustments), run the payroll calculation and confirm the payroll? Do users have access to their own HR and payroll records?					AI1 AI2 DS5
3.2	***Access to online checks is restricted appropriately.***					
3.2.1	Who has access to create and process online checks? Are these appropriate members of the payroll function?					DS5
3.3	***Access to the banking process is restricted appropriately.***					
3.3.1	Who has access to the bank control run process? Are these users appropriate? Who has access to the EFT file? Where is the file downloaded? Is it a secure location, and is access restricted to only those users who require it? Is the file encrypted?					DS5 DS11

	Control Objective/Test	Response Yes	Response No	Response N/A	Comment	CobiT References
3.	**Calculating and Disbursing Payroll *cont.***					
3.3.2	Does the organization utilize a special bank application to transfer the payment file to the bank? Who has access to this application? Are logical access controls in place when logging onto the bank transfer/interface application (e.g., password and user ID combinations)? Are audit trail reports maintained to log all user activity on the bank transfer/interface application?					AI1 DS5 DS13
3.4	***Discrepancies and exceptions are reviewed and corrected.***					
3.4.1	Are payroll processing procedures and security design documentation in place and approved by management? Are the processing statistics reviewed after each Global Payroll run to identify errors? Are errors from the Payroll Error Message for Employees report (PAY011) reviewed, investigated and resolved?					AI4 DS8 DS10 DS11

	Control Objective/Test	Response			Comment	CobiT References
		Yes	No	N/A		
3.	**Calculating and Disbursing Payroll *cont.***					
3.4.1 *cont.*	Is the Payroll Precalculation Audit SQR (PAY035) run and reviewed prior to the payroll calculation stage to identify possible errors due to lack of data integrity?					
3.5	***Edit and validation rules are in place to identify errors in the payroll.***					
3.5.1	Are the errors from the processing statistics reviewed, investigated and resolved? Are errors from the Payroll Error Message for Employees report (PAY011) reviewed, investigated and resolved?					DS11
3.6	***Payroll runs are reviewed and approved by the payroll administrator/manager.***					
3.6.1	Are the errors from the processing statistics reviewed, investigated and resolved? Are errors from the Payroll Error Message for Employees report (PAY011) reviewed, investigated and resolved? Do outstanding exceptions have the OK to Pay flag set to No to remove the paylines from the final pay confirmation?					DS10 DS11 DS13
3.6.2	Are the following reviewed prior to final processing and authorization of the payment file: • General deductions by recipient					DS11

	Control Objective/Test	Response: Yes	Response: No	Response: N/A	Comment	COBIT References
3.	**Calculating and Disbursing Payroll *cont.***					
3.6.2 *cont.*	• Individual deductions by recipient • Employee net pay					
3.7	***Interface controls are in place for EFT.***					
3.7.1	Are interface controls in place for the download and transfer of payment files? Are header and trailer records used? How does the organization ensure that the bank receives the complete and accurate file? Are reconciliations performed? Is the payment file encrypted?					DS5 DS11 DS13
3.7.2	Is there a time delay between processing the payment file in PeopleSoft and the transmission to the bank? Where is the file located during the delay? Is it secure and accessible only to appropriate personnel?					DS3
4.	**Reporting and Reconciliation**					
4.1	***Access to GL run control processes is restricted appropriately.***					
4.1.1	Does the security design documentation define the access requirements for individual jobs in the Payroll function? Is this documentation approved by management?					PO10

Control Objective/Test		Response: Yes	Response: No	Response: N/A	Comment	COBIT References
4.	**Reporting and Reconciliation *cont.***					
4.1.1 *cont.*	Who has access to update the GL with payroll data via the GL run control process? Are these users appropriate?					
4.2	***Access to PeopleSoft reporting is restricted appropriately.***					
4.2.1	Does the security design documentation define the access requirements for individual jobs in the Payroll function? Is this documentation approved by management? Who has access to PeopleSoft reports? Are these users appropriate?					DS5
4.3	***GL reconciliations are performed at period-ends.***					
4.3.1	Has the payroll processing and period-end time table been defined and approved? Have the specified dates for the execution of the GL Run Control process been defined and approved? Are reconciliations performed between the Payroll module and the GL? Are these reviewed and approved?					DS13

Control Objective/Test		Response			Comment	COBIT References
		Yes	No	N/A		
4.	**Reporting and Reconciliation *cont.***					
4.4	***Bank reconciliations are performed at period-ends.***					
4.4.1	Have month-end procedures been documented and approved? Are reconciliations performed between the GL and the relevant bank statements for all source bank accounts?					AI4 DS11

Appendix G—Security Administration Cycle Audit Program

Control Objective/Test		Documentation/ Matters Arising	COBIT References
Preliminary Audit Steps			
Gain an understanding of the PeopleSoft environment.			
a.	Determine what version and release of the PeopleSoft software has been implemented (by holding Ctrl-J on any PeopleSoft page). If multiple versions, document the various versions.		AI2
b.	Obtain details of the following: • Operating system(s) and platforms • Total number of named users (for comparison with limits specified in contract) • Number of PeopleSoft instances • Database management system used to store data for the PeopleSoft system • Location of the servers and the related LAN/WAN connections (need to verify security and controls, including environmental, surrounding the hardware and the network security controls surrounding the connectivity). If possible, obtain copies of network topology diagrams. • Listing of business partners, related organizations and remote locations that are permitted to connect to the PeopleSoft environment • Various means used to connect to the PeopleSoft environment (e.g., dial-up, remote access server) and the network diagram if available • The firewall protection, if any, where remote access is provided		AI2 DS11

Control Objective/Test		Documentation/ Matters Arising	COBIT References
Preliminary Audit Steps *cont.*			
c.	Determine whether separate systems for development, test and production were implemented and whether each instance is a totally separate system or within the same system. Determine that all systems are segregated and access to these is segregated as necessary. Specifically, note the access the database administrators and operating system administrators have to which environments. These should be restricted to the production environment only.		DS9
d.	Determine whether the PeopleSoft production environment is connected to other PeopleSoft or non-PeopleSoft systems. If so, obtain details as to the nature of connectivity, frequency of information transfers, and security and control measures surrounding these transfers (to ensure accuracy and completeness).		DS13
e.	Identify the modules that are being used.		AI2 AI3
f.	Identify whether the organization has implemented any of the following new e-enabled solutions: • Supply chain management • Supplier relationship management • Customer relationship management • Enterprise performance management • Enterprise service automation		PO4
g.	Determine whether the organization makes use of any other e-enabled functionality. If so, describe functionality and purpose.		PO3 DS9

	Control Objective/Test	Documentation/ Matters Arising	COBIT References
Preliminary Audit Steps *cont.*			
g. *cont.*	Always understand the robustness of the network protection to ensure that it is tightly controlled to minimize any potential external attacks on the PeopleSoft system.		
h.	Determine whether the organization has created any locally developed reports or tables. If so, determine how these programs/reports or tables are used. Depending on the importance/ extent of use, review and document the development and change management process surrounding the creation/ modification of these programs/reports or tables.		DS11
i.	Obtain copies of the organization's key security policies and standards. Highlight key areas of concern, including: • Information security policy • Sensitivity classification • Logical and physical access control requirements • Network security requirements, including requirements for encryption, firewalls, etc. • Platform security requirements (e.g., configuration requirements)		DS5
j.	Obtain information regarding any awareness programs that have been delivered to staff on the key security policies and standards. Consider specifically the frequency of delivery and any statistics on the extent of coverage (i.e., the percentage of staff that has received awareness training).		DS7
k.	Maintain permission lists, roles and user profiles.		AI4 DS11

<table>
<tr><th colspan="2">Control Objective/Test</th><th>Documentation/ Matters Arising</th><th>COBIT References</th></tr>
<tr><td colspan="4">Preliminary Audit Steps cont.</td></tr>
<tr><td>k.
cont.</td><td>Determine whether job roles, including the related transactions, have been defined and documented.

Determine whether procedures exist for maintaining (creating/changing/deleting) permission lists and whether they are followed.</td><td></td><td></td></tr>
<tr><td>l.</td><td>Adequate access administration procedures should exist in written form. Determine whether any of the following procedures exist within the organization:
• Procedures to add/change/delete User profiles
• Procedures to handle temporary access requests
• Procedures to handle emergency access requests
• Procedures to remove users who have never logged into the system
• Procedures to automatically notify the administration staff when staff holding sensitive or critical positions leave the organization or change positions

If so, document the process and comment on compliance with the policies and standards, and the adequacy of resulting documentation.</td><td></td><td>DS5</td></tr>
<tr><td>m.</td><td>Obtain copies of the organization's change management policies, processes, procedures and change documentation. Consider specifically:
• Development and migration processes and procedures
• Emergency change processes and procedures</td><td></td><td>AI6</td></tr>
</table>

	Control Objective/Test	Documentation/ Matters Arising	COBIT References
Preliminary Audit Steps *cont.*			
m. *cont.*	• Development standards, including naming conventions, testing requirements and move to production requirements		
n.	Determine whether the organization has a defined process for creating and maintaining instances. If so, obtain copies and documentation related to the creation and maintenance of instances.		DS3 DS9
o.	Review outstanding audit findings, if any, from previous years. Assess impact on current audit.		ME1 ME4
Identify the significant risks and determine the key controls.			
p.	Obtain details of the risk assessment approach taken in the organization to identify and prioritize risks.		PO9
q.	Obtain copies of and review: • Completed risk assessments impacting the PeopleSoft environment • Approved requests to deviate from security policies and standards • The impact of the above documents on the planning of the PeopleSoft audit		PO9 ME4
r.	If a recent implementation/upgrade was completed, obtain a copy of the security implementation plan. Assess whether the plan took into account the protection of critical objects within the organization and segregation of duties. Assess whether an appropriate naming convention (e.g., for profiles) was developed to help with security maintenance and comply with required PeopleSoft naming conventions.		AI2 AI4 AI5 AI7 DS5

<table>
<tr><th colspan="2">Control Objective/Test</th><th>Documentation/ Matters Arising</th><th>COBIT References</th></tr>
<tr><td>1.</td><td colspan="3">Development and Integration Tools</td></tr>
<tr><td>1.1</td><td colspan="3">Access to development and integration tools is restricted to authorized users and segregated from incompatible duties.</td></tr>
<tr><td>1.1.1</td><td>Review access security matrices and access assignment documentation to gain an understanding of the security design. Corroborate this understanding by generating lists of users with access to the Application Designer and Application Engine menus and reviewing their level of access by writing and executing the following query in PeopleSoft Query Manager:
SELECT A.OPRID, A.OPRDEFNDESC, A.ACCTLOCK, B.ROLENAME, C.CLASSID, D.MENUNAME, D.BARNAME, D.BARITEMNAME, D.PNLITEMNAME, D.DISPLAYONLY, D.AUTHORIZEDACTIONS

FROM PSOPRDEFN A, PSROLEUSER B, PSROLECLASS C, PSAUTHITEM D

WHERE A.OPRID = B.ROLEUSER AND B.ROLENAME = C.ROLENAME AND C.CLASSID = D.CLASSID

Order by A.OPRID, B.ROLENAME, C.CLASSID, D.MENUNAME to ensure that the user IDs (OPRID), roles (ROLENAME), permission lists (CLASSID) and components (MENUNAME) are listed in alphabetical order.</td><td></td><td>DS5</td></tr>
</table>

Control Objective/Test		Documentation/ Matters Arising	COBIT References
1.	**Development and Integration Tools *cont.***		
1.1.1 *cont.*	The column D.AUTHORIZEDACTIONS will contain values that represent the action types that the user is authorized to perform. A listing and description of these actions are detailed at the end of this chapter. Note: The auditor should determine which of all the values are considered high risk within the organization. The D.DISPLAYONLY column will have a value of 0 or 1. A value of 1 means all fields in the page are display-only to the user, and a value of 0 means this setting is turned off and the action type codes indicate the level of access granted. A.ACCTLOCK will have a value of 0 or 1. A value of 1 means the user ID is locked from system entry, and a value of 0 means the user ID is available for use. Use caution if filtering users who are locked out. Users can be temporarily locked out for an excessive number of incorrect password attempts. As such, users with access to sensitive pages should not be discounted from the above query until it is confirmed they no longer require access to PeopleSoft. In addition to locking the account, it is good practice to remove all roles and permission lists from a user profile when that access is no longer required.		

Control Objective/Test		Documentation/ Matters Arising	COBIT References
1.	**Development and Integration Tools *cont.***		
1.2	***Security documentation is available for object security and is in line with management's intentions.***		
1.2.1	Review security documentation to gain an understanding of the definition security design. Corroborate by generating a list of users with access to definition groups. This can be generated by writing the following query in Peoplesoft Query Manager: SELECT A.OPRID, A.OPRDEFNDESC, A.ACCTLOCK, B.CLASSID, B.OBJGROUPID, B.DISPLAYONLY FROM PSOPRDEFN A, PSOPROBJ B WHERE A.OPRCLASS = B.CLASSID; Note: In the event that a user belongs to multiple definition groups and more than one group provides access to a definition, the level of access provided to the user is determined by the definition group with the highest level of access. Generate a list of definition groups and the definitions defined in them by writing the following query in Query Manager: SELECT A.OBJGROUPID, A.ENTTYPE, A.ENTNAME FROM PSOBJGROUP A Alternatively, the following query could be used for increased detail: SELECT PSOPRDEFN.OPRID, PSOPRDEFN.OPRDEFNDESC, PSOPROBJ.CLASSID, PSOPROBJ.OBJGROUPID, PSOPROBJ.DISPLAYONLY, P SOPROBJ.VERSION, PSOBJGROUP.ENTTYPE,		DS13

	Control Objective/Test	Documentation/ Matters Arising	COBIT References
1.	**Development and Integration Tools *cont.***		
1.2.1 *cont.*	PSOBJGROUP.ENTNAME, PSOBJGROUP.VERSION, PSOPRDEFN.ACCTLOCK, PSOPROBJ.CLASSID FROM PSOBJGROUP INNER JOIN (PSOPROBJ INNER JOIN PSOPRDEFN ON PSOPROBJ.CLASSID = PSOPRDEFN.OPRCLASS) ON PSOBJGROUP.OBJGROUPID = PSOPROBJ.OBJGROUPID; At a minimum, join the PSOPRDEFN and PSOPROBJ classes to obtain a report on user IDs with the definition groups they have been assigned. Review the output from both queries to determine appropriateness and compliance with security documentation. Generate a list of users with access to PeopleTools menus via the query detailed in chapter 10, 1.1.1 Development and Integration Tools: Testing Techniques.		
2.	**Data Management Tools**		
2.1	***Access to sensitive pages in production is restricted to authorized users and segregated from incompatible duties.***		
2.1.1	Review access security matrices and access assignment documentation to gain an understanding of the security design. Corroborate this understanding by generating lists of users with access by running the SQL query detailed in chapter 10, 1.1.1 Development and Integration Tools: Testing Techniques, and review users with access to the previously discussed menus and pages.		AI4 DS5

	Control Objective/Test	Documentation/ Matters Arising	COBIT References
2.	**Data Management Tools *cont.***		
2.1.1 *cont.*	Review security procedures created by management that identify whether the SQR Alter tool and DDDAudit.SQR and SYSAudit.SQR reports are run and independently reviewed and investigated by management. Corroborate this by selecting a sample of reports and reviewing for evidence of independent review and follow-up of exceptional items.		
3.	**Operations Tools**		
3.1	***Access to the process schedule manager functions is restricted to authorized users.***		
3.1.1	Review the system design documentation relating to access security (design of roles and permission lists) and any established policies, procedures, standards and guidance related to the maintenance of roles/ permission lists, in particular the design and assignment of process scheduler access, process groups and process profiles. Corroborate this understanding by generating and reviewing a list of user IDs with access to functionality under the Process Scheduler menu. The list can be generated by writing the following query in PeopleSoft Query Manager: SELECT A.OPRID, A.OPRDEFNDESC, A.ACCTLOCK, B.ROLENAME, C.CLASSID, D.MENUNAME, D.BARNAME, D.BARITEMNAME, D.PNLITEMNAME, D.DISPLAYONLY, D.AUTHORIZEDACTIONS		PO9 AI1 AI4 DS5

	Control Objective/Test	Documentation/ Matters Arising	COBIT References
3.	**Operations Tools *cont.***		
3.1.1 *cont.*	FROM PSOPRDEFN A, PSROLEUSER B, PSROLECLASS C, PSAUTHITEM D WHERE A.OPRID = B.ROLEUSER AND B.ROLENAME = C.ROLENAME AND C.CLASSID = D.CLASSID Order by A.OPRID, B.ROLENAME, C.CLASSID, D.MENUNAME to ensure that the user IDs (OPRID), roles (ROLENAME), permission lists (CLASSID) and components (MENUNAME) are listed in alphabetical order. The authorized actions column will contain values that represent the action types. These values are detailed at the end of chapter 10. Generate and review a list of process group permissions assigned to user IDs by writing the following query: SELECT A.OPRID, A.OPRDEFNDESC, A.ACCTLOCK, B.PRCSGRP FROM PSOPRDEFN A, PSAUTHPRCS B WHERE A.OPRCLASS = B.CLASSID Order by A.OPRID to ensure that the user IDs (OPRID) are listed in alphabetical order. Generate and review a list of process group permission contents by writing the following query: SELECT A.PRCSTYPE, A.PRCSNAME, A.PRCSGRP FROM PS_PRCSDEFNGRP A		

	Control Objective/Test	Documentation/ Matters Arising	COBIT References
3.	**Operations Tools *cont.***		
3.1.1 *cont.*	Generate and review a list of users and their process profile configurations by writing the following query: SELECT A.OPRID, A.OPRDEFNDESC, A.ACCTLOCK, B.CLASSID, B.SRVRDESTFILE, B.SRVRDESTPRNT, B.CLIENTDESTFILE, B.CLIENTDESTPRNT, B.OVRDOUTDEST, B.OVRDSRVRPARMS, B.RQSTSTATUSUPD, B.RQSTSTATUSVIEW, B.SRVRSTATUSUPD, B.SRVRSTATUSVIEW, B.MVSJOBNAME, B.MVSJOBACCT, B.RECURUPD FROM PSOPRDEFN A, PSPRCSPRFL B WHERE A.PRCSPRFLCLS = B.CLASSID Order by A.OPRID to ensure that the user IDs (OPRID) are listed in alphabetical order. Note: The Process Scheduler Admin role grants users access to override controls established via Process Profile permission lists; therefore, the following query should be executed to identify users that have been assigned this access: SELECT A.OPRID, A.OPRDEFNDESC, A.ACCTLOCK, C.ROLENAME, C.DESCR FROM PSOPRDEFN A, PSROLEUSER B, PSROLEDEFN C WHERE A.OPRID = B.ROLEUSER AND B.ROLENAME = C.ROLENAME AND C.ROLENAME = 'ProcessSchedulerAdmin'		

	Control Objective/Test	Documentation/ Matters Arising	COBIT References
4.	**Security Administration Tools**		
4.1	***Security administration profiles are segregated and assigned to system management staff.***		
4.1.1.	Determine that the security administration functions have been assigned appropriately. The following menu names are associated with security administration: • MAINTAIN_SECURITY • DEFINITION_SECURITY • TREEMANAGER • UTILITIES The migration of objects among database instances (DEV to TST to PROD) requires access to the Application Designer. The relevant menu names (components) for migration are: • APPLICATION_ DESIGNER • DATA_MOVER Determine whether the security administration functions have been assigned appropriately and administrator tasks are segregated. Review access security matrices and access assignment documentation to gain an understanding of the security design. Corroborate this understanding by generating lists of users with access to the above menu names and reviewing their level of access by performing the test described in chapter 10, 1.1.1 Development and Integration Tools: Testing Techniques.		PO4 AI6 DS5 DS13

	Control Objective/Test	Documentation/ Matters Arising	COBIT References
4.	**Security Administration Tools *cont.***		
4.1.1 *cont.*	If full segregation is not possible due to resource issues, consider one of the following scenarios: • The ability to create/maintain roles or permission lists and assign them to user profiles is included in the user profile of Security Administrator 1. The ability to migrate roles, permission lists and user profiles to the production instance is contained in the user profile of Security Administrator 2. • The ability to migrate roles and permission lists into production and assign authorization profiles to user master records is included in the user master record of Security Administrator 1, and the ability to create/maintain activity groups or authorization profiles is contained in the user master record of Security Administrator 2. This scenario is acceptable, but may cause some control concerns, as it may be more difficult to implement appropriately. If this segregation of duties options is practicable, assess hard copies of reports detailing changes to security tables (e.g., PSROLEUSER, PSROLECLASS, PSAUTHITEM, PSOPRCLS, PSOPRDFN) and changes to user profiles (via the audit tab) for evidence of review and action by management. Note: The review of changes to security tables assumes that logging of activity on specific tables has been set up.		

	Control Objective/Test	Documentation/ Matters Arising	COBIT References
4.	**Security Administration Tools *cont.***		
4.2	***PeopleSoft access security design is documented and signed off by management during the implementation.***		
4.2.1	Review the system design documentation relating to access security (design of roles and permission lists) and any established policies, procedures, standards and guidance related to the maintenance of roles/ permission lists and the list of roles/ permission lists and their assignment to user IDs defined in the system. Ascertain from management whether this documentation has been maintained accurately since implementation. Perform two tests to corroborate the understanding gained through review of the documentation to ensure the accuracy of the documentation and the effectiveness of compliance with the established policies: • Generate a list of user IDs, roles, permission lists and subsequent menu items assigned to them by writing the following query in PeopleSoft Query Manager: SELECT A.OPRID, A.OPRDEFNDESC, A.ACCTLOCK, B.ROLENAME, C.CLASSID, D.MENUNAME, D.BARNAME, D.BARITEMNAME, D.PNLITEMNAME, D.DISPLAYONLY, D.AUTHORIZEDACTIONS FROM PSOPRDEFN A, PSROLEUSER B, PSROLECLASS C, PSAUTHITEM D		PO4 PO5 AI2 DS5

	Control Objective/Test	Documentation/ Matters Arising	COBIT References
4.	**Security Administration Tools *cont.***		
4.2.1 *cont.*	WHERE A.OPRID = B.ROLEUSER AND B.ROLENAME = C.ROLENAME AND C.CLASSID = D.CLASSID Order by A.OPRID, B.ROLENAME, C.CLASSID, D.MENUNAME to ensure that the user IDs (OPRID), roles (ROLENAME), permission lists (CLASSID) and components (MENUNAME) are listed in alphabetical order. • Further investigation on an individual user profile basis should be performed manually or externally in Excel, MS Access or ACL. Alternatively, to identify users and roles only, use the following query: SELECT A.ROLEUSER, A.ROLENAME, A.DYNAMIC_ SW FROM PSROLEUSER A Take a representative sample of user profiles from the system and confirm them against the original documentation. Resolve any discrepancies with management. Test changes to roles, permission lists and user profiles since the implementation of the system. Changes to tables in PeopleSoft are reflected by the addition of a new row if they are specifically set to be audited. This applies only to effective-dated data—this does not apply to security changes unless the security tables are specifically audited.		

	Control Objective/Test	Documentation/ Matters Arising	COBIT References
4.	**Security Administration Tools *cont.***		
4.2.1 *cont.*	Note: A query would have to be written to download the Security table to be reviewed (e.g., PSAUTHITEM). This involves taking a sample of changes from the system and tracing them back to current documentation. Management should also be able to provide source documentation for the authorization of these changes. The effectiveness of this test is dependent on management implementing the system audits on the relevant tables. See also chapter 10, Security Administration Tools: Risks, 4.9 Table Logging and Audit Trails.		
4.3	***SYSADM password capabilities and permissions are adequately reviewed and controlled.***		
4.3.1	Review the PeopleSoft administrator password to ensure that it has been changed from the default. Alternatively, attempt to sign on to the system using the PeopleSoft administrator's password, and observe the success or failure of this attempt. Generate lists of users with access to the above menu names by writing the query detailed in 1.1.1 (under Development and Integration Tools Testing Techniques) in PeopleSoft Query Manager. Review the output for appropriateness of the access provided, focusing on user IDs with combinations of the menu names detailed.		DS5 DS11

	Control Objective/Test	Documentation/ Matters Arising	COBIT References
4.	**Security Administration Tools *cont.***		
4.3.1 *cont.*	Alternatively, run the following query on the PSROLEUSER table to identify users with access to the PeopleSoft Administrator role: SELECT A.ROLEUSER, A.ROLENAME, A.DYNAMIC_SW FROM PSROLEUSER A WHERE A.ROLENAME = 'PeopleSoft Administrator'		
4.4	***Default PeopleSoft passwords for the superuser IDs have been changed and access appropriately restricted.***		
4.4.1	Determine the policies and procedures in place regarding the use of the default user IDs and changing the default passwords. Attempt to gain access to the PeopleSoft system using the default user IDs and passwords.		DS5
4.5	***Access to powerful profiles is restricted.***		
4.5.1	Generate lists of users and their access by writing the query detailed in chapter 10, 1.1.1 Development and Integration Tools: Testing Techniques, in PeopleSoft Query Manager. Review the output for appropriateness of the access provided, focusing on user IDs containing the powerful roles and permission lists. The user list identified by this test should be checked to ascertain whether individuals who have access to the above-mentioned functionality require this access based on their job responsibilities and established policies, procedures, standards and guidance.		DS5 DS11
4.6	***Password parameter controls are established and adhered to by the organization.***		
4.6.1	Gain an understanding of the authentication techniques and controls by reviewing documented security policies governing password controls and required parameter settings.		PO9 DS5

	Control Objective/Test	Documentation/ Matters Arising	COBIT References
4.	**Security Administration Tools *cont.***		
4.6.1 *cont.*	Corroborate this understanding by reviewing the password parameter settings configured on the system (Home→PeopleTools→Security→ Password Configuration→Password Controls): • Check the ENABLE SIGNON PEOPLECODE box to see if it is checked. • Review the parameter settings for compliance with security policies and standards and against accepted best practice. The following SQL can be used to report on password controls that have been configured: SELECT A.PSWD_CNTRL_ON, A.PSWDEXPIRESDAYS, A.PSWDWARNDAYS, A.MINPSWDLENGTH, A.PSWDREQSPECIAL, A.PSWDREQDIGITS, A.ALLOWOPRID, A.LOGINATTEMPTS, A.LOCKOUTDURATION, A.PURGE_DAYS, A.PASSWORD_ HISTORY FROM PSSECOPTIONS A It is also worth noting that organizations may integrate PeopleSoft with LDAP directories to store user IDs and passwords; therefore, these directories also need to be audited to determine the level and adequacy of password controls.		

	Control Objective/Test	Documentation/ Matters Arising	COBIT References
4.	**Security Administration Tools *cont.***		
4.6.1 *cont.*	Select a sample of permission lists (Home→PeopleTools→Security→ Permissions & Roles→Permission Lists) and review the time-out values under the General Attributes page for compliance with security policies. Alternatively, write the following query in Query Manager to obtain a list of sign-on times by user ID: SELECT B.OPRID, A.DAYOFWEEK, A.STARTTIME, A.ENDTIME FROM PSAUTHSIGNON A, PSOPRDEFN B WHERE B.OPRCLASS = A.CLASSID Order by A.OPRID to obtain an output with the user IDs (OPRID) in alphabetical order. Note that the DAYOFWEEK code range is 0-6, corresponding to Sunday to Saturday, and the start time of 0 = 00:00 hrs and end time of 1439 = 23:59 hrs.		
4.7	***Security policies and procedures are in place and include specific guidance on the use of correction mode.***		
4.7.1	Review security documentation to gain an understanding of the policy regarding the use of Correction Mode. Generate lists of users with access to the above menu names by writing the query detailed in chapter 10, 4.1 Security Profiles, in PeopleSoft Query Manager. Review the output for appropriateness of the access provided, focusing on user IDs with authorized actions values of 8, 9, 10, 11, 12, 13, 14, 15, 136, 137, 138, 139, 140, 141,		PO8 AI2

	Control Objective/Test	Documentation/ Matters Arising	COBIT References
4.	**Security Administration Tools *cont.***		
4.7.1 *cont.*	142 and 143. A detailed list of authorized actions and their values is provided at the end of chapter 10. Alternatively, the following query could be used: SELECT A.OPRID, A.OPRDEFNDESC, A.ACCTLOCK, B.ROLENAME, C.CLASSID, D.MENUNAME, D.BARNAME, D.BARITEMNAME, D.PNLITEMNAME, D.DISPLAYONLY, D.AUTHORIZEDACTIONS FROM PSOPRDEFN A, PSROLEUSER B, PSROLECLASS C, PSAUTHITEM D WHERE A.OPRID = B.ROLEUSER AND B.ROLENAME = C.ROLENAME AND C.CLASSID = D.CLASSID AND D.AUTHORIZEDACTIONS BETWEEN 7 AND 16 OR D.AUTHORIZEDACTIONS > 135 Determine whether these users should have Correction Mode access as part of their roles and responsibilities. Match all user IDs to relevant HR records to determine staff position and currency of service. This will also assist in identifying redundant users.		
4.8	***Security documentation is defined in query-level security design, and policies and procedures are aligned with management's intentions.***		
4.8.1	Review security documentation to understand the intended query security design: • Generate a list of users with access to the Query Manager menu utilizing the query detailed in chapter 10, 1.1.1 Development and Integration Tools: Testing Techniques.		AI4 DS5 DS11

	Control Objective/Test	Documentation/ Matters Arising	COBIT References
4.	**Security Administration Tools *cont.***		
4.8.1 *cont.*	• Generate a list of query profiles using the following query: SELECT A.OPRID, A.OPRDEFNDESC, A.ACCTLOCK, B.ROLENAME, C.CLASSID, E.CLASSID, E.VERSION, E.QRY_RUN_ONLY, E.QRY_CREATE_PUBLIC, E.QRY_CREATE_WFLOW, E.QRY_MAX_FETCH, E.QRY_MAX_RUN, E.QRY_ADV_DISTINCT, E.QRY_ADV_ANY_JOIN, E.QRY_ADV_SUBQUERY, E.QRY_ADV_UNION, E.QRY_ADV_EXPR, E.QRY_MAX_JOINS, E.QRY_MAX_IN_TREE, E.QRY_OUT_LISTBOX, E.QRY_OUT_NVISION, E.QRY_OUT_CRYSTAL, E.QRY_ADM_AUTOPUBLIC, E.QRY_ADM_AUTOPRIV, E.QRY_ADM_LIMUNAPPRV, E.QRY_ADM_UNAPP_ROWS FROM PSOPRDEFN A, PSROLEUSER B, PSROLECLASS C, PS_SCRTY_QUERY E WHERE A.OPRID = B.ROLEUSER AND B.ROLENAME = C.ROLENAME AND C.CLASSID = E.CLASSID • Generate a list of user access to query trees and the access groups assigned to them by writing the following query in Query Manager: SELECT A.OPRID, A.OPRDEFNDESC, A.ACCTLOCK, B.ROLENAME, C.CLASSID, D.CLASSID, D.TREE_NAME, D.ACCESS_GROUP, D.ACCESSIBLE FROM PSOPRDEFN A, PSROLEUSER B, PSROLECLASS C, PS_SCRTY_ACC_GRP D		

	Control Objective/Test	Documentation/ Matters Arising	COBIT References
4.	**Security Administration Tools *cont.***		
4.8.1 *cont.*	WHERE A.OPRID = B.ROLEUSER AND B.ROLENAME = C.ROLENAME AND C.CLASSID = D.CLASSID This determines the tables that a user may access when maintaining their queries.		
4.9	***Policies and standards are documented to define the critical records and record fields that are to be logged for changes.***		
4.9.1	Review security procedures created by management that identify what critical records and fields are being logged and how often these logs are reviewed by management. For the critical records and record fields identified, check that the following audit settings have been configured appropriately in Application Designer: • Record-level auditing—Choose the Objects workspace and open the record. Check Use Properties, and review the audit options selected: – Audit Record Add—Inserts an audit table row whenever a new row is added to the table – Audit Record Change—Inserts one or two audit table rows whenever a row is changed on the table – Audit Record Selective—Inserts one or two audit table rows whenever a field that is also included on the record definition for the audit table is changed – Audit Record Delete—Inserts an audit table row whenever a row is deleted from the table		DS5 ME1

Control Objective/Test		Documentation/ Matters Arising	COBIT References
4.	**Security Administration Tools *cont.***		
4.9.1 *cont.*	• Record field-level auditing—For the record fields chosen, check the Use Properties of the different field type (character, number, data/time) options, and review the audit options selected: – Field Add—Audits this field whenever a new row of data is added – Field Change—Audits this field whenever the contents are changed – Field Delete—Audits this field whenever a row of data is deleted by management. For the critical records and record fields identified, check (via Home→ PeopleTools→Application Designer) that the audit settings have been configured appropriately.		

Default User IDs

PeopleSoft comes delivered with default user IDs, providing superuser-type access to specific applications within the system. **Figure 10.4** lists some of the more powerful user IDs that should be removed from production:

Figure 10.4—HRMS Default User IDs

BELHR	GER	PSESP	UKHR
CAN	GRHR	PSFRA	UKNI
CFR	JCADMIN1	PSGER	USA
CNHR	NLDHR	PSINE	USHR
ESP	PS	PSJPN	WEBGUEST
FRA	PSCFR	PSPOR	WEBMODEL
FRHR	PSDUT	TIME	

PeopleSoft is delivered with a number of default permission lists providing superuser-type access to various applications in the system. These permission lists that should be removed from production are shown in **figure 10.5**.

Figure 10.5—HRMS Default Permission Lists					
HHR_TRN	HHR_VC04	HPI_KCI001	HTL	PSAPPS	PSQRY
HHR_VC01	HHR_VC05	HPY	KRONOS	PSBASS	
HHR_VC02	HPA	HPYCFR	MOBILE	PSDEV	
HHR_VC03	HPI	HST	PS	PSEM	

Appendix H—Security Administration Cycle Audit ICQ

	Control Objective/Test	Response			Comment	COBIT References
		Yes	No	N/A		
1.	**Security Administration**					
1.1	***Access to development and integration tools is restricted to authorized users and segregated from incompatible duties.***					
1.1.1	Does the organization have separate database instances for production (PROD) and development (DEV)? Are development and maintenance of PeopleSoft objects and functions performed in the development instance? Does the organization utilize the following tools: • Application Designer • Application Engine • Workflow Administrator • Business Process Designer Is access to the development and integration tools in the production environment restricted to authorized users and segregated from incompatible duties?					AI2 DS5 DS13

Control Objective/Test		Response: Yes	Response: No	Response: N/A	Comment	COBIT References
1.	**Security Administration** ***cont.***					
1.2	***Security documentation is available for object security and aligned with management's intentions.***					
1.2.1	Has security documentation been compiled to define the PeopleTools object-level security design and procedures for creation and modification of object definitions, in line with management's intentions? Has object security been implemented to restrict access to object definitions via Application Designer, Application Engine, Workflow Administrator and Business Process Designer, and has every object been assigned to an object group?					PO7 DS5
2.	**Data Management Tools**					
2.1	***Access to sensitive pages in production is appropriately restricted to authorized users and segregated from incompatible duties.***					
2.1.1	Who has access to the database and PeopleTools? Are these users appropriate? What is the process for modifying object definitions? Are the following data management tools used by the organization, and is access to these appropriate: • Data Mover • Import Manager • Mass Change • Cube Manager • Application Designer					DS5 DS13

	Control Objective/Test	Response			Comment	COBIT References
		Yes	No	N/A		
2.	**Data Management Tools *cont.***					
2.1.1 *cont.*	Does management generate and review the reports DDDAudit.SQR and SYSAudit.SQR?					
3.	**Operation Tools**					
3.1	***Access to the process schedule manager functions is restricted to authorized users.***					
3.1.1	Who has access to the Process Schedule Manager? Do they require this access? Have process security groups and process profiles been established and assigned to permission lists that are aligned with the security design and management's intentions? Are there documented procedures for the maintenance of roles/ permission lists and, in particular, the design and assignment of process scheduler access, process groups and process profiles?					PO4 DS5
4.	**Security Administration Tools**					
4.1	***Security administration profiles are segregated and assigned to system management staff appropriately.***					
4.1.1	Who has access to the security administration functions, and are these persons appropriate? Are security administration profiles segregated and assigned to system management staff appropriately?					DS5

	Control Objective/Test	Response			Comment	CobiT
		Yes	No	N/A		References
4.	**Security Administration Tools** ***cont.***					
4.2	***PeopleSoft access security design is documented and signed off by management during the implementation.***					
4.2.1	Was documentation developed that describes the design and assignment of permission lists and roles, and was a procedure developed for the maintenance of this documentation? Did management sign off for this documentation during the implementation? Has a copy of the documentation been kept offsite for use in the event of a disaster?					AI2 DS4 DS5 DS11
4.3	***SYSADM password capabilities and permissions are reviewed and adequately controlled.***					
4.3.1	Has the SYSADM default password been changed? Is access to ALLPNLS and PSADMIN permission lists restricted to only those who require it? Is a formal approval required for assigning the above permission lists to end users?					DS5 DS13
4.4	***Default PeopleSoft passwords for the superuser IDs are changed and access restricted.***					
4.4.1	Has the default PeopleSoft password for superuser IDs been changed and restricted to appropriate individuals for specific situations only?					DS5 DS11

	Control Objective/Test	Response			Comment	COBIT References
		Yes	No	N/A		
4.	**Security Administration Tools *cont.***					
4.4.1 *cont.*	Is the SYSADM password stored in a safe for emergency access only?					
4.5	***Access to powerful profiles is restricted.***					
4.5.1	Who has access to the powerful profiles? Are these users appropriate? Is the assignment of powerful permission lists restricted in line with approved security design documentation and management's intentions?					DS5 DS9 DS11
4.6	***Password parameter controls are established and adhered to by the organization.***					
4.6.1	Have password controls been established to support the confidentiality of user passwords and restrict unauthorized access? Are there standards/ guidelines in place that are communicated to end users to ensure that users have security awareness? Has password control management been implemented in PeopleSoft through the password parameter settings?					AI3 AI4 DS5
4.7	***Security policies and procedures are in place and include specific guidance on the use of correction mode.***					
4.7.1	Do the security policies and procedures include specific guidance on the use of correction mode?					PO10 AI4 DS5

Control Objective/Test		Response			Comment	COBIT References
		Yes	No	N/A		
4.	**Security Administration Tools *cont.***					
4.7.1 *cont.*	Is approval required for users who require Correction Mode?					
4.8	***Security documentation is defined in query-level security design, policies and procedures in line with management's intentions.***					
4.8.1	Has the security documentation defined query-level security design, policies and procedures in line with management intentions? Has this documentation been formally approved? How is query security set up?					AI4 DS5 DS11
4.9	***Policies and standards are documented to define the critical records and record fields that are to be logged for changes.***					
4.9.1	Have policies and standards been documented, and do they include defining the critical records and record fields that should be logged for changes? Have the PeopleSoft auditing system capabilities been extended to include tracking changes to security tables? Are these logs reviewed on a regular basis as part of the security procedures for the organization?					AI4 DS12 ME1

Appendix I—CobiT Control Objectives

CobiT 4.0 was released in 2005 by the IT Governance Institute (ITGI). This release was a major upgrade from CobiT 3rd Edition. However, the new release does not contain any changes that invalidate the previous framework. The chart below indicates the CobiT 4.0 control objectives used in the reference column of the PeopleSoft Security Administration internal control questionnaires and audit programs.

Domain		Process
Plan and Organize	PO1	Define a strategic IT plan.
	PO2	Define the information architecture.
	PO3	Determine technological direction.
	PO4	Define the IT processes, organization and relationships.
	PO5	Manage the IT investment.
	PO6	Communicate management aims and direction.
	PO7	Manage IT human resources.
	PO8	Manage quality.
	PO9	Assess and manage risks.
	PO10	Manage projects.
Acquire and Implement	AI1	Identify automated solutions.
	AI2	Acquire and maintain application software.
	AI3	Acquire and maintain technology infrastructure.
	AI4	Enable operation and use.
	AI5	Procure IT resources.
	AI6	Manage changes.
	AI7	Install and accredit solutions and changes.

Domain		Process
Deliver and Support	DS1	Define and manage service levels.
	DS2	Manage third-party services.
	DS3	Manage performance and capacity.
	DS4	Ensure continuous service.
	DS5	Ensure systems security.
	DS6	Identify and allocate costs.
	DS7	Educate and train users.
	DS8	Manage service desk and incidents.
	DS9	Manage the configuration.
	DS10	Manage problems.
	DS11	Manage data.
	DS12	Manage the physical environment.
	DS13	Manage operations.
Monitor and Evaluate	ME1	Monitor and evaluate IT performance.
	ME2	Monitor and evaluate internal control.
	ME3	Ensure regulatory compliance.
	ME4	Provide IT governance.

References

Anderson, Lynn; *Understanding PeopleSoft*, Sybex, Cap Gemini and Ernst & Young US LLC, USA, 2001

Bilbrey, Darrell; *PeopleSoft Administrator's Guide: The Essential Resource for Implementation and Administration*, Sybex Inc., USA, 1999

Gillespie, Richard; JoAnn Gillespie; *PeopeSoft Developer's Handbook*, McGraw Hill, USA, 1999

Greenberg, Paul; Michael Fauscette; Scott Fletcher, *et al*; *Special Edition Using PeopleSoft®*, Que, USA, 2000

ISACA, *Security, Audit and Control Features SAP® R/3®: A Technical Risk Management Reference Guide, 2nd Edition*, USA, 2005

Mirani, Jagdish; Anne Ozzimo; "Oracle Applications: Committed to Your Success," Oracle, USA, 2006

Oracle, "Oracle Fusion Architecture and Oracle Fusion Applications: Technology," USA, 2006

PeopleSoft, *Peoplebook Library, http://ps8dweb1.vccs.edu:6001/sa80books/eng/psbooks/index.htm*

Index

K

L

M

N

O

P

Q

R

S

T

U

W

Other Publications

All publications come with detailed assessment questionnaires and work programs. For further information, please visit www.isaca.org/bookstore or e-mail *bookstore@isaca.org*.

Security, Audit and Control Features Oracle® Applications: A Technical and Risk Management Reference Guide, 2nd Edition

This guide provides frameworks and methodologies for auditing and testing in an Oracle environment using Release 11*i*. It is written with the business manager in mind, as well as the IT and assurance professional and has been updated to address:

- Third-party audit tools, e.g., BrainTree, Deloitte
- ACL' s CCM technology
- New Oracle Applications facilities:
  - Management of whistle blower complaints to support Sarbanes-Oxley section 301
  - Management of capital and risk for Basel II
  - Support for greater levels of financial control, transparency and accountability to support various regulatory requirements, including Sarbanes-Oxley and International Financial Reporting Standards (IFRS)
- Audit programs and internal control questionnaires cross-referenced to CobiT 4.0
- Impact of Oracle Corporation's Project Fusion

2006

IT Control Objectives for Sarbanes-Oxley, 2nd Edition

This second edition, which provides CIOs, IT managers, and control and assurance professionals with scoping and assessment ideas, approaches and guidance in support of the IT-related Committee of Sponsoring Organizations of the Treadway Commission (COSO) internal control objectives for financial reporting. A streamlined road map is provided to help turn compliance into a competitive challenge. Lessons learned and sustaining ideas are also included. The second edition is updated for recent Security and Exchange Commission and Public Company Accounting Oversight Board guidance related to entity level controls, risk based/top down approach, application controls and evaluation of deficiencies, as well as an update for CobiT 4.0 references. 2006

Information Security Governance: Guidance for Boards of Directors and Executive Management, 2nd Edition

This book discusses why information security governance is increasingly important and outlines questions to ask and steps to take to ensure an effective information security governance programme within an enterprise. 2006

CobiT® Mapping: Mapping of PRINCE2 With CobiT 4.0
Projects in Controlled Environments (PRINCE) is a structured method for project management. The PRINCE method was first established in 1989 by the UK Central Computer and Telecommunications Agency (CCTA), now the UK Office of Government Commerce (OGC). The detailed mapping consists of the information requirements of PRINCE2 as mapped to each CobiT control objective. The structure follows the domains, processes and control objectives of CobiT. 2006

CobiT Mapping: Mapping of PMBOK With CobiT
This publication contains a detailed mapping of A Guide to the Project Management Body of Knowledge (PMBOK© Guide) with CobiT, as well as the classification of the standards discussed in this paper, as presented in *CobiT Mapping: Overview of International IT Guidance*, 2nd Edition. 2006

CobiT® Mapping: Mapping of SEI's CMM for Software With CobiT 4.0
The Software Engineering Institute (SEI) Capability Maturity Model (CMM) is a set of best practice descriptions for software development that can be used to improve the IT organization's performance. The impact of SEI CMM performance is broadly leveraged across the CobiT domains. Almost all of the SEI key practice areas (KPAs) are applicable to the CobiT processes.

This detailed mapping references the CMM key activities and measurement sources of commonality for each CobiT detailed control objective. The structure follows the domains, processes and control objectives of CobiT, and the mapping shows the coverage by SEI CMM KPAs within each SEI maturity level. 2006

CobiT Mapping: Mapping of ISO/IEC 17799:2000 with CobiT, 2nd Edition
This publication contains a detailed mapping of ISO/IEC 17799:2000 with CobiT, as well as the classification of the standards discussed in this paper, as presented in *CobiT Mapping: Overview of International IT Guidance,* 2nd Edition. 2006

CobiT Mapping: Overview of International IT Guidance, 2nd Edition
This publication focuses on the business drivers for implementing, as well as the risks of non-compliance with, the CobiT guidance. It contains a classification, short overview of the content, and an explanation of how the following guidance align or map to CobiT:
- COSO
- ITIL®
- ISO/IEC 17799:2005
- FIPS PUB 200
- ISO/IEC TR 13335
- ISO/IEC 15408:2005/Common Criteria/ITSEC
- PRINCE2®
- PMBOK©

- TickIT
- CMMI
- TOGAF 8.1
- *IT Baseline Protection Manual*
- NIST 800-14

2006

CobiT 4.0

Control Objectives for Information and related Technology (CobiT) is an IT governance framework and supporting tool set that allows managers to bridge the gap between control requirements, technical issues and business risks. CobiT enables clear policy development and good practice for IT control throughout organisations. It emphasises regulatory compliance, helps organisations to increase the value attained from IT, enables alignment, and simplifies implementation of the CobiT framework. 2005

CobiT *Online*

CobiT Online is, as its name suggests, an online offering of CobiT, including full browsing and searching capabilities, benchmarking functions, downloads, a discussion area, and the capacity to customise and create the user's own version of CobiT. 2006, 2003

Security, Audit and Control Features SAP®R/3®: A Technical and Risk Management Reference Guide, 2nd Edition, 2005

This guide provides frameworks and methodologies for auditing and testing in an Oracle environment using Release 11*i*. It is written with the business manager in mind, as well as the IT and assurance professional and has been updated to address:

- Third-party audit tools
- Investigatory tools, such as ACL's CCM technology
- New Oracle Applications facilities:
  - Management of whistle blower complaints to support Sarbanes-Oxley section 301
  - Management of capital and risk for Basel II
  - Support for greater levels of financial control, transparency and accountability to support various regulatory requirements, including Sarbanes-Oxley and International Financial Reporting Standards (IFRS)
- Audit programs and internal control questionnaires cross-referenced to CobiT 4.0
- Impact of Oracle Corporation's Project Fusion

Managing Risk in the Wireless Environment: Security, Audit and Control Issues

Val IT *Enterprise Value: Governance of IT Investments*

Information Security Governance: Guidance for Boards of Directors and Executive Management, 2nd Edition

Aligning CobiT, ITIL and ISO 17799 for Business Benefit

Security Awareness: Best Practices to Serve Your Enterprise
Cybercrime: Incident Response and Digital Forensics
Information Security Harmonisation—Classification of Global Guidance
IT Governance Domain Practices and Competencies series:
- *Information Risks: Whose Business Are They?,* 2005
- *Optimising Value Creation From IT Investments,* 2005
- *Measuring and Demonstrating the Value of IT,* 2005
- *Governance of Outsourcing,* 2005
- *IT Alignment: Who Is in Charge?,* 2005

Managing Information Integrity: Security, Control and Audit Issues, 2004
COBIT® *Security Baseline™*, 2004
Control Practices, 2004
IT Control Objectives for Sarbanes-Oxley, 2004
Oracle® Database Security, Audit and Control Features, 2004
OS/390—z/OS: Security, Control and Audit Features, 2003
IT Governance Implementation Guide, 2003
COBIT *Quickstart™*, 2003
Risks of Customer Relationship Management: A Security, Control and Audit Approach, 2003
Board Briefing on IT Governance, 2nd Edition 2003
Security Provisioning: Managing Access in Extended Enterprises, 2002
Electronic and Digital Signatures: A Global Status Report, 2002
Virtual Private Network—New Issues for Network Security, 2001
E-commerce Security series:
- *Securing the Network Perimeter,* 2002
- *Business Continuity Planning,* 2002
- *Trading Partner Authentication, Registration and Enrollment,* 2000
- *Public Key Infrastructure,* 2001
- *A Global Status Report,* 2000
- *Enterprise Best Practices,* 2000

Control Objectives for Net Centric Technology (CONCT), 1999
Digital Signatures—Security and Controls, 1999

Web Postings (*www.isaca.org/research*)

Security Critical Issues, 2005
Information Security Governance—Top Actions for Security Managers, 2005
Enterprise Identity Management: Managing Secure and Controllable Access in the Extended Enterprise Environment, 2004
Peer-to-peer Networking Security and Control, 2003